Praise for
The Last Flight of the Scarlet Macaw

"Not even Hollywood could invent Sharon Matola. The plucky American arrived in Belize in the '80s, founded a popular zoo, and became an expert on the scarlet macaw, an increasingly rare rainbow-colored parrot. When the Belizean government proposed erecting a dam in pristine macaw habitat, she leapt to the bird's defense. This fascinating account of the resulting battle touches upon greed, corruption, and the legacy of colonialism. While the outcome is sobering, there's a glimmer of hope for imperiled species everywhere in feisty irritants like Matola."
—*Entertainment Weekly*

"[A] stunning and significant piece of environmental journalism."
—*USA Today*

"A dynamic cast of characters buoys the story . . . With a plot so multilayered and dramatic that readers will need to remind themselves it's a true account, the narrative achieves the depth of a case study and the accessible intimacy of a short feature. Throughout, Barcott's relaxed, lucid writing and inventive descriptions . . . place readers firmly on the side of Matola and the birds."
—*The Miami Herald*

"A gripping account . . . A seasoned journalist, Barcott ably handles this wide-ranging, multifaceted story. Employing novelistic scene-setting, pithy detail and crisp dialogue, he covers cumbersome legal hurdles, arcane international legalities and raucous public hearings with the graceful ease of a long-distance runner. . . . Through tough reporting, colorful travel writing and a touch of natural history, Barcott has elevated an obscure environmental struggle to epic status." —*The Seattle Times*

"Barcott brings a fresh, urgent view." —*The Washington Post*

"Well-reported and often compelling . . . Barcott deserves much praise for the diligence and thoroughness of his reportage." —*The Seattle Post-Intelligencer*

"A meticulous and evocative story . . . Barcott is a wonderful writer, clear and unadorned . . . who is able to cram a great deal of information . . . into a fascinating and increasingly tense detective story, profile in courage and political thriller." —*The Sunday Oregonian*

"[Barcott] spins a fast-paced, wide-ranging tale that reads like a thriller with plenty of unexpected twists yet delivers a powerful message about the monuments we build and what they say about us." —*Fast Company*

"Hiaasen-esque, but real life." —*New York Post*

"Matola's personality, persistence and wit coupled with Barcott's language and storytelling make *The Last Flight of the Scarlet Macaw* a thrilling and gripping book." —*Milwaukee Journal Sentinel*

"A sympathetic saga of eco-activism with a cast of unforgettable characters . . . Matola is a journalist's dream. . . . Well worth reading." —*Natural History*

"Superbly written by Bruce Barcott, [*The Last Flight of the Scarlet Macaw*] describes in compelling detail the unsuccessful fight against the Chalillo dam. . . . A brave and informative book." —*Owen Sound Sun Times* (Ontario, Canada)

"An enthralling saga, expertly told." —*Marin Independent Journal* (California)

ALSO BY BRUCE BARCOTT

The Measure of a Mountain: Beauty and Terror on Mount Rainier

Northwest Passages: A Literary Anthology of the Pacific Northwest from Coyote Tales to Roadside Attractions

The Last Flight of the Scarlet Macaw

THE LAST FLIGHT OF THE

Scarlet Macaw

One Woman's Fight to Save

the World's Most Beautiful Bird

BRUCE BARCOTT

RANDOM HOUSE TRADE PAPERBACKS

New York

2009 Random House Trade Paperback Edition

Published in the United States by Random House
Trade Paperbacks, an imprint of The Random House
Publishing Group, a division of Random House, Inc.,
New York.

RANDOM HOUSE TRADE PAPERBACKS and colophon are
registered trademarks of Random House, Inc.

Originally published in hardcover in the United States
by Random House, an imprint of The Random House
Publishing Group, a division of Random House, Inc.,
in 2008.

LIBRARY OF CONGRESS CATALOGING-IN-
PUBLICATION DATA
Barcott, Bruce
The last flight of the scarlet macaw: one woman's fight
to save the world's most beautiful bird/Bruce Barcott.
p.   cm.
Includes index.
ISBN 978-0-8129-7313-6
1. Scarlet macaw—Conservation—Belize.   2. Wild bird
trade—Belize.   3. Cage bird industry—Belize.
4. Matola, Sharon.   I. Title.
QL696.P7B27   2008
333.95'871097282—dc22   2007019954

Printed in the United States of America

www.atrandom.com

9 8 7 6 5 4 3

Book design by Simon M. Sullivan

To Claire, with all my heart

Contents

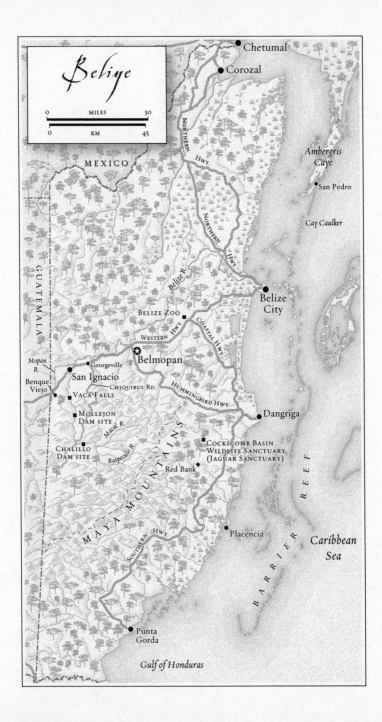

Belize

MILES	
0	30
0	45
KM	

Chetumal

Corozal

MEXICO

Ambergris Caye

San Pedro

Cay Caulker

GUATEMALA

NORTHERN HWY

NORTHERN HWY

Belize R.

BELIZE ZOO

COASTAL HWY

WESTERN HWY

Belize City

Mopan R.

Georgeville

Belmopan

San Ignacio

CHIQUIBUL RD.

Benque Viejo

VACA FALLS

HUMMINGBIRD HWY

MOLLEJON DAM SITE

Macal R.

CHALILLO DAM SITE

Raspaculo R.

Dangriga

COCKSCOMB BASIN WILDLIFE SANCTUARY (JAGUAR SANCTUARY)

Red Bank

MAYA MOUNTAINS

B A R R I E R   R E E F

SOUTHERN HWY

Placencia

Caribbean Sea

Punta Gorda

Gulf of Honduras

THE SCARLET MACAW LOOKS like a creature dreamed up by Dr. Seuss. It's a red parrot with wings tipped buttercup yellow and royal blue. Its black beak hooks around its jaw like a saber tooth. Its eyes are the color of egg yolks. Its tail shoots out of its body like a torch. A macaw is about the size of a housecat. It possesses a bill capable of cracking bones and a tongue as dextrous as a human thumb. Macaws mate for life, and those lives can be incredibly long—fifty years or more. They travel in large packs, dozens strong, and when they gather to eat seeds their bodies speckle the canopy like plump red cherries. If birds formed villages, a town of macaws would thrum with happy marriages and lively conversation.

Few creatures can match the macaw's powers of enchantment. The bird possesses a childlike, inquisitive nature and an uncanny ability to mimic human speech. Its powers of reason and memory mark it as one of the smartest birds alive. For more than five hundred years we've stolen macaws from the wild and made them our pets, jungle souvenirs squawking on perches in our dining rooms and parlors. Columbus brought back a pair from the New World as a gift for Queen Isabella and King Ferdinand. In sixteenth-century Flemish paintings, they appeared as symbols of romantic love. Today they are travel brochure superstars, icons of tropical beauty beckoning tourists to hop a southbound plane.

For thousands of years, a handful of charismatic animals have captured the human imagination through their combination of beauty, elusiveness, and ferocity. In aboriginal cultures they're honored with special respect and reverence. In modern society they serve as embodiments of untrammeled wilderness. North America has the bear and the eagle. Central and South America have the jaguar and the macaw. When I see macaws in the wild, a ripple of joy runs through me. Macaws reassure us. Wherever they fly, raw jungle still survives.

They won't fly much longer. Scarlet macaws are disappearing from Central America. In most countries they're down to one or two populations. Belize has two hundred wild scarlet macaws. So does Guatemala. Mexico has less than a hundred. El Salvador has none. The macaws are vanishing quickly and quietly. Only a few field biologists understand the extent of the loss. The bird's disappearance in Central America has been masked by its relative abundance in South America. Healthy populations in the Amazon basin keep the scarlet macaw off international endangered species lists. Meanwhile, the bird winks out in Mesoamerica, a region that reveres the macaw as much as Americans cherish the bald eagle.

Scarlet macaws aren't the only creatures in trouble, of course. Many scientists believe we're in the midst of the sixth great extinction, a massive species snuff-out of a magnitude that happens every hundred million years or so. Of the 40,177 species assessed in 2006 by the World Conservation Union, 16,119 were listed as threatened with extinction. Despite the best efforts of conservationists, the rate of biodiversity loss is speeding up. Over the past five hundred years, most extinctions have been limited to oceanic islands. Over the past twenty years, continental extinctions have become as common as island extinctions. Of the world's ten thousand species of birds, about one thousand are expected to die out within the next three human generations. Nearly three-quarters of the world's commercial fish stocks are overfished or have collapsed completely. Scientists give large carnivores—tigers, lions, grizzlies—one more century to live, two at most.

We kill some animals outright, but mostly we just destroy their homes. Scarlet macaws are dying out in Central America because the region lost one-fifth of its forest cover between 1990 and 2005. Climate change is increasing the rate of that loss. It's already making it tougher for animals to live in the Arctic, and it's expected to do the same in Central America and the rest of the world. The U.N. Intergovernmental Panel on Climate Change estimates that 20 to 30 percent of plant and animal species will face an increased risk of extinction because of global warming. Many of those could be lost within the next fifty years. In the Native American mythology of the Pacific Northwest, colorful tales are often set in the time before the coming of the people, when characters like Coyote and Turtle had the planet blissfully to themselves. We may well be living in the time before the leaving of the animals.

When trouble seems intractable, sometimes the best thing to do is go somewhere else and see how other people work the problem. Finding a spot isn't difficult. The same story of species loss unfolds in the rain-soaked mountains of Kauai, the Andean highlands of Peru, and the windswept taiga above the Arctic Circle. In my case, fate brought me to a tiny Central American country often ignored by the rest of the world. I watched as the forces of global capitalism and international environmentalism battled for six years over the survival of the last scarlet macaws in Belize. At the center of it all was a woman who ran a charming little zoo.

Part I

*I*F YOU FEEL A NEED to escape the law, elude creditors, hide assets, or shed the skin of your humdrum life, you could do worse than run away to Belize. Belize is a tiny nation tucked between Guatemala, Mexico, and the Caribbean Sea. It's firmly attached to Central America but considers itself a Caribbean island, like a chicken that thinks it's a duck. For more than a hundred years Belize was known as British Honduras, one of the most remote outposts of the British Empire, which explains why it's the only Latin American nation to embrace English as its official language.

It's difficult to overstate the smallness of the place. Imagine a country the size of Massachusetts with the population of Corpus Christi, Texas. Give it an army of seven hundred soldiers and a seat in the United Nations and you start to get an idea of Belize. Centuries ago more than one million Maya populated this part of Central America. Today fewer than three hundred thousand Belizeans spread themselves among the country's river towns and tin-shack villages. Two-thirds of the country is covered by jungle.

Belize goes unnoticed by the rest of the world, and over the years the country has parlayed its obscurity into an attractive asset. For those shipwrecked on the shoals of life, Belize offers a new beginning. The country teems with adventurous refugees who've set up shop in the middle of the Central American jungle. British innkeepers, Mennonite farmers, Chinese shopkeepers, Lebanese entrepreneurs, American missionaries, Canadian aid workers, and Dutch scientists live peacefully alongside the nation's longer-established residents, the Garifuna artists, Maya cacao growers, Mestizo plantation managers, and Creole politicians who make up the majority of the country's population. Belize draws the eccentric, the madcap, and the downright mad. In this colorful human menagerie it takes some doing to stand out, but there is one woman who manages to delight, enrage, captivate, frustrate, and inspire her fellow Belizeans more than anyone else. She's the proprietor of the Belize Zoo. Her name is Sharon Matola.

Sharon shares her office with a three-legged jaguar named Angel. When the screen door bangs, Angel limps up a cleated ramp that connects the jaguar habitat to the office, a plywood shack on stilts. When she sees Sharon, Angel rolls over and stretches like a dog wanting its belly scratched. Sharon will toss Angel a piece of chicken through the wire fence that separates them. The jaguar catches the meat in her jaws with a *clop*. Visitors to Sharon's office often ask to pet Angel, which Sharon discourages. "Never pet a jaguar," she once told me, "unless you're willing to feed her your hand."

Sharon speaks fluent Russian and once worked as a lion tamer for a traveling Mexican circus. She sings to wild jaguars to soothe them. As a young woman she married a dentist and lived in a tidy house in Iowa City. When she grew restless she started hopping freight trains to Florida. She once smuggled a spider monkey across the Mexican border by swimming the Rio Grande with the animal balanced on her head. She's an expert in mycology, the study of fungi, and is considered one of the world's foremost authorities on both the scarlet macaw and the Baird's tapir, a three-toed ungulate with a ridiculous floppy snout. Most of that knowledge she picked up while walking through the Central American jungle carrying little more than a machete.

Sharon is more at home in the jungle than most of us are in our mother's kitchen. An American by birth, she's spent the past quarter century in the raw tropical landscape of Central America. In the fall of 1982 she left the United States to work as an assistant on a nature documentary being filmed in Belize. At the end of the shoot, the director left her in possession of a jaguar, two macaws, a ten-foot boa constrictor, and seventeen other animals. "Once you domesticate wild animals, they can't care for themselves in the wild," Sharon told me. "If you turn them out they'll starve." So she painted a sign that said BELIZE ZOO and stuck it beside the lonely road that runs from Belize City to the Guatemalan border. People came.

Today the zoo exhibits 125 individual animals and hosts more than seventy thousand visitors every year—more than one-quarter of Belize's entire population. It is the country's most visited tourist attraction and one of the region's most prestigious scientific research stations. Belizean children idolize Sharon Matola. She invites them to the zoo and holds a tarantula in her palm, wraps a boa around her leg, and speaks to April the tapir as her friend. In the eyes of children she lives a magical life, padding through her own zoo like Willy Wonka strolling the chocolate factory floor. Sharon often buzzes through the countryside on a Kawasaki 650 motorcycle, and when children see her coming they jump and wave and shout her name: *Zoo Lady!*

I met Sharon in 2002 on a reporting trip to Belize. Ari Hershowitz put me on to her. Hershowitz is a scruffy, bearded guy I met years ago while writing a story about a gray whale nursery in Mexico. A multinational corporation wanted to build a salt factory in a calving lagoon. Hershowitz, an organizer for the Natural Resources Defense Council (NRDC), was one of the people who stopped it. Over the years we kept in touch. One day I called and found him in an expansive mood. He had a new project. An international energy company wanted to build a dam that would flood one of the last great sections of unbroken jungle in Central America. "It's a small dam but the damage would be enormous," he said. "This river valley is like a cradle of life. It's filled with jaguars, tapirs, scarlet macaws. They'd all be wiped out by the dam."

"Where's the river?" I asked.

"Belize."

I fumbled for an atlas. "Belize?" I said, flipping to the index. "What part of Belize?"

"Middle of the country, about ten miles from the Guatemalan border," Hershowitz said. "Seriously, you should go check it out. It's a two-hour flight from Houston." He paused. "It's a former British colony. Everybody speaks English."

"Who's fighting the dam?"

"We're working with a coalition of groups down there, but there's one woman who's spearheading things. Her name's Sharon Matola. She's kind of the Doctor Doolittle of Belize."

I reached for a pen. "Any other interesting characters?"

Hershowitz chuckled. "How much time you got?"

Later that week I made a few phone calls to Belize, which is an experience not unlike playing the slots. You dial and dial, and once
in a while the call goes through. Everyone I talked to either loved
or despised Sharon Matola. "She's our Joan of Arc," one woman
told me. Another man practically spat when he mentioned "that
woman." A little online research revealed that the Belizean newspapers were equally divided. Some praised the Zoo Lady and her
anti-dam crusade. Others blamed her for all of the nation's ills.
Banks wouldn't lend Belize money because of Sharon Matola.
Children went hungry because of Sharon Matola. The *Belize Times,*
the Belizean government mouthpiece, called her a modern-day
colonialist and a traitor to the nation. A government spokesman
labeled her "an enemy of the people."

It was that phrase—"an enemy of the people"—more than anything else, I think, that convinced me to fly to Belize and track
down the Zoo Lady. Over the next six years I would come to ap-
preciate Sharon Matola in all her complexity. She is a strange and
enchanting woman. She can display more tenacity, courage, generosity, and love than seems possible for one person. She can be
warm, goofy, and funny. She can also be impossibly stubborn and
self-righteous. I didn't know that at the beginning. All I knew was
that if any government hated and feared a woman that much, I
wanted to meet her.

According to the World Conservation Union (IUCN),* the most
respected scientific organization tracking species extinction, one
in every four mammal species and one in eight bird species face a

---

*Although its full name is the International Union for the Conservation of
Nature and Natural Resources, the IUCN is commonly known as the World
Conservation Union.

high risk of extinction in the near future. Plants and animals are disappearing at a rate at least a hundred times the planet's natural, or background, extinction rate. The problem has become known as the "sixth extinction crisis" because it follows previous waves of species disappearance in the Ordovician, Devonian, Permian, Triassic, and Cretaceous periods. Those extinctions happened over geologic time. This one is happening in the blink of an eye.

At times the earth's fate seems so dire and inexorable that I'm tempted to throw up my hands and say to hell with it. The forces driving the sixth extinction possess so much money and power that fighting them requires a willing suspension of disbelief. The odds are so long that if you look at them too hard you'll lose your mind. Every once in a while, though, I meet a rare subspecies of human who offers hope. It's almost never a politician or a scientist. It's almost always a woman without credentials. They're often self-taught researchers who become experts through years of hard experience and close observation. They're the ones who scoop up a jar of brown water from a ditch and ask impertinent questions about what's in it. Because they don't know protocol they barge in and do what nobody else has the courage to do. They don't ask permission. When government authorities demand to know what gives them the right to speak, they don't flash advanced degrees. They straighten their shoulders and say, I have the right because I walk on this earth and I breathe this air.

My first phone conversation with Sharon fell short of dazzling. I caught her on her way out of town, and over a crackly connection she gave me the quick-and-dirty info most reporters require. We agreed to talk later at length. Weeks passed. We didn't talk. And then one day she called back and said she was going into the field in a few weeks to track the migration of scarlet macaws across the Maya Mountain divide. "I can't take you on the whole trip but you can come along on the first few days if you want," she said. "We'll be going up the river that would be destroyed by the dam."

"What should I bring?" I asked.

She thought for a second. "Bug repellent," she said.

The Chalillo Dam was a proposed 150-foot-high concrete impoundment dam that would block the Macal River, the main artery draining the western slope of the Maya Mountains. The dam would produce 6 megawatts of electricity, enough to power at least six thousand households. A deep reservoir would rise behind the dam and turn twelve miles of the Macal and six miles of its tributary, the Raspaculo, into a bathtub. Drowned in that tub would be a valley teeming with tapirs, jaguars, peccaries, and scarlet macaws. The macaws would feel the brunt of it, according to the dam's opponents. A rare subspecies nests in trees near the river and nowhere else in Belize. Proponents of the dam argued that the birds would simply make new nests in trees above the floodline.

The corporation developing the dam was Fortis, a power company based in Newfoundland, Canada. In 1999, Fortis purchased Belize's electrical utility, Belize Electricity Limited (BEL), as part of the Belizean government's privatization program. Fortis planned to spend $25 million to build the dam.

I called Sharon from an airport pay phone. She was too busy to see me. "I'm showing Prince Andrew around the zoo," she said. She wasn't kidding. Members of the royal family sometimes stop by during tours of the former colony. "Why don't you come by tomorrow morning?"

I made my way by rental car to Belize City, the nation's largest city and notoriously dangerous cultural capital. The sign on the outskirts of town read BELIZE CITY, POPULATION 70,000: WORKING FOR A BETTER CITY. Founded 350 years ago in a mosquito-ridden swamp near the mouth of the Belize River, the city exists because seventeenth-century sea merchants found it a convenient spot to anchor while loading timber. Today Belize City is a teeming town of stilted wood houses pinched together along narrow broken streets just inches above sea level. The land is so saturated that the dead lie entombed in surface vaults at the edge of town.

I turned on the radio. "No suspect has been identified in the pedal-by shooting that left one man dead in Belize City yester-day. . . ." A string of soccer scores followed, and then a public service announcement. "The Belize dollar is *strong*," declared the announcer. "Show your pride. Purchase your goods in Belizean dollars and exchange American currency at the official rate of two Belizean dollars for one American." There are few things in this world that can be called dead certainties. One is that when the government starts running ads boasting of the local dollar's strength, the local dollar is about as mighty as a kitten in a river.

I switched off the radio and took in the scene around me. Uni-formed schoolchildren walked along the curb. Stately black women crossed the street holding umbrellas like shields against the sun. Shirtless men with long dreadlocks wove their bicycles among streetside fruit vendors. Deep gutters and open canals crosshatched the city, filled with turbid water and menacing, well-muscled crabs.

The streets of Belize City are laid out like a tangle of snakes. Most are unmarked. There is no commercially produced map, al-though a crude letter-size rendering of the city's layout circulates around the city like tourist samizdat. If you are lucky enough to acquire a blurred photocopy, you may learn to guard it as you do your passport.

I cut across a canal, caught a whiff of its stink, and turned left, scanning for a street sign. An old man with gray dreadlocks wan-dered into the middle of the street, barked something hostile, then continued on his way. I tugged at my shirt, sodden from the tropical heat. Another turn. Didn't I just cross this bridge?

At an abandoned Texaco station I approached a man squatting beside a display of carved wooden dolphins on a filthy blanket. "I'm trying to find the Chateau Caribbean," I said. "I wonder if you—"

"Where you goin', mon?"

"The Chateau Caribbean."

He cocked his head and squinted at me.

"No, no. Don' know it, mon."

I glanced at the map. "It looks like it's near the Radisson."

"Radi-*sown*?" he said, and grunted. The Radisson Fort George is the only business-class hotel in Belize City. In a country where a government job pays twenty dollars a day, tips from a tourist's pocket can support an entire family. The Radisson supports a micro-economy of taxi drivers, tour guides, diving charters, and folk artists. Everyone knows where the Radisson is.

"Yeh mon, shtret down heah, keep di rye, you see di weh," he said. Belize's first language is English. Belize City's first language is an English dialect so thoroughly mashed with Creole that it's difficult to understand.

The Chateau Caribbean was a once-grand seaside hotel that glory had long since abandoned. One of the *b*'s had fallen off its sign. Its pink paint curled. Inside, nothing moved. Not the bellhop, not the ceiling fans, not the air.

"Credit machine not working today," said the desk clerk. She was a heavyset woman who, like the dolphin salesman, avoided direct eye contact. "You can pay cash?"

"Sure," I said, unzipping my sweat-soaked money belt. "Belizean or U.S.?"

As the evening sun fell into the sea, I strolled around a peninsula jutting into the warm Caribbean Sea. Above me frigate birds spread their great wings and rode the wind to distant homes in the cayes, the tiny offshore islands that form the Western Hemisphere's largest barrier reef. Belize has a strange relationship with the sea. In proclamation and lore, Belizeans are forever declaring their love for the Caribbean. In Belize City, which is dominated by the descendants of black Caribs, to be Belizean is to be Caribbean. The national anthem hails Belize as the "land of the free by the Carib Sea." Yet when it comes to the sea itself, the Caribbean is merely the place where the city ends. It's less a shoreline than a giant curb. Again and again I tried to walk the land's margin and failed. The sidewalk disintegrated into jagged concrete. A skim of plastic bags, used condoms, and empty bottles floated on the tide. Foamy gutter runoff streamed around breakwater boulders. I kept to the shore until I was stopped by a fence topped with razor wire. I cut back to the hotel through a rusty playground.

Outside the Chateau Caribbean, a column of smoke caught my eye. It was a fire in the cayes. I walked to a nearby pier, where an old Creole man stood staring out at the water.

"What do you suppose is burning out there?" I asked.

"Where?" he said.

"Out there in the cayes. The smoke."

He looked to where I was pointing. After a moment he turned to me and said, "No smoke, sir. They clouds."

"No, no. Not the puffy white things. Look *there*. Black smoke coming up. See where it hits the pressure layer and spreads south?"

He looked again. He frowned. It was as if he had been trained to deny evidence of calamity for fear of scaring the tourists.

"No fire," he insisted. "Clouds."

Back at the Chateau, I rinsed off the day's sweat and fell into bed. In the middle of the night I rose from a fitful sleep and switched on the light. The room stayed dark. I tried another light. It didn't work either. I turned over and went back to sleep. In the morning I awoke to find both lights burning.

CHAPTER 2

*T*HE ZOO WASN'T HARD TO FIND. I aimed the car west toward Guatemala and drove about thirty miles before spotting a crudely fenced compound in the middle of a tropical savannah. BELIZE ZOO, the sign said. A HAVEN FOR WILDLIFE. I checked in at the front gate and waited for Sharon.

It was still early, but the warm breath of the day already dampened my shirt. Blackbirds made a sound like water dripping, *quirt quirt,* in the trees. I glanced at the framed photos and letters hanging on the concrete wall: naturalist Gerald Durrell playing with the monkeys, thank-you notes from Harrison Ford and Dolly Parton.

Sharon swept around the corner. "Sorry to keep you waiting," she said. "We had a new tapir come in this morning. He was hit by a car. Blind in both eyes. Don't ask me where we're going to put him. Plus the e-mail's not working and I've got an urgent message to get to the vet. Oh, and four busloads of tourists are coming in an hour."

"I'm Bruce," I said, holding out my hand.

"Oh. Right. Sharon," she said, and looked down at her hands. They held a bucket of raw chicken. She was on her way to feed the animals.

"Why don't you follow me," she said.

A tall woman with a lightly freckled face and wide, strong shoulders, Sharon possessed a rugged beauty that hadn't deserted her in middle age. Her forearms were crosshatched with scars. "Jaguars and pumas," she explained. "Something startles them, they tense and sink their claws, and you have to pry them off." She wore black gumboots smeared with mud.

I followed her to the tapir pen. A peculiar-looking relative of the horse and rhinoceros, the tapir is sometimes called a living fossil because it stopped evolving about fifty-five million years ago. "We can get right in with them, it's okay," she said. Sharon threw one leg over the fence and hopped into the soft mud. I'd seen tapirs before, at Seattle's Woodland Park Zoo. Their sharp teeth and stupendous girth had always impressed me. "I'll hang back here," I said.

"Hey, Bullet!" she cried.

A male tapir trotted up to her. Sharon pulled a carrot out of her back pocket. The tapir used its snout to pull it into its jaws. He munched contentedly.

Sharon explained that years ago the tapir had been shot in the head and left to die. A local man found him and brought him to the zoo. The bullet is still there. "That's why he's named Bullet Head," she said. "He's a little brain-damaged."

"Where's April?" Sharon called out to the female. April the tapir is the zoo's most famous resident. Shortly after Sharon started the zoo in 1983, a hunter discovered a young tapir dying in the bush. A parasite known as a screwworm had burrowed under its hide and was eating the tapir alive. The hunter hoisted the tapir into the bed of his truck and drove it to the zoo. "A screwworm is nasty," Sharon said. "It'll bore straight for the brain and make a huge wound. When she came to me I could stick my entire fist inside her body." Tapirs are notoriously shy around humans. Like most Belizeans, Sharon had never actually set eyes on one.

"I decided I wasn't going to let her die," she recalled. Using a cattle bottle, she fed the tapir banana milk shakes spiked with vitamins and medicine. Sharon slept next to the tapir in her own room. The home remedy worked. The screwworm died. The tapir lived. Sharon named it April to mark the month the animal arrived.

The Belize Zoo is filled with Aprils and Bullet Heads: misfits, poaching casualties, orphans, abandoned pets, and problem jaguars who developed a taste for cattle and household pets. None of the animals were snatched from the wild. There are no penguins or tigers or bears. Every species in the zoo occurs naturally in Belize.

At the spider monkey exhibit, the sight of the Zoo Lady sent the primates into a frenzy. One young monkey leapt from the crown of an oak tree and caught a lower branch in a perfect tail-hook landing. Swaying from his tail, he looked at Sharon hopefully. She gave him what he wanted. "Whoa! My goodness. You showoff! You big baby showoff!" she said. With the animals, the Zoo Lady can be coy, she can scold, she can gush. She's a flirt.

We strolled past a small green pond, and I pointed out a crocodile sunning itself on a rock. "Morelet's croc," Sharon said, referring to the species. "That girl's a volunteer."

"She escaped *into* the zoo?"

"Yep. She can leave. She's got the option."

"Why does she stay?"

"Food, I imagine," Sharon said. "The eating's good here. She's got fish in the pond and at five o'clock the agoutis start bouncing around." Five o'clock is closing time at the zoo. Once the humans depart, a swing shift of agoutis roams the gravel paths. Agoutis are rodents the size of small dogs. They look like a cross between a rat and a pot-bellied pig. They are as ubiquitous in Belize as squirrels are in the United States, and their local name—"bushrabbit"— indicates that humans as well as crocodiles find them good eating.

We came to the tayra, a rat-eating weasel. "Hello, sugar," Sharon said. The tayra trundled up to the fence and sniffed for handouts. "Sweetheart." Sharon tossed it a bloody chicken part. Despite her cooing tone, the Zoo Lady was feeling disenchanted with tayras. During a recent field trip to study scarlet macaws, she watched two young macaws take their first leap out of the nest. "A nesting pair will work all year just to bring one or two chicks to the point of fledging," she said. "And there are only two hundred macaws in all of Belize. The entire species is struggling to hold on. That's one of the main reasons I'm fighting the dam." Sharon recounted how she watched through binoculars as the two fledglings tumbled out of their nest and fluttered awkwardly to the jungle floor. Waiting below, a tayra tracked each macaw's arc like a center fielder running down a fly ball. The fledglings were eaten immediately. The memory made Sharon fall silent for a moment. Then she spoke. "Bam! Two wiped out just like that," she said. "It's a hard life out there."

Without thinking, I moved my hands toward the tayra's cage. Sharon caught me. "You don't want to be stupid and put your fingers there," she said. "You don't know how strong those claws are."

A crackle came from the radio at Sharon's hip. One of the keepers had a question about stringing aviary nets. Sharon murmured an answer as we moved down the path past the keel-billed toucan. I'M YOUR NATIONAL BIRD, read the sign outside the toucan's netting. AREN'T YOU PROUD THAT I'M A BELIZEAN TOO?

Around the next corner we came upon a muddy pen of about thirty white-lipped peccaries. Central America's version of a wild boar, peccaries travel in enormous packs sometimes a hundred strong. They are dirty, ornery beasts. Their hair is as long and coarse as pine needles. An open gland on their back secretes a musky oil that the peccaries continually rub over themselves, their packmates, and any nearby tree or stump. All that gland-rubbing produces a powerful stink. "Do you smell it?" Sharon asked.

I did. Pungent. I inhaled a little deeper. "Wait for it," she said. "When the wind—"

"Oh! Jesus!" My head jerked back.

"—shifts."

"I used to be able to reach in and pet these guys," she said. But peccaries live in a strict social structure ruled by an alpha male, and the new alpha male was a boar who didn't tolerate petting. "That's him," she said, pointing to an angry beast clacking his jaws.

"Does he have a name?"

"Saddam," she said. Saddam flashed his teeth. "Oh, stop it, you lovely thing," Sharon said. "Look, Saddam, Bruce doesn't think you're disgusting. Bruce thinks you're fascinating." Saddam paid no mind to me. It was Sharon he wanted to intimidate. She turned to leave. "If we're reincarnated," she said, "I want to come back as a peccary. Nice life."

On the way to Sharon's office, we stopped to see a jabiru stork named Boomer. At five feet tall, jabiru storks are the tallest flying birds in the Americas. Their height isn't the first thing you notice about them, though. It's the beak: a medieval dagger half as long as the bird's body. "Boomer's parents were shot back in '93 near Burrell Boom," a village between Belize City and the zoo, she said.

"Does he go after fish?" I asked.

"Fish?" Sharon said. "Fish nothing. This guy's a killer."

A few years ago Sharon walked past the jabiru exhibit and noticed a tall German tourist standing on the pier that juts into the stork's habitat. He shuffled about looking for the bird. Sharon glanced above him and, to her horror, saw Boomer perched on the pier's topnetting, jabbing like a spear fisherman at the man's head. "Boomer was trying to skewer the poor guy," she said. "Weren't you? Weren't you, Boom?" The bird eyed us warily. "The guy wasn't even aware of it. The only thing that saved him was the fact that he kept moving, just slightly, just enough to make the bird miss." I looked up. The net had been replaced by corrugated tin.

Sharon kept two offices at the zoo. She shared her official office near the front gate with the zoo's business manager, Claudia Duenas. Her second office was a staff secret. Sharon called it her *oficina*. It was a little hut hidden under fan palms back by the commissary. She went there to think, write, and escape the incessant demands of the zoo. "I like it here," she told me. I did too. During afternoon squalls, raindrops drummed against the tin roof. The floor's wooden planks offered up an oddly comforting groan. The office looked like a diorama of Sharon's life. Expedition tents, mud-caked sneakers, sleeping bags, water bottles, and plastic five-gallon buckets hung from the rafters. Plain wooden shelves sagged under thick books with titles like *Behavior of Captive Wild Animals* and *Checklist of the Vascular Plants of Belize*. Research papers sprouted between the books like white weeds. On an ice chest sat a rock hammer and a tapir skull. The ice chest was labeled "Field Samples—Do Not Eat." Angel the three-legged jaguar paced behind chicken wire at the far end of the *oficina*. A doggie door let Angel come and go as she pleased. Sharon's desk was buried under a landslide of reports, papers, and field notes. Above it she'd pinned a newspaper clipping: "KEEPER LOSES ARM IN ATTACK BY ZOO ANIMAL." Near the door hung a poster for a Belizean politician named Ralph Fonseca. Over everything, as if tipped from a giant salt shaker, were insect droppings, termite wings, and the spun-glass husks of dead spiders.

Sharon rummaged through a bin of rolled maps. She found a

British Forces survey of the Chalillo area and spread it on the ice chest. It had a lot of green space and very few roads. The legend indicated the green stuff was "medium jungle," a technical classification for subtropical forests sixty feet high.

"Let's get one thing straight," Sharon said. "I'm not against all dams. They want to build a fifty-meter-high dam. With a dam that big you're usually talking about hundreds of megawatts. If it were giving that much power, as much as you need for all of Belize, I wouldn't stand in the way. But we're talking about *six* megawatts!"

She pointed to the river, a kinked hose that separated the arid Mountain Pine Ridge from the damp, medium-jungly Chiquibul Forest Reserve. "That's where we're headed tomorrow," she said. Through a fortuitous combination of geography, soil conditions, and weather patterns, the Macal River valley had been left untouched by human development for nearly a thousand years. As vast swaths of Central American jungle fell to slash-and-burn agriculture, the valley remained a secret sanctuary for the region's endangered species. Tapirs abounded there. Jaguars thrived. Scarlet macaws nested in ceiba trees on the banks of this river and in no other place in Belize. "I've been all over Central America," Sharon told me. "Nothing matches the abundance and the biodiversity of this place. It's like nature on overdrive."

That night I stayed up late reading books purchased at the zoo's gift shop. *The Mammals of Belize, The Birds of Belize,* and *The ABC's to the Vegetation of Belize* were hand-stapled field guides illustrated with clip art and crude drawings. The author of all three was Sharon Matola. When I asked her about it later, she told me she'd gotten fed up with the fact that Belizean students learned biology from hand-me-down British textbooks. "Belizean kids can read all about rabbits in Wales but don't have any books that tell them about the agoutis in their own backyard," she said. "So I wrote them myself." The mammal guide explained how animals in North America and South America evolved separately for 130 million years until the Isthmus of Panama rose from the sea about seven million years ago. That land bridge allowed anteaters, possums, monkeys, and rodents to migrate north from South America, and let peccaries, brocket deer, and other mammals come south from North America. Scientists call it the great faunal interchange. "What lives in Belize today," Sharon wrote, "is largely a result of this animal walkabout."

In the morning, Sharon and I lashed tents, supply bins, and food to the top of a Land Rover. The plan was for me to accompany her for the first few days of a two-week expedition to the Maya Mountain divide, where she hoped to confirm the daily migration route of the scarlet macaws.

A few others joined us. Tony Garel, the zoo's reptile expert, hoped to get a close-up look at the crocodiles and snakes lurking in the Macal Valley's lush green shadows. A wiry mestizo with a pencil mustache, Garel was the zoo's longest-tenured employee. He often ran day-to-day operations when Sharon was away. Brian Holland, a geologist who owned a dolomite mine in the southern town of Punta Gorda, came along to examine the bedrock exposed along the riverbank. Holland was an expatriate American with a cheerful mien and a disarming smile. Naturalist Chapal Bol worked at a field station operated by London's Natural History Museum. The museum owned one of the few vehicles rugged enough to get us to the river, and Sharon had talked Bol into driving us to our put-in spot. Greg Sho, a short, powerfully built Maya, was known as one of Central America's greatest woodsmen. He often trained British commandos to survive in the jungle. Sho was there to make sure we all came back alive.

We jammed ourselves and our gear into the Rover and set out. By midmorning the sun was already beating the country into submission. We rolled down the Western Highway with the windows open, shouting to be heard over the breeze.

"I hear you had a run-in with a tommygoff last month, Chapal," Holland said. In Belize, "tommygoff" is slang for a deadly snake, in this case the fer-de-lance. Named for its spearpoint head, the fer-de-lance is the most lethal snake in Central and South America. Its venom contains both an anticoagulant and a necrotizing agent, which means it rots the flesh of its victims and causes massive internal bleeding simultaneously. It's a nasty way to go.

"Not me," said Bol. "Forestry logger. Out working the chainsaw. Snake bit him in the upper thigh. Man chainsawed the snake's head off."

"How'd the logger turn out?" I asked, looking for reassurance.

"Not too good," said Bol. "He survived three days. His head swelled up like this"—Bol took both hands off the wheel in order to approximate the size of a basketball—"and his arms turned purple."

"Didn't have a doctor around?" said Holland.

"Yeah, doctor came," said Bol, "but did him no good. Doctor just watched him die." I glanced at my bare legs. I was the only one in the Rover wearing shorts.

"Did you bring a hat, Bruce?" Sharon said.

I shook my head.

She shot me a look of concern. "Maybe we can find one for you," she said. "I never go into the field without a hat. Do you know about botflies?"

Greg Sho, who had to this point spoken not a single word, chuckled. "The botfly," he said, almost fondly.

"Here's the deal with botflies," said Sharon. "They're the size of house flies. They lay their eggs on the legs of mosquitoes. When the mosquito lands on you to take a bite, the botfly eggs attach to your skin. Your body heat triggers the eggs. They hatch and the maggots burrow into your skin. They stay there for like forty-two days eating your flesh."

"And you know this because—?" I said.

"I had five in my head one time."

I caught Greg Sho's eye. He gave me a head nod like "Welcome to Belize."

"Here's the bad news about botflies," Sharon said. "When the maggots get in there it feels like someone is trapped in your head with an ice pick trying to break out."

"How do you get them out?" I asked. "Surgery?"

"Tobacco," said Sho. "They have breathing holes. You wet the tobacco and put it over the holes."

With the tobacco poultice in place, Sharon said, you just had to wait twelve hours. Then you could squeeze them out like maggoty blackheads.

A silence fell over the car. As we rolled westward toward the Maya Mountains, the serene pine savannah gave way to thicker, darker forest interrupted by clearings of green pasture. Well-kept barns and farmhouses replaced the plywood shacks that line the highway outside Belize City. This was the Cayo district, Belize's pastoral Bible belt. Belize's tropical climate, English tongue, and entrenched poverty brought a lot of Christian missionaries from the United States. Attracted by the sunshine, cheap land, and freedom, many of them stayed here and set up little churches. In Cayo, low-watt radio stations broadcast sermons from the American South, and iguanas sun themselves on billboards quoting scripture.

At the village of Georgeville, we turned onto the Chiquibul road and climbed into the Maya Mountains. Chapal Bol tested the Land Rover's springs on a road cratered like the moon. Brian Holland smiled. "Now we're really getting bakabush," he said.

I braced against the roof to keep from knocking my skull. The jungle around us rose three stories tall, broken now and then by lonely outposts of civilization. We drove by a farm run by a German religious institute. I asked Holland about it. "Belize tends to become a black hole for odd foundations, little religious sects, and strange people," he said. "I had a neighbor in Punta Gorda a couple years ago. Nice guy, late thirties, American. Said he was a screenwriter. He'd come over and do yoga with my wife. He kept a low profile, but it wasn't like he was hiding out or anything. And then one day he just up and vanished. Turned out he *was* hiding out. The guy was on the FBI's Ten Most Wanted list."

The Mosquito Coast was shot here back in the mid-eighties, and during my sojourns in Belize it often seemed like the movie had never wrapped. The film's main character, Allie Fox, played by Harrison Ford, escaped the crass commercialization of America by moving his family to the Central American bush. "The jungle," Fox said. "It would take courage to go there. Four o'clock in the morning courage." Belize is chockablock with Allie Foxes. Some run Chinese groceries, others make a go at ecotourism, Internet gambling, online drug sales, or banana farming. A few lie low and hope not to be found by the DEA or the FBI. Belize sells its sovereign-nation services to any who can pay the price. Among shipping merchants Belize is renowned for offering one of the world's cheapest flags of convenience. The country's passports move in a notoriously open market. Asian immigrants trying to slip into the United States often use Belizean passports, which can be bought over the Internet for $15,000 to $40,000. Questions are rarely asked. In 1999, an accused Sikh terrorist sitting in a Toronto jail wired $40,000 and a passport application to Belize. Passport officials banked the money and mailed the man proof of his Belizean citizenship. Canada returned the favor by deporting the accused troublemaker to Belize City.

Some days Belize feels like an old Caribbean port town: poor, forgotten, engulfed in an aura of postcolonial decay. Other days it's the Wild West, a frontier land not yet harnessed by the reins of regulation, lawsuits, safety, and decorum. A local man once told me, "There's a kind of freedom in Belize that doesn't exist anywhere else in the world." In Belize you're on your own.

Five miles upstream from the dam site, we shoved off in kayaks. Our route would take us up the Macal to its confluence with the Raspaculo. From there we'd push up the smaller river to the limit of the proposed reservoir's reach. "If Chalillo goes up, everything we see will be inundated," Sharon said.

During the dry season, the Macal is a gentle river. In its fattest sections it stretches as wide as the length of three pickup trucks. As we paddled upstream, I dangled my legs over the side to cool off. The river was so shallow that my feet bounced along the rocky bottom.

Sharon scanned the treetops for birds. Nothing yet. She zigzagged shore to shore looking for tapir and jaguar tracks. At a big boulder she leaned out and grabbed something. "Otter scat!" she called, like a child finding a penny on the sidewalk.

The density of the forest around us was astonishing. In places the ridge seemed to rise straight up from the river like a green curtain ten stories tall. Thick tangles of vine-covered trees, shrubs, and tall grasses heaved out over the water. Green iguanas sat motionless on overhanging limbs and watched our curious yellow boats pass beneath them. Known in Belize as "bamboo chicken," iguanas constantly fend off a forestful of creatures bent on eating them. Hanging out over the river gives them an easy escape—they plop into the water and swim away.

At one point the river took a turn and spread itself thin over smooth pebbles. Our kayaks nudged to a halt. "Time to haul," said Tony Garel. We each grabbed a rope line and dragged the boats over the shallows.

Brian Holland, the geologist, came alongside me. "Come back in six months and you won't recognize the place," he said. "This'll be under fifteen, twenty feet of water." He looked behind him. "Isn't that right, Sharon? Gotta time this river right."

"Brian, where's your sense of adventure?" she said. Clearly this was an inside joke. Holland filled me in. Years ago he accompanied Sharon on a research expedition up this same river. Except it wasn't the same river at all. It was the Macal in the rainy season. "River was so high we couldn't get near it," he said. "Whole trees were clogging the water." The expedition team ended up cutting their way through the tall cane grass along the riverbank. "Sounds fine, right?" said Holland. "Except that grass will cut you up. Like paper cuts. Full of ticks, too."

As I bent down and took a sip from a cupped hand, I caught a glimpse of Sharon paddling to the shore. She waved me over. "Tapir tracks," she said. A muddy opening in the bank held the tapir's distinctive three-toed imprint. "Fresh ones. Probably came down to drink and swim. Poop, too. Tapirs like to poop in the river."

Tony Garel paddled past us. "Croc," he said. "Small one." He indicated a snaggle-toothed beast sunning itself on a rock twenty yards away. Garel approached with stealth and speed but the crocodile spotted him and slid into the river.

My eyes adjusted to the wildlife around us. Oropendola nests, grass pouches woven by the cinnamon-colored relative of the blackbird, teardropped from the branches of giant fig trees. Otter scat stained riverside boulders. A gray plumbeous kite dueled a short-tailed hawk for a disputed piece of prey. Their enraged shrieks and high-pitched growls rang over the water.

Greg Sho paddled ahead and returned with exciting news. "Scarlet macaws," he said. "Fifteen or more. In a fig tree."

We stroked upriver and scanned the canopy. The birds perched on the open branches of a massive fig. They put out an awful racket. The scarlet macaw sounds like one of nature's chain-smokers, their cry a throaty, blaring *rrrra*. Sharon pointed out seven more in a quamwood tree. "Two pair and one trio," she said. "If it's three, it's a family." From a hundred yards the bird's markings were unmistakable. There was the yellow of a rain slicker, the blue of indigo dye, the red of an Irish pub door.

The macaws remained in constant motion. They bobbed, they clucked, they swiveled their heads and preened one another like teenagers parked on a Saturday night. Four flew overhead in tight formation.

To see a scarlet macaw in flight is to catch a glimpse of some top-secret aircraft on a test run. Its body seems too big and its tail too long to stay aloft. Nevertheless, macaws are able fliers. Sharon had organized this expedition, in fact, to document the birds' daily commute from these nests to a feeding ground near the village of Red Bank, twenty-five miles away on the other side of the Maya Mountains. Macaws don't spend a lot of time flitting about. It takes a lot of energy to get that big body flying. They prefer to find a sturdy branch and crack seeds all afternoon. We sat for a long while and watched.

"The power company says the macaws will fly to other trees and build other nests," Sharon told me. "They make me crazy with comments like that."

It seemed a tough argument to refute. Birds nest in trees. Belize is full of trees. The trouble, Sharon said, was that the natural world holds more complexity than most of us can see with our untrained eyes. "Do you see this?" she said. She held her hand up to a clump of overhanging branches.

I saw nothing peculiar. "What am I supposed to be seeing?"

"Look closer," she said. "How do you think that log got there?"

Fifteen feet above the water, a section of pine as thick as my leg nestled in the branches of a fig tree. I scanned downriver. All along the same elevation were small twigs, pieces of grass, and clumps of leaves. It slowly dawned on me what I was seeing. "It's a tide line," I said.

"Exactly," said Sharon. During the rainy season the Macal swelled into a muddy torrent capable of ripping up large trees and stripping bank grasses clean. Because only trees with broad roots and buttresses, such as figs and ceibas, can survive such a flood, they flourish while other species are swept out to sea. Most years the lower ceiba and fig branches can withstand the high floods, but some years they can't. Some years the flood rips a branch out of its socket. That injury eventually turns into a cavity, which scarlet macaws find ideal for nesting.

"The macaws are here because of the river, but they never actually visit the river," Sharon told me. "It's too dangerous. Tayras, jaguars, pumas, ocelots. Lots of predators on the ground. Macaws drink rainwater that collects in the hollow crotches of trees." The ceibas and figs grow strong and tall with enormous smooth trunks. Their lowest branches start forty feet in the sky, an ideal setup for nest security. Without low branches, predators can't gain purchase on the tree. If intruders do find a way to climb up, the macaws will see them coming long before they reach the nest.

"The macaws don't just need trees," Sharon told me. "They need *these* trees."

Macaws aren't the flood's only beneficiaries. The surging river strips away the valley's dense grasses and shrubs, but the plants survive thanks to their dense root mats, which hold the valley's soil intact and capture the sediment turbing in the river. When the flood recedes, the combination of moist rich soil and abundant sunshine triggers explosive growth. The grasses and shrubs resprout within days and turn the valley into a natural greenhouse. During the dry season, when grasses, fruits, berries, and seedlings desiccate and wither elsewhere in the forest, the Macal River valley remains abundant. When food grows scarce, animals from all over western Belize migrate to the valley. The grasses attract tapir and brocket deer; the seeds and insects draw birds; the fruits and nuts bring peccaries and agoutis. They come to feed, and in turn become food. High-level predators come to eat those below them on the food chain. Acre for acre, there isn't a spot in Central America that thrums with more life and death than the Macal Valley. "Everything out here is driven by one thought: Eat now," Sharon told me. "It's all about food. The trees reach for the sun and throw all their leaves up top in the crown to feed on the sun. The peccaries come for the grubs, the deer come for the grass, the jaguars come for the peccaries and the deer. Eat and don't get eaten. That's the game."

We pitched our tents that night at Crocodile Camp, a riverside clearing where the water branched into dark eddies that crocodiles used for nesting. While Sharon took notes on the macaws, I followed Greg Sho across the river on a peccary quest. He'd caught a whiff of them earlier that afternoon and suspected they might be watching us through the trees.

Using a machete, Sho cleared a path to a small bog. "They're rooting," he said. I knelt down and saw fresh hoofprints in the mud. Peccary stink hung in the air. "Wait here," Sho said. He crept after the hoofprints and disappeared into the bush. I waited and listened. Three minutes later Sho reappeared at a trotting pace. He didn't stop when he reached me. "They are coming," he said.

I stood there for a moment, letting the information sink in. Meanwhile, Sho beat it to the river. I turned heel and ran as fast as I could. Vines and branches whipped my face. My feet hit the river and kept on running.

The tropical sun dipped below the trees and released its grip on the day. Freshets of cool air curled off the river. Darkness began pooling in the forest beyond camp.

Brian Holland appeared with an armload of rocks. I asked him what he was finding.

"About what I expected," he said. "Plenty of limestone and shale but no granite." Holland, a gallant geologist with silver-tipped hair, was a reluctant soldier in Sharon's anti-dam crusade. Like a lot of people I met, he was led to Belize by a series of happenstance events. He fled the United States for Sweden at the height of the Vietnam War. A consulting job brought him to Belize, where he discovered a little slice of paradise in Punta Gorda, a fishing town near the country's southern border. Sharon hadn't really recruited him, Holland told me. He'd discovered on his own that the company building the dam had no idea what kind of rock they were building the dam upon. "They're saying the river's full of good solid granite," he said, "but I've never found granite out here."

"Could dam builders make such a basic mistake?"

"Contractors are human," he said. "Engineers make mistakes. The only problem is that there's a town of fifteen thousand people living directly downriver from the dam. If the dam fails, that mistake could wipe them out in a matter of seconds."

After dinner, I picked seed ticks out of my leg. Sharon kept me company. "That's not so bad," she said, noting the dots moving up my shin. A few years ago, she told me, she and Greg Sho went on an expedition into the Bladen River Nature Reserve, a rugged forest on the western slope of the Maya Mountains. Through a series of mishaps involving tropical storms and killer bees, they found themselves ration-poor and miles off course. After traversing muddy slopes and hacking through bush, they made camp by a small creek at dusk. Dinner consisted of three soggy crackers. Sharon rolled into her hammock, exhausted and famished. But sleep wouldn't come. In the moonless night dozens of seed ticks scrabbled across her skin and probed for blood. "I switched on my headlamp and it was like I had the measles," she said. "These guys were everywhere." She decided to ignore them. Mind over matter. But the itching grew worse. "And then I thought, Wait a minute!

Ticks are crustaceans, right? Related to crabs and lobsters."
(They're arachnids, actually, related to scorpions and spiders.) A
proud smile spread across her face. "So I turned the light back on
and began picking them off my skin and popping them into my
mouth."

Brian Holland grimaced. "Ugh! Sharon."

"Took me about forty-five minutes. Ate every last one, rolled
over, and went to sleep."

"How'd they taste?" I asked.

"Like nothing," she said. "Like tasteless little pinpricks."

Later that night, around a fire, we passed a bottle of whiskey and
talked about the dam. "What are the politics of this thing?" I
asked.

"Complicated," said Tony Garel. The party currently in power,
the People's United Party (PUP), wanted the dam built. Prime
Minister Said Musa had become the project's cheerleader in chief.
The opposition United Democratic Party (UDP) had taken a
halfhearted stand against the dam, mainly because whatever Musa
and the PUP stood for, the UDP opposed.

"This is a country of two hundred and fifty thousand people,"
Sharon said. "Politics here is heavy-blooded."

"Blooded," I said. "As in violent?"

"No, no," she said. "Belizeans aren't politically violent. Especially compared to the rest of Central America. There's apathy
here. Peace, too—there's never been a civil war or kidnappings or
any of that. People have been conditioned to expect that the government will do what it wants and there's not much an average
person can do about it. I mean 'blooded' as in bloodlines. There's
an old Creole saying: 'Blood falla vein.' Blood follows the vein.
Relatives look out for one another here. There are a number of
prominent families and everybody knows whether they're PUP or
UDP because they've been that way for generations."

"Like the guy on the poster in your office?"

"Ralph Fonseca?" she said. "I don't want to talk bad about
Ralph. But yes, his family. They're old PUP. Ralph's the finance

minister and pretty much runs the country. Ralph's brother is the mayor of Belize City."

I asked her how she came to be labeled an enemy of the people.

"So you saw Norris Hall's column," she said. I nodded. She rested her head on her hand and sighed. "Norris . . ." she said. "Norris is kind of like the government's attack dog. He says what the ministers would like to say but can't because it would be too unseemly."

"Who does he work for?"

"You should ask him," she said. She grew quiet. She reached for the whiskey bottle. A reflection of the dying fire flickered in the glass. "Retribution can be tough," Sharon said.

"You want to tell me about it?" I said.

"Another time," she said. "I gotta turn in. Big day tomorrow." She rose and turned and walked into darkness.

The next morning we pushed into a river shrunk by a rainless day. As we made our way upstream the shallows came more often. We dragged the boats over stony shoals. Greg Sho told me we were lucky to hit any depth at all. "Later in the season you don't paddle," he said. "Just walk."

We came to the confluence of the Macal and the Raspaculo, a wide stretch of calm water. Sharon led us south up the Raspaculo. "In case you're thinking it might get deeper," she said, "Raspaculo means 'scrape your butt' in Spanish."

The slopes and ridges grew steeper the farther we traveled up the Raspaculo. In the distance we heard the roar of a British Forces jet. Brian Holland looked up but couldn't spot it behind the clouds. "Those BEL geologists would read that as a volcano stirring," he said, chuckling. "Of course these mountains haven't been active since the Permian." Geologist humor.

The most effective survival tool in the jungle isn't a set of sharp claws or teeth. It's camouflage. What can't be seen won't be eaten. The Maya Mountains have practiced this ancient strategy for more than a thousand years. The low, densely forested range runs eighty miles down the southern half of Belize and into northern

Guatemala. It's virtually unknown to tourists and scientists alike. There's no signature feature to draw the eye, no Matterhorn or El Capitan piercing the sky. The range excels at drawing no attention to itself. During the height of the Mayan empire the mountains held hundreds of settlements, including the city-state of Caracol. But when the Mayan city-states began their decline, humans faded away and didn't return for nearly a thousand years. Bereft of gold or silver, the hills held no allure for the Spanish conquistadors. Geological explorers discovered no coal or oil. Nineteenth-century British cartographers left the area blank except for the words "Mountainous Country Unexplored or Inhabited." The mountains called no attention to themselves. The place was invisible, left uneaten by the modern world.

The mountains were so ignored, in fact, that the first scientific exploration of the Raspaculo River basin took place only at the close of the twentieth century. In 1991 a joint scientific-military operation mounted by the Natural History Museum of London and the Royal Marines sent sixteen soldiers and scientists up the river. Sharon Matola was among them.

"The first time we came up here I didn't know what to expect," she told me as we paddled slowly upstream. "What we found just blew me away. Jaguars, pumas, river otter, howler monkeys. Keel-billed motmots and scarlet macaws. The place was like a Noah's Ark for all the endangered species driven out of the rest of Central America. There was so much life! I could barely sleep at night. Seriously. Tapirs would wander past us like they'd never seen humans before.

"That expedition was when I first saw the macaws," she continued. Sharon and Elizabeth Mallory, an American biologist on the expedition, watched as the parrots soared overhead in twos and threes. Over the next decade Mallory and the Zoo Lady returned to the Macal and Raspaculo rivers and produced some of the first field studies on scarlet macaws in the wild. It was Mallory who came up with the theory of the long-distance commute. "Elizabeth suspected that the birds were nesting here and flying over the Maya Mountain divide to feed on nuts and berries on the eastern slope," Sharon said. "Two years ago Greg and I went up to the divide and saw that it was true. The macaws crossed over the spine." The current trip was an attempt to confirm the route and prove that their earlier sighting wasn't a onetime event. "In a couple of days we should be able to see them there again."

The sun broke through the clouds at midday. We stopped to find some shade and make camp. After pitching our tents, Sharon, Brian Holland, and I wandered upstream to a crystalline waterfall. It was like nothing I'd ever seen. A small creek tumbled down an embankment into a series of gleaming bone-white pools. Each was a little bigger than the one above it: teacup to soup bowl, washbasin to bathtub to swimming hole. "Travertine," Holland explained. "The water carries calcium carbonate in solution. It mineralizes once it stops flowing." I hoisted myself over the rim of one, then another and another. The rock offered such easy grip— it was practically sticky beneath my fingers—that I felt I could spider straight up the wall. I stripped down and let the turquoise water take me. I floated for a while. A hummingbird darted around my nose. Fig branches and palm fronds swayed gently overhead.

Sharon sat on the edge of the cup. "We're still not above the reservoir," she said. "The dam would flood all this."

The next morning we went our separate ways. Sharon and Greg Sho continued upstream to the Maya Mountain divide. Brian Holland, Tony Garel, and I paddled downriver to our put-in spot where Chapal Bol waited with the Land Rover. Before we departed, Sharon told me something. "There's so much more to this than you can understand in one trip," she said. "But I know you've got a deadline and you'll do the best you can."

"What more is there?" I said.

"Come back sometime and I'll show you," she said.

CHAPTER 3

S HARON GREW UP STARVED FOR WILDLIFE. As a young girl she spent hours watching butterflies flicker in the trees outside her row house in Baltimore. She trained a squirrel named Willie to beg for peanuts at her back door. Then she taught Willie to sit on her knee. "Squirrels are rodents, they're pretty smart," she told me. In human society the term *rodent* naturally correlates with *vermin*. In Sharon's world the first thing that comes to mind is *high intelligence*.

Her father worked at a brewery. Her mother was a college administrator. They raised Sharon and her sister and brother in a city riven by the racial strife of the sixties. One of her earliest memories is of her best friend's mother throwing herself against the elementary school door to keep black children from entering. When she was in high school, the city exploded in a five-day riot following the assassination of Dr. Martin Luther King, Jr. Amid all the human strife, animals distracted and consoled her. She sneaked birds and bugs into her room, to the horror of her mother. At the library she happened upon *My Family and Other Animals,* Gerald Durrell's memoir of his animal-obsessed childhood. The book was a revelation. She read it straight through and then read it again. "I thought I was the only person in the world who'd ever lived with animals like that," she told me, "and here was a whole book written about it."

In junior high school she bought a mouse at a pet shop for a quarter. She named it Dolly. Every afternoon she raced home from school and shut herself in her room with the mouse. Hour after hour, she trained the rodent to run an elaborate maze of ladders, slides, and obstacles. The setup won first prize at a school science fair and gave Sharon the chance to enter a citywide competition. Like a coach keeping a champion sprinter in shape, Sharon ran

Dolly through the course every day leading up to the competition. Then, the night before the contest, Sharon took Dolly outside to clean her cage. The little mouse slipped through her fingers and scurried across the street. A neighbor's dachshund spotted the mouse and, as Sharon watched, the dog caught Dolly in its little teeth and ate her. "That was an early lesson in the workings of nature's food chain," Sharon told me. "The big things eat the little things."

She joined the Air Force after high school. It was 1973, and the end of the draft had the military scrambling to recruit an all-volunteer force. The Air Force responded by raising its glass ceiling, putting women in command positions and in the cockpit (though not in combat), and declaring that it would double the number of women in uniform in four years. "The recruiters were desperate for strong women who could pass the physical," Sharon recalled. "They really liked the looks of me." She signed up for a four-year stint. After basic training she volunteered for a jungle survival course. "I liked to go camping," she said, "so I figured why not?" Three weeks later she was on a military transport to Panama.

The idea was to teach pilots to survive after they were shot down over Vietnam. Sharon and seven pilots, all men, were dropped into the middle of the Central American jungle with nothing but a radio. They were told to expect a food drop in three days. It never came. "The first couple days we ate fruit and berries," she recalled. "And then when we realized the drop wasn't coming, things kind of broke down." The men around her began to wither. Some curled up and cried. Sharon didn't. "I started hunting lizards," she said. She found raw iguana protein-rich and tasty. Her comrades were less enthusiastic. "Most of them couldn't eat it," she said. The squad eventually walked out of the jungle. The men emerged haggard and shaken by the experience. Sharon loved every minute of it.

That first taste of the jungle hardwired something in her. "It was a revelation," she told me. "I fell in love with the tropical forest."

She didn't move to the jungle right away. First she tried normalcy. During her stint in the Air Force she fell in love with a dentist from Iowa. They got married and settled down in Iowa City. She gave two years to midwestern domesticity. Her husband was an avid reader who loved to hike and camp. He pulled teeth while Sharon studied Russian and wildlife biology at the University of Iowa. It might have been an ideal setup for someone. It wasn't for Sharon. Her husband wanted to have kids. She didn't. Iowa was too flat and too dry, with too much sky. She felt her future closing in on her. Sharon panicked. One afternoon when her husband was away, she spied an empty boxcar on an eastbound freight and climbed aboard.

Two days later the train rolled to a stop in Florida. Sharon hopped out and started her life over again. She found a college in Sarasota and enrolled in a biology course that required her to complete an independent study of animal behavior. As it happens, Sarasota is the winter home of Ringling Bros. and Barnum & Bailey circus. Animal trainers from all over the world live there. One day Sharon barged into a circus compound and watched a Romanian tiger tamer work with a cageful of cats. The old man had flowing gray hair and spoke so softly he could barely be heard. At the end of the session Sharon introduced herself. "I'd like to be your apprentice, if you'll have me," she said.

The old man sized her up. The prospect couldn't have been unappealing. Pictures of Sharon in her twenties show a slim, athletic woman with an easygoing California smile.

The tiger tamer rolled up his sleeves. He held his arms to the light to make sure Sharon saw every blemish. "If you want to work for me," he said, "go home, take off your clothes, and stand before a mirror. Look yourself in the eye and say, 'If I am going to work with wild animals, I am going to get scarred.' And if you are comfortable with that, then return to me tomorrow morning at eight o'clock." She did as she was told. The next day she was there at seven forty-five.

In the tiger training trade there are a few basic rules. Never show fear. Never be afraid of getting hurt—because you will. And never, ever, turn your back on the animals. "He had a simple, soothing vocabulary with the animals," Sharon recalled. "Outside the ring he was perfectly capable of carrying on a sophisticated conversation. But when he got in to work with the tigers he said the same things over and over again. Simple commands. Rewards. 'Gooood boy,' 'That's my baby girl.' He combined that with positive reinforcement—pieces of meat. He never raised his voice to them."

The Romanian and his tigers departed in the spring. Sharon stayed in school. She loved working with animals but wanted to live under an open sky, not a canvas tent. Looking for a field that would get her back to the jungle, she hit upon the study of fungi. Mycology was a young science. Researchers had only recently proved that mushrooms were neither plants nor animals but something halfway between. Gaps in knowledge waited to be filled by scientists willing to crawl through forest, field, and jungle. It sounded perfect to Sharon.

A mycology professor agreed to take her on as his graduate student. Months of study ensued. Sharon spent her days shuttling between library and lab. As much as she enjoyed learning about hyphae, septa, and mycelia, she grew restless. She wanted to get out in the field. One day at lunch she opened the help-wanted section of the *Tampa Tribune*. "Girls wanted for Mexican circus," she read. "Good pay, much travel." Sharon dialed the number.

A gruff voice answered. Yeah, the job was open, the man said. The circus was looking for tall white women. He had a hard time keeping them because all they had to do was dance at night. Mornings and afternoons were their own. "The girls get bored," he said.

Two words occurred to Sharon: *Mexican mushrooms*. She could use the traveling circus as Charles Darwin used the *Beagle*. All morning and afternoon off? A new town every day? Imagine the fungi she could collect!

Plus, she loved to dance.

Two weeks later she met the circus owner and his wife at 4 A.M. in an International House of Pancakes parking lot. Sharon and four other girls piled into a van and set out for El Paso, where they planned to cross the border into Juárez. On her lap Sharon clutched a dissecting kit, two rolls of wax paper, research notebooks, and *The Biology of the Fungi*. The other girls carried makeup kits. "Not to be unkind, but they were basically strippers looking for a ticket out of Tampa," Sharon recalled.

They eyed the college girl with suspicion. "Honey," one of them said, "are you sure you're on the right bus?"

When they got to Juárez, the circus manager gave Sharon a red sequined bikini. "Here's your costume," he said. "You're going to learn the lion and tiger act."

The cats liked her and she liked the cats. The old Romanian's method of positive reinforcement worked well with the felines, who were accustomed to harsh commands and poor treatment. Sharon's natural rapport with animals didn't go unnoticed. By the time the circus opened in Chihuahua, the show's advance men were papering villages with posters promoting her as the daughter of the legendary trainer Gunther Gebel-Williams. Every morning Sharon prowled the stalls of the village market, quizzing vendors about the mushrooms they sold. In the afternoon she ventured into the nearby hills and filled her collecting kit with fresh samples. In the evening she donned makeup, false eyelashes, silver stilettos, fishnet stockings, and sequined bikini and danced in the spotlight with lions and tigers. Every third day the circus folded its tents and moved on.

Over time Sharon befriended a fellow circus member, a spider monkey named Rocky. Once a star performer, Rocky had tried the patience of his trainer one too many times. When word went around camp that Rocky was about to go missing, permanently, Sharon took him in. She and the monkey got along well. She and the humans, not so much. Midway through the tour Sharon complained that some of the animals were being mistreated. Words escalated into threats, and Sharon found herself out of a job. She gathered her mushroom samples, stuffed Rocky in a backpack, and made her way north. A train got her as far as Juárez. Then there was the problem of the spider monkey and the border. "I couldn't exactly board an airplane wearing Rocky as a hat," she told me. So she found a coyote—a border smuggler—willing to guide the two of them across the Rio Grande. His price: ten dollars.

After dark the coyote led Sharon and Rocky through a maze of back alleys and abandoned lots and into the dark ravines of the Chihuahuan desert. With every step she grew more certain that the coyote was about to rob her, stab her, and leave her to die in the desert. But he kept his word. With Rocky on her shoulders, Sharon jumped the border fence, swam across the Rio Grande, and ran like hell for America. "I didn't stop until I looked up at a street sign and it said Ninth Avenue—not Calle Nueve," she said. "That's when I realized we'd made it to El Paso."

Famished and soaked, Sharon tucked Rocky into her jacket and strolled into an all-night diner. The waitress had seen plenty of illegals dampen her counter. But never a white girl. "*¿Cómo usted hizo una mojada?*" she asked. How'd you get to be a wetback?

Sharon unzipped her jacket and let Rocky poke his head out. The waitress shrieked. Then she laughed and poured Sharon a cup of coffee on the house.

It took her four days to hitchhike from El Paso back to Sarasota. "I could've made it in half the time without the monkey," she said. Waiting for her in Florida was a letter with an unfamiliar return address: "R. Foster, Belize City." She opened it.

The letter was from documentary filmmaker Richard Foster. "You don't know me, but you've been highly recommended by a mutual friend," he wrote. Foster was shooting a nature film involving jaguars and tapirs in Central America, and he desperately needed an assistant. Would she consider coming down for three months?

An airplane ticket dropped out of the envelope.

Foster was a classic Belizean type. An unflappably cheerful Englishman, he arrived in Belize in the mid-seventies as the hired captain of a rich man's yacht. After teaching himself to shoot film on a hand-wound Bolex, Foster sold a nature short to a producer in London and left the yachting life forever. By the time he contacted Sharon, Foster had established a rudimentary film studio on twenty acres of tropical savannah between Belize City and the capital, Belmopan.

Sharon abandoned her plans to return to school. "Work with wild animals in the Central American jungle? I was there!" she told me. After finding a home for Rocky in a monkey sanctuary, she took a bus to Miami and caught a flight to Belize City. It was her first time in the country. Foster picked her up in a dusty truck. As they drove to his compound, near where the zoo sits today, a feral landscape rolled past her window. She inhaled the warm wet air. It was the autumn of 1982. Belize still glowed with the euphoria of independence. Great Britain had cut the colony loose the previous year and the tiny nation faced nothing but the blue skies of a self-determined future. Sharon saw mangrove swamps and grassy savannah run uncut to the horizon. Jabiru storks soared overhead like paper kites. "I thought it was the most perfect place I'd ever seen," she told me.

Foster's film, called *Selva Verde* (Spanish for "green forest"), explored the complex relationships between animals in the subtropical forest. When he filmed the jaguars and pumas, Foster armed himself with a fire extinguisher and a Smith & Wesson .44 handgun. If things turned ugly he could disarm the cat with a blast from the extinguisher. If that didn't work, the gun was backup. (He never had to use it.)

Finding enough animals was never a problem. Foster's on-screen talent consisted of orphans that local Belizeans had adopted as pets and discarded when they started shredding the furniture. "Once people heard what we were doing out there, they started showing up with ocelots, jaguars, and curassows they didn't want anymore," said Foster, who still lives in Belize and shoots nature documentaries around the world.

When *Selva Verde* wrapped, Foster packed his cameras for an assignment in Borneo. On his way out of town, he offered to let Sharon stay at his place while he was gone. She asked him what to do about the animals. "Keep them or turn them out in the bush," he said. "Whatever you like."

Sharon took stock of her situation. She was alone in the jungle, low on cash, and without a job. The leftovers in Foster's fridge would last her a week, two at most. Her only assets were a jaguar, an ocelot, a puma, and a handful of exotic birds. That's when inspiration struck. What would Gerald Durrell do in her situation? He'd start a zoo.

She found some yellow paint and scrap wood and fashioned a sign: BELIZE ZOO. The next morning she nailed it to a post and pounded it into the ground with a rock. Then she walked to J.B.'s, a roadside cantina three miles down the Western Highway. "Hey, J.B.," she told the owner. "If people stop by the bar and get bored, send them down to Richard's place. Because now it's a zoo."

She made no money at first. Zilch. A few curious Belizeans turned off the highway now and then. Maybe ten in a week. Anyone who showed up got a personal tour from Sharon. She survived by selling eggs and sometimes the chickens too. She fed the animals with spoilage from local restaurants and scraps from a butcher at the British Forces base. She slept in a spare room at Richard Foster's place. When money ran out, she begged. She showed up at cocktail parties and charmed donations out of diplomats. When she didn't have the correct attire, she improvised. One evening she found herself in Belize City drenched and muddy and due at an ambassador's reception. She threw herself on the mercy of a friend. An hour later Sharon turned up at the party in a dress made entirely from the woman's curtains. As the astonished guests looked on, Sharon threw her hands in the air and declared, "Scarlett O'Hara, eat your heart out."

She had no long-term plans for the zoo. And then one day an old man from Belize City came out to see the animals. He was a rickety fellow with hair gone white with age. His dark Creole features had been weathered by decades spent squinting into the Belizean sun. He walked slowly with a dignified gait. It took him nearly forty-five minutes to shuffle down the dusty half-mile road that spurred off the Western Highway to the zoo. It was late afternoon. Sharon was shutting down for the day.

"Hello, miss," he said. "I heard this is the place to see the animals."

"It is, but I'm so sorry," she said. "We're closed for the night."

"I understand. I am sorry too."

She looked at the man's face and considered the bus ride and long walk he'd just endured.

"Okay, come on in," she said. "I'll show you around."

Twilight cast long shadows as they strolled the grounds. Sharon led the tour but the old man did most of the talking. As they stood before the curassow the man said, "If they see a curassow, dogs will attack it and eat it and go crazy." When they came to the anteater's cage he said, "Dogs will attack an anteater, but the anteater will stick its tongue up the dog's nose and suck out its brains." It went on like that. For every animal the man had a folk tale about how a glance from its eyes or the touch of its snout could render a man impotent or drive dogs insane. When they neared April the tapir, the man veered away. He refused to look at it. To do so, he said, risked blindness.

Then they got to the jaguars. Maya and Pinto, two old orphaned cats, tussled in the fading twilight. Sharon and the old man stood and watched them. A tear ran down his cheek.

"I am sorry, miss," he said. "I've lived my whole life in Belize. This is the first time I have seen the animals of my country."

She sat up late that night, thinking. The old man was no aberration. She'd run enough Belizeans through the zoo to realize that most locals saw the wild animals around them as either dog-killers, eye-blinders, or supper. Bush myths about the supernatural powers of tapirs and jaguars instilled fear in people, which fed the instinct to shoot first and ask questions later. Belizeans lived in one of earth's great cradles of wildlife, yet most knew almost nothing about it. They didn't even know any names! Jaguars were called tigers. Pumas were called red tigers. Ocelots were called tiger cats.

"I decided that night that no matter what, I was going to make a go of it at the zoo," she told me. She turned to Gerald Durrell for guidance. A proper zoo shouldn't be a mere amusement park, Durrell wrote in *The Stationary Ark*. It should combine the highest levels of animal care and scientific research with a mission to educate the public and conserve the diversity of wildlife in the world. Durrell founded his zoo, the Jersey Wildlife Preservation (now the Durrell Wildlife Conservation Trust), on Jersey, an island in the English Channel, because it was, he wrote, "a place which was small and made its own rules." Sharon would make Belize her own Jersey.

Tony Garel was her first employee. He started coming around to see the animals not long after Sharon started the zoo. A nineteen-year-old kid from Belize City's tough Southside district, Garel was soft-spoken and street-smart. He spent much of his childhood catching snakes and crocodiles in the mangrove swamps around Belize City. Garel knew more about local reptiles than most experts in the field. He had three times as many vipers and coral snakes stashed in his mother's house than Sharon had at the zoo. When she offered him a job, she warned him: "I can only pay you for two days a week."

"Okay," he said. "I be there." Twenty years later, he still hadn't left. Sharon's hiring practices haven't changed much either. Most zoo employees got the job by showing up at the front gate and asking for work. New hires usually start out on the groundskeeping crew. "If they want to work with the animals, after a while they'll assist one of the keepers," Sharon told me. "My senior keepers will let me know who's got the potential to be in animal management." Two of her best keepers got their start raking leaves. A few expat Americans and Brits have worked there over the years, but for the most part the staff is Belizean. It's a good job, and most who work there consider themselves lucky to have the gig. There's no 401(k), but benefits come in unconventional ways. When a staff member's kid got sick, or someone struggled to make rent, the Zoo Lady discreetly provided a little help. One morning Sharon picked me up for a long drive down to southern Belize. We'd agreed to meet at six but she banged on my door at five. "Sorry, but I've got to make a stop on the way," she explained. "Here, hold this." She handed me a chocolate cake. We drove to the house of a zoo staffer. At the door, she stuck five candles in the cake and lit them. She knocked on the door, roused the household, and sang "Happy Birthday to You" to a wide-eyed five-year-old boy. Then we left and continued with our day. Sharon didn't say another word about it.

The zoo has never purchased or captured an animal for its collection. Often they just appear at the front gate. Amy Bodwell, an American who now works at Chicago's Brookfield Zoo, apprenticed under Sharon in the late eighties and early nineties. "You never knew what you were going to find when you came to work in the morning," Bodwell told me. "One morning there would be a box sitting there and inside was a baby margay cat. Or a jar with a fer-de-lance."

Zoo escapes aren't as common as you might think. "The zoo is their territory, it's what they know," John Foster once told me. Foster (no relation to Richard Foster) was a zookeeper who'd come to Belize as a British soldier in the 1970s. "If they get out, they usually don't go far."

That's not to say escapes never happen. "One time the puma got loose," Richard Foster recalled. Foster and his wife, Carol, struggled to help Sharon keep the zoo together in its early years. "The only way we could get it back was by tying a live chicken on a string and dragging it in front of the puma. Carol got up on the roof and directed us—'The cat's over here!'—and I'd pull this bloody chicken through the yard until the puma started chasing me. Finally the cat ran after me into a pen, I ran out the other side, and Tony shut the gate." The chicken did not survive.

When food didn't work, Sharon turned to other lures. April the tapir ran to bush once when Richard Foster was filming her for a nature documentary. "It was dusk," Sharon recalled. "We called and called, we screamed her name. Darkness came. We thought we'd never see her again. Then I thought of a trick that might bring her back. When she was a baby and had that screwworm, I had to stay up late every night to nurse her with the bottle. I'd crank the music to keep myself awake. So that night I put a tape in my boom box. I think it was the Doors. So I'm standing there holding the boom box, blasting 'Light My Fire' into the jungle. And guess what: Here comes April, trotting right back to me."

Other escapees ran themselves to ground. "The king vulture got out one day and we spotted him circling above the zoo," John Foster recalled. "Having a grand time, he was. After about fifteen minutes of flying, though, he had to land and catch his breath. The

bird was absolutely knackered! He hadn't flown like that in years."
Foster didn't even have to use a net. "He flew another ten minutes,
then had to rest. Then five and a rest. Finally he just stood there
and let us pick him up and take him back home."

John Foster once told me about the time he taught the otters to
swim. "One day we got these orphaned pups dropped off, no more
than a couple weeks old," he said. "They could no more swim than
you or me at that age." He started them off in a mixing bowl with
two inches of water. They progressed to a kitchen sink. *Teach* may
be a strong word—otters will learn to swim on their own. Foster
was merely leading them to water. "Then I took them to the pond
behind Richard's house. I waded in a bit and coaxed them to follow. After a while they discovered there were fish in the pond, and
that they could eat the fish, and from there it was Bob's your
uncle."

It was that kind of bakabush ingenuity that gave the zoo its sto-
rybook flavor. The animals were cripples and orphans, the keepers
castaways and dreamers, the signs hand-painted. The whole place
ran on spit, muscle, and a three-dollar gate fee. For Sharon it was
a dream come true. When she wasn't hanging out with the animals, she was leading groups of schoolchildren through the zoo,
opening the eyes of an entire nation to the marvels around them.
Word of the wondrous little zoo began to spread. Gerald Durrell
himself stopped by and spent a day strolling the grounds.

Not everybody was impressed, though. Five years after the
zoo's founding, Sharon met officials from the American Association of Zoological Parks and Aquariums during a fund-raising
swing through the United States. The AAZPA (now known as the
Association of Zoos and Aquariums, AZA) is the accrediting
agency and trade group for American zoos. Sharon invited them
down for a visit. They came and toured the zoo, which was still a
chicken-wire-and-mud-path operation.

The AAZPA men weren't pleased with what they saw. At
breakfast the next morning the association's president gave Sharon
a dressing-down she'd never forget.

"I'm going to tell you something about your so-called zoo," he
said. "If you were in the U.S., I'd shut you down tomorrow. If you

can't operate a world-class zoo, you need to get out of the business."

Sharon nearly threw up her eggs.

As it happened, Sharon was scheduled to speak at the AAZPA's annual conference in Columbus, Ohio, later that fall. Instead of canceling her appearance, she scrapped her planned lecture and prepared a new slide show.

In Columbus she played to a packed house. Word had gotten around about this Belizean Calamity Jane and her charming little zoo. After a brief overview of the zoo's history, she repeated the AAZPA's president's line about shutting her down. Then she flashed a series of slides showing what life was like in Belize: tin roof shanties, milpa farms, dirt roads. "I have a question for all of you," she said. "What do you think Belizeans are going to think about a 'world-class zoo' "—she put up a slide of a shiny multi-million-dollar American zoo—"in a country where the prime minister's house looks like this?" Up came a picture of then prime minister Manuel Esquivel's house, a rickety perch on wooden stilts in the middle of Belize City.

"This is our hospital," she said, and showed a slide of Belize's cinder-block clinic. "Does the Belize Zoo exist for these people"— a slide of the AAZPA officials—"or for these people?" She brought up her final slide, a picture of an old Creole woman cackling at having one of Tony Garel's snakes draped over her shoulders.

"You can have this," Sharon said, unpinning her AAZPA badge. "Because I'm not a member of your organization anymore." Leaving the image of the old woman on the screen, Sharon stormed out of the room.

"From that point on," she told me, "I was a rogue operator."

CHAPTER 4

*B*ELIZE IS THE YOUNGEST COUNTRY in the Western Hemisphere, but you'd be hard-pressed to find a nation more firmly gripped by history. Its recent past—those 350 years of British rule—hangs over the country like an unhappy childhood. The ghosts of colonialism haunt Belize as much as any African nation. One of the many ironies about the place is that so little has been written about this period. The complete roster of historians producing serious work about Belize contains only two names.* If you want to know what happened here two thousand years ago, though, you'll have entire libraries at your disposal. From A.D. 220 to the mid-900s, about the time the Saxons were running the Celts through with iron-tipped pikes, present-day Belize hosted one of the most powerful, sophisticated, and enigmatic civilizations of the first millennium: the Maya.

Images of Mayan temples are so ubiquitous in Belize that it's hard to imagine a time when cities like Tikal, Xuantunich, Lubaantun, and Caracol lay buried under centuries of forest deadfall. Yet those ruins remained little known to the outside world until John Lloyd Stephens and Frederick Catherwood came to Central America in 1839.

Stephens was the Paul Theroux of his day, the author of a bestselling travel book set in the Arabian Peninsula. Catherwood was an architect who had spent years sketching Egypt's mosques and pyramids. They met by chance in London and struck up a friendship over their interest in ancient relics. At the time, rumors circulated around London about lost cities hidden in the jungles of

* They are O. Nigel Bolland, a sociology professor at Colgate University, and Assad Shoman, a Belizean scholar, diplomat, and longtime adviser to Prime Minister Said Musa.

Mesoamerica. A dispatch from a Central American army officer published by France's Société de Géographie fired speculation about what ruins lay yet undiscovered. "These accounts," wrote Stephens, "however vague and unsatisfactory, had roused our curiosity." Enticed by the promise of discovery, the amateur explorers hatched a plan to find the ancient city of Copán in what is now northern Honduras.

In October 1839, Stephens and Catherwood sailed from New York to Belize City. Upon their arrival they found a city not entirely unlike the one that exists today: houses built on pilings, roads ankle-deep in mud. "Balize," as Stephens called it, had about six thousand inhabitants, two-thirds of them recently emancipated slaves. As a citizen of the slaveholding United States, Stephens was amazed at Belize City's racial integration. Passing throngs of well-dressed dark-skinned Belizeans along the town's waterfront, he remarked, "I might have fancied myself in the capital of a negro republic."

There were no roads to the interior—"only wilderness unbroken by even an Indian path," Stephens noted—so the pair continued down the coast via steamboat. They turned inland up Guatemala's Rio Dulce and trekked overland to a Mayan village near Copán, just across the Honduran border. The local alcalde, or village leader, received Stephens and Catherwood coolly. (Their arrival, it turned out, had delayed his attendance at a cockfight.) When they asked about the lost city, the alcalde waved his hand dismissively and murmured something about the old ruins on the other side of the river. The next day the two men rode mules through cornfields to the river. Gazing across the water, they saw a limestone wall cut sharp and straight. The wall's top was overgrown with a furze of giant ceibas, palms, and vines. "This was part of the wall of Copán," wrote Stephens, "an ancient city on whose history, books throw but little light."

Until that moment, the civilized and scholarly world considered the history of the Americas to be largely a tale of mud huts and hunting. The standard text of the day, William Robertson's *History of America,* portrayed the New World's inhabitants as living in a state of "primeval simplicity." Stephens and Catherwood's scramble up the wall changed all that. With a Maya guide leading the way, the pair strolled through the forested ruins in amazement. They found altars and stelae "in workmanship equal to the finest monuments of the Egyptians." They marked out broad terraces as perfect as Roman amphitheaters. They climbed pyramids buried in soil but still bearing a few telltale stone steps. By the early afternoon, Stephens and Catherwood realized they had discovered not merely ruins but evidence of an entire civilization. "We sat down on the very edge of the wall and strove in vain to penetrate the mystery by which we were surrounded," Stephens wrote. "Who were the people that built this city?"

More than 165 years later, volumes of deciphered hieroglyphs and historic re-creations of daily life around the plazas have answered Stephens's question, but what's striking is how much we still don't know about how the great Mayan empires faded away. Archaeologists still spend summers uncovering fresh ruins in Central America, and climatologists pull ice and sediment cores from mountains and lakes hoping to gain new insights into environmental changes that might have doomed the ancient cities. In the annals of lost civilizations, the Maya occupy a special place. As Jared Diamond wrote in *Collapse,* his exploration of the demise of civilizations, "All of us love a romantic mystery, and the Maya offer us one at our doorstep." Who were they? Corn farmers, mostly. If you travel through the Mayan districts of Belize today, you won't get far beyond the village square before running into a high patch of maize. These are small family plots growing corn to be ground into meal and plated as tortillas. If you wandered through the same districts two thousand years ago, you'd see the same kind of people doing the same kind of work.

Mesoamerica, a region that encompasses Mexico's Yucatán Peninsula, Guatemala, Belize, and parts of northern Honduras and El Salvador, welcomed the first Maya sometime prior to 3500 B.C. By and by those early kinship tribes banded together in hamlets, which became villages, which became towns. People in one town made products that people in other towns desired. Trade ensued. Around the time of Christ's birth, well-established trade routes veined Mesoamerica, moving salt and seashells west from the Caribbean coast and green obsidian south from modern-day Mexico. Mayan city-states rose where inland trade routes converged. The greatest of them all was Tikal, located about thirty miles across the Belizean border in Guatemala. At the height of its power the royal city held as many as fifty thousand people, with a hundred thousand more tending small farms in the surrounding countryside.

We often speak of the "Mayan empire," but there was never a single unified empire. The situation was more akin to the city-states of ancient Greece or the fractured kingdoms of Renaissance Italy. More than fifty Mayan cities were spread across Mesoamerica. Some coalesced into small kingdoms that warred with their neighbors. As anthropologists unearth more and more hieroglyphs, a clearer picture is emerging of a region beset by political intrigue, minor wars, puppet kings, matrimonial alliances, and palace gossip.

Tikal's eternal rival was Calakmul, a city to the north in the present-day Mexican state of Campeche. After skirmishing over trade routes for nearly 150 years, the conflict came to a head in the middle of the sixth century, when Tikal mounted a military assault against Calakmul. The raid, only partially successful, weakened Calakmul's military power but strengthened its resolve. For the next six years Calakmul's king restocked his armory and plotted revenge. Caracol, a city-state near the Chalillo dam site, had been a longtime rival of Tikal's as well. Calakmul and Caracol allied their forces and struck back, overrunning Tikal in a spectacularly bloody "star war," so called because battle leaders chose the day of attack based on astrological alignment.

That should have been the end of Tikal, but in A.D. 692, a new strongman named Hasaw Chan K'awil, "Heavenly Standard-Bearer," led a resurgent Tikal in its own star war against Calakmul. Hasaw took the city, killed its king, and oversaw what archaeologists discreetly term a "bloodletting ceremony." The victory inaugurated a second renaissance at Tikal. Hasaw revived the kingdom's building program, directing his architects to build

Temple I and Temple II, the magnificent pyramids that stand
today as the most recognizable icons of Mayan civilization. Historians once more struck stone with chisels. Musicians played ancient melodies on ceramic flutes, bone whistles, and drums.
Artisans crafted necklaces and vessels out of jade. Mayan ateliers
turned out fabulous ceremonial robes and headdresses.

And then it all stopped. Sometime around the beginning of
the ninth century, royal dynasties began to disappear across Mesoamerica. The last inscription at Tikal was carved in A.D. 869. After
that, nothing. Major cities were abandoned with no evidence of
hasty flight or violent destruction. They became terrestrial ghost
ships. And it wasn't just the cities. In what archaeologist David
Webster calls "one of the great demographic transformations in
history," an entire region lost most of its people. At the height of
Classic Mayan civilization, an estimated three million people lived
in the region controlled or influenced by Tikal and Calakmul. Another million lived in the area stretching from present-day Belize
down to Copán in Honduras. Population levels across Central
America are just now returning to Classic Mayan levels, more
than a thousand years after the empire's fall. Modern-day Belize
supports only one-quarter of the population it did during the heyday of Tikal.

What most likely happened, many Mayan scholars contend, is a
combination of drought and agricultural exhaustion. City-states
expanded beyond the capacity of their natural resources. Data
drawn from lakebed cores suggest that Central America experienced one of its worst megadroughts between A.D. 800 and 1000.
Lakes and rivers dried up. Crops failed. Drought-induced famine
would have put the authority of kings and priests in double jeop-
ardy. The great stone plazas at cities like Tikal were designed to
channel wet-season rainfall into reservoirs where the water would
be stored for use during the dry season. At its core, the power of
rulers like Heavenly Standard-Bearer relied on water control.
With crops failing and the reservoirs drained, the great leaders
would have been hard-pressed to justify their rule. Two lean years
would have been tough. But twenty? Fifty? Compounding the
problem was the concept of personal accountability. "Fundamen-

tal to the Classic Mayan world view was the idea that collective ills or misfortunes resulted from personal and moral rather than systemic failings, whether the persons were gods, ancestors, or semidivine rulers," writes David Webster. "In times of trouble, in other words, people did not ask, 'What is the problem,' but rather 'Who is the problem?' " Under this theory the Mayan collapse was a chain reaction of failure: first the rain, then the food, then the kings, then civilization itself.

The surviving Maya dispersed into small villages and lived peacefully for the next 650 years. Then in 1519 the Spanish showed up and broke hell upon the land.

Lured by reports of gold jewelry spotted on natives of what is now Mexico, Spanish adventurer Hernán Cortés landed a force of 530 men at a village on the Gulf of Mexico and led them on an eight-month march to the Aztec capital of Tenochtitlan, located at what is now Mexico City. On November 1, Cortés and his conquistadors rode down from the flanks of the volcano Popocatepetl into one of the greatest cities in the world. With a population of 225,000, Tenochtitlan boasted more people than London and Paris combined. Aztec kings ruled from dazzling white palaces and strolled through elaborate gardens and aviaries. Fresh spring water flowed through one of the world's most elaborate aqueducts. Wealth came to the city on a timetable: A supply convoy laden with sixty bowls of gold dust—tribute from the provinces—arrived every eighty days. Fired by opportunity and greed, Cortés kidnapped the Aztec leader Moctezuma and demanded the king's ransom in gold. A few months later Cortés invited Aztec nobles to the city's central plaza for a traditional feast. With the nation's leaders unguarded and unarmed, Cortés unleashed his horses, swords, and cannons—technology unknown in the New World—and killed them all. After that, the conquest of Mexico was a mop-up operation.

The Maya of modern-day southern Mexico and Belize turned back Spain's early forays into their territory, but by the 1540s Spanish settlers had pushed into the Yucatán and looked to con-

tinue their southward expansion. The Spanish viceroy sent soldiers into the Central American mainland as far as the Bay of
Honduras. Their ostensible mission was "the pacification and
baptism of these people," but the real motive was gold.

The troops who blazed through present-day Belize were a particularly vicious crew. When they encountered the Maya, the conquistadors killed those they could and "pacified" the rest. A
Spanish bishop who witnessed pacification firsthand described
Spanish soldiers "cutting off noses, arms and legs, and the breasts
of women; throwing them into deep lagoons with gourds tied to
their feet; stabbing the little children because they did not walk as
fast as their mothers; and if those whom they drove along, chained
together around the neck, fell sick or did not move along as fast as
the others they cut off their heads, so as not to stop and untie
them."

Over the course of the sixteenth century, Spain established
modest outposts in and around what is now Belize, but the country never outgrew its status as a colonial backwater. From Mexico
and latter-day Peru the conquistadors looted enough gold and silver to turn Spain into the superpower of the seventeenth century.
Mayan Mesoamerica provided no precious metals and plenty of
irritation. In 1638, the Maya residents of Tipu, a town on the
Macal River a few miles downstream from the Chalillo Dam site,
rebelled against the Spanish. The rebellion was typically Mayan:
The locals faded into the forest, one by one. The Spanish sent
word into the woods that those who returned would not be pun-
ished. A few came back to Tipu, where they were bound and
whipped, and the rebellion soon turned from flight to fight. Locals
bashed and burned the "reduction towns" established by the
Spanish. The Spanish governor sent a party of Franciscan friars to
quell the uprising, which began spreading from Tipu to other out-
lying villages. The friars met a war party armed with machetes.
"Let the governor come," the rebel Maya leader told the priests.
"Let the king come. Let the Spanish come. We are ready to fight
them."

The Maya were ready but the Spanish were not. The friars advised the governor that a military campaign was the only way to quell the rebellion. The governor considered the cost of sending troops, building forts, and capturing thousands of natives in the formidable tropical forests, and must have asked himself a question that prime ministers, generals, and CEOs would ask many times over the next 350 years: What are we doing in Belize?

The Maya were not alone in their harassment of the Spanish. Piracy had been a problem in the Caribbean from the earliest days of Spanish rule. In 1523, Hernán Cortés loaded part of his stolen treasure on a galleon bound for Spain. The boat never made it to the open sea. Pirates led by a Frenchman named Jean Florin captured the vessel, murdered her crew, and made off with the booty. Florin's success encouraged others to follow him into the sweet trade, and for more than a century the Caribbean Sea hosted a never-ending scrum between Spanish galleons, fat with silver and pearls, and pirate vessels, prowling like wolves.

Faced with unruly Maya on land, bloodthirsty pirates at sea, and little financial incentive to remain, the Spanish all but abandoned their settlements near the Bay of Honduras. For the region's Maya population, as for all indigenous Americans, the Spanish century had been catastrophic. Battle casualties, enslavement, and imported diseases such as smallpox combined to reduce the number of Central American Maya from more than two million in 1523 to less than half a million fifty years later.

If there is credit or blame for the British settlement of Belize, it must be laid at the foot of the fashion industry. In the sixteenth century, Spanish settlers in the Yucatán discovered a crooked swamp-loving tree known as logwood. The tree's heartwood boiled down into a blue-black dye that offered an alternative to indigo. The timber sold for £100 per ton in England, which meant a three-foot section of logwood sold for as much as a skilled tradesman could make in a year. Pirates caught on to its value when they saw it stacked as ballast in plundered ships. Not long after, they observed thickets of logwood growing in the swamps north of the Bay of Honduras. Logging, they realized, held all the profit potential of piracy without the occupational hazards. The pirates began wading ashore.

Legend has it that a Scottish pirate named Peter Wallace founded Belize when he established a logging camp at the mouth of the Belize River around 1638. Historical records indicate that such a pirate did exist, but it's anybody's guess whether Wallace actually set up there. Some historians dismiss the Wallace story as so much creation-myth fiction, and doubt the local belief that *Belize* came from a corrupted version of Wallace's surname. Wallace . . . Walliz . . . Balliz . . . Belize. It's a stretch.

Spain, which still claimed the territory, sent military ships to roust the British loggers, who called themselves Baymen. The Spanish met with little success, as the Baymen knew how to defend themselves. They were, after all, former pirates.

Spain and England squabbled over the Bay of Honduras off and on for the next century, but the Spanish claim was doomed by one simple fact: The Spanish didn't want to live there, and the British did. In 1755, a party of Spanish soldiers came ashore to burn and pillage Belize City. They left soon after the sacking was done, proclaiming the miserable swamptown fit only for Englishmen. The rivalry came to an end in 1798 when a motley militia of crown-loyal Baymen and their slaves defeated a Spanish force of thirty-one vessels and twenty-five thousand soldiers in the Battle of St. George's Caye. How the settlers overcame such odds— they're said to have fought from logwood rafts—is a subject widely mythologized by Belizeans, who for many years celebrated the battle's anniversary as the colony's birthday.

The history of the British in Belize can be summed up in a sentence: They came for the wood, and when they took the last tree, they left. The Baymen enjoyed handsome profits on their logwood exports until the late 1760s, when their greed and lack of foresight caught up with them. "The settlement at the Bay of Honduras," as Belize was then known, started shipping more logwood than European dyers wanted. Predictably, oversupply depressed the market price. Just as predictably, the Baymen responded by ramping up production. On any given day, forty to seventy-five ships lay anchored at the mouth of the Belize River waiting to fill their holds with logwood. As those ships reached London, the price for logwood spiraled toward zero. Fortunately for the Baymen, they had more luck than market sense. Just as the logwood market crashed, a master craftsman named Thomas Chippendale ignited a home furnishings craze among England's aristocracy. Chippendale's exquisite tables and high-backed chairs spawned an industry of imitators and fueled an insatiable demand for mahogany. Belize was lousy with the stuff. The Baymen swapped logwood for mahogany and retained Belize's position as England's lumberyard.

Subtropical logging was hot, rough, dangerous work. Logging teams bushwhacked through swamps and jungles teeming with ticks and vipers. As soon as they could afford to, the Baymen began purchasing black Africans from the Jamaican slave markets. In 1745, black slaves outnumbered white Englishmen two to one. By 1790 slaves made up three-quarters of the population. Most were owned by the dozen powerful Baymen who amassed so much timberland that historian O. Nigel Bolland described the situation as "a forestocracy."

Belize remained that way for most of the next two hundred years, with power and wealth concentrated in the hands of a small clique of white landowners while the rest of the country remained ignorant, docile, and poor. England abolished slavery throughout the empire in 1838, but Belize's forestocracy preserved its pool of cheap labor by buying up all the land, thus preventing the possibility of small-acreage agriculture. A few acres of land offered a wage laborer the chance to farm on the side. A strong crop might allow him to quit the mahogany gang, which would drive up the cost of labor. The whole thing was a devious reversal of Jeffersonian democracy. If, as Thomas Jefferson believed, the strongest democracy would emerge from a nation of independent farmers, then surely the inverse must be true: Keeping mahogany cutters dependent on low-wage jobs would consolidate the power of the elite. In 1862, Great Britain declared the settlement a colony and named it British Honduras. In the classic colonial dynamic, British Honduras existed to supply the mother country with raw material and to purchase England's finished goods. To that end, England continued the anti-farming regime and kept the forestocracy in control. Homegrown Belizean food, after all, meant fewer purchases of imported British fare. And the more wild acreage that was cleared for crops and pasture, the less that existed for mahogany. "For most of its history," wrote Bolland, Belize "could be simply but not inaccurately described as a trading post attached to a timber reserve."

The British took the wood and left Belize with no railway, two dirt highways, and a handful of colonial administration buildings. That's the modern Belizean take on things, but it's not entirely fair. Belize wasn't much to begin with. One colonial governor arrived in Belize City in 1934 to find that he had two transportation choices: horseback or canoe. England's Colonial Office earmarked some funds for road construction and drainage, but the mother country never saw the point of investing in infrastructure. The cutters who felled mahogany stacked the wood on the riverbanks and let the rainy season floods flush the timber to Belize City. Why build roads when Mother Nature delivered it for free?

Basic utilities like electricity, water service, and telephone lines were left in a similarly sorry state. The water system leaked like a sieve. Phone connections were fickle. The nation's power grid wasn't a grid at all. Each town was powered by its own diesel generator. Many villages had no power at all.

The old system creaked along for decades. On September 21, 1981, Great Britain handed over the reins of power to George Price, Belize's founding prime minister. Price's main concern wasn't power and water but the Guatemalan army, which routinely threatened to invade Belize. Then the late 1980s hit the country. Computers, compact disc players, and satellite TV arrived in Belize City. Appliance stores sold refrigerators, microwave ovens, and washer-dryer sets. Government and business offices replaced typewriters with personal computers. Power lines and streetlights crept out to rural districts. Tourism boomed. Forty thousand visitors came to Belize in 1985. Five years later that figure had swelled to a hundred thousand. Those tourists arrived with high expectations. They wanted air conditioners, not ceiling fans. Soon the locals wanted them too. Belize needed more power.

Officials at the state-owned electric utility didn't have many options. Belize has no coal. Small pockets of oil and natural gas lie deep within the country's bedrock, but no local refineries exist to turn the raw material into retail product. Nuclear plants cost too much to build. For political reasons, government officials were reluctant to buy power from Guatemala or Mexico. When power company officials surveyed their choices, they focused on the one thing Belize had in abundance: rivers.

For most of the year, water drains slowly from Belize. In the northern half of the country the movement is almost imperceptible. Rainfall bleeds away into lagoons, marshes, and rivers that meander across lowlands to reach the sea. In the south, however, the Maya Mountains split the country in half. Water rushes down the eastern half of the Mayas in short, steep rivers. On the western slopes most tributaries drain into the Macal River, which runs west toward Guatemala before curving around in a sweeping C and joining the Belize River in a deep, slow push to the Caribbean Sea.

The best place to build a hydroelectric dam is in a deep canyon where the existing walls form a natural bathtub. Belize has no deep canyons, but there are a few places along the Macal River where the ridges rise high enough to hold a reservoir. In 1995, the state electric utility built a 25-megawatt dam at a place called Mollejon, an eleven-mile drive into the jungle from Benque Viejo, a town near the Guatemalan border. There was only one problem with the Mollejon Dam: It was a run-of-the-river structure, which meant it didn't back up any water. It could produce power only as long as the river flowed. The Macal River, like most rivers in Belize, shriveled to a trickle during the dry season. And the dry season—December through May—was high season for tourism. Every year the Mollejon powerhouse shut down just when Belize most needed its electricity.

To solve the problem, power company officials conceived of a second dam. The upstream structure, considerably bigger than

Mollejon, would block the river and store the rainy season runoff in a reservoir twelve miles long. During the dry season the second dam would draw down the reservoir and provide Mollejon with a steady stream of turbine-turning water. The place they chose to build the second dam was an abandoned jungle camp known as Chalillo.

CHAPTER 5

SOME DAYS SHARON RUNS around the zoo dressed like a crazy person. She'll pair a green button-down shirt with snakeskin-patterned lycra pants, the kind worn by heavy-metal guitarists in the eighties. Other times she'll come to work in camouflage pants and a purple tank top. Converse All-Stars— canvas Chuck Taylors—are her preferred shoes. "They're cheap and they have these holes that let river water drain," she explains. Her sunglasses are cracked, taped, and unfashionable. Sometimes I think Sharon dresses this way to heighten her colorful profile. Other times I think she's truly blind to color and pattern in human attire.

I don't know what Sharon was wearing on the day she first heard about Chalillo. I've asked her. She hasn't the foggiest clue. She does know it was a Monday, the first day of February 1999. Monday is the zoo's slowest day. It's when the keepers and the animals recover from the weekend crowds and the maintenance crew fixes whatever's been broken.

She arrived just after dawn. In the cement-block commissary a few of the keepers were chopping mangoes and watermelons for the birds. Sharon grabbed a mug of coffee and a wrinkled copy of *Amandala,* the largest of Belize's four weekly papers, and headed to the back office. Angel heard her rubber boots on the wooden steps and came running. "How's my baby today?" Sharon said. The jaguar pawed the floor.

Sharon sipped coffee at her desk and flipped past the usual front page mayhem. Belize City is a moderately dangerous place, but the local papers can make it seem like bedlam. *Amandala* is the liveliest of the bunch. Machete fights and pedal-by murders are chronicled in screaming headlines. "A ROTTING CORPSE IN A COUNTRYSIDE LATRINE" and "MACHETE VIC TAKES SIX CHOPS—

AND LIVES!" are typical. She skimmed past tamer features: scholarship winners, soccer scores, another American on the lam fighting extradition. Then a story buried in the back pages caught her eye. "CABINET RE-THINKS HYDRO HOLDING RESERVOIR CONSTRUCTION SITE," it said. Prime Minister Said Musa and his cabinet ministers had agreed to move the site of a proposed hydroelectric dam from Rubber Camp, an abandoned rubber tappers' station, to a spot lower on the Macal River: Chalillo.

"All interested parties are invited to submit suggestions or objections," the government said.

Sharon clutched her head in her hands. She'd just returned from a field study at Chalillo. The last scarlet macaws in Belize nested at the bottom of the planned reservoir.

"Oh, no," she said.

She picked up the phone.

"Meb, it's Sharon at the zoo," she said after the beep. "Listen, what do you know about this dam at Chalillo? Please call me back as soon as you can."

Meb Cutlack was an old Fleet Street muckraker living out his golden years in the tropical swelter of Central America. Perpetually rumpled, Cutlack had great saggy jowls and spoke in the mixed-up vowels of his native Australia. His left eye floated independent of his right. Some days he wore an eye patch, which gave him the look of a shambly pirate. He could often be seen roaring down the Western Highway in a rusty Chevy Geo, chasing scoops for his column in *The Reporter.*

Sharon pulled out a map of the Macal River valley. Her finger traced the veiny river upstream from Chalillo. Depending on how high the dam was, it could flood miles of the Macal—and possibly the Raspaculo too.

The phone rang.

"Look, here's what I know," Cutlack told her. "This thing has been on the drawing board for years but now they're finally going to build it."

"How big a dam are we talking about?" said Sharon.

"Nothing's certain at this point," Cutlack said. "They're dis-

cussing a thirty-meter dam with a reservoir about twenty kilometers long."

She measured the distance on her map. "My god. That would
wipe out that whole section of river. How could they do this?"

"Give them some credit, Sharon," said Cutlack. "They were
going to put it up at Rubber Camp, which would have inundated
much more acreage."

"Come on, Meb. You're going to give these guys *credit*?"

"I told them I'm with them as long as they can prove it's economically feasible."

"You did *what*?"

"Calm down, Sharon. They cannot ever prove that. I've seen
their reports. The economics simply don't work out."

"Who's pushing this? Is it Musa?"

Said Musa was elected prime minister the previous year. His
name reflected the Lebanese heritage of his father, but Musa was
Belizean-born, raised in the country's rural west and educated in
England at Manchester University. Like many of his generation,
Musa's political history traced an arc from socialist firebrand
(1970s) to reluctant capitalist (1990s). With his scholarly glasses
and shock of white hair, Musa governed with the affect of a strict
yet loving grandfather.

"Said? Not so much. Honestly, I think he's still on the fence."

"Then who's behind it?"

Cutlack paused. "Ralph wants it," he said.

Sharon's spirit had been sinking since she read the story in
Amandala. Now it hit bottom.

"Ralph," she said. "Of course."

Ralph Fonseca went by many names in Belize. The Big Wheel.
King Ralph. The Minister of Everything. A large man with a
sloped forehead, Fonseca possessed the cunning of Iago and the
silhouette of Alfred Hitchcock. He was Said Musa's finance minister. The title barely hinted at his power. Fonseca's father—*blood
falla vein*—was finance minister to George Price, Belize's founding
father, and the younger Fonseca was raised in the bosom of the
PUP. He cut his teeth as a money manager for Barry Bowen, the

biggest landowner in Belize. He rose to power by masterminding the PUP's two previous national victories. The party won control of the government in 1989 and 1998 by overwhelming its rival, the UDP, with buckets of campaign money. Belize has no campaign finance laws, so nobody knew exactly where the money came from. But everybody knew it was raised by Ralph.

By the late 1990s, Fonseca had become Belize's own Cardinal Richelieu. He oversaw the privatization of the country's public utilities. He negotiated and signed secret contracts that ceded control of the nation's rivers and ports to foreign corporations. When the country ran short of cash, Fonseca went to the money markets to peddle more Belizean bonds. If it had to do with the government or money, it didn't happen without the Big Wheel's approval.

Sharon fed the jaguars their morning chicken. She tossed an unlucky mouse to the king vultures. She talked to the animals as always, but she couldn't stop thinking about the dam. Back at her office she reread the article.

. . . all interested parties are invited to submit suggestions and objections. . . .

Well, that was a place to start. She sat down and wrote a letter to Prime Minister Musa.

Her note was two parts flattery, one part complaint. In Belize there are two cardinal sins: confrontation and disrespect. Airing disputes in public is considered poor etiquette. It's an attitude born of Belize's insularity. In a nation of 275,000 people, members of the chattering class all attend one another's parties, openings, and ceremonies. Their children go to school together. Social grace helps everyone get along. As for respect, it was the most essential attitude a foreigner like Sharon could possess. It had to be given, given again, and given some more. Having endured the arrogance of colonial governors for more than two hundred years, Belizean leaders were highly attuned to the slightest hint of disrespect from an outsider. And make no mistake: Sharon Matola was an outsider. Her twenty years at Mile 29 couldn't bring her inside. Neither could her Belizean citizenship. By virtue of her American birth and white skin she would always be an outsider.

A letter of protest, therefore, had to be prefaced with a few lines of tribute and praise. With those out of the way, Sharon got to her point. The proposed dam, she wrote, would wipe out the single most important habitat for endangered species in Belize. "We are gambling with our natural resources, treasures that are not duplicated anywhere else in the region," she wrote. "This is not a sound move." She slid the note into an envelope, hopped on her motorcycle, and rode the twenty-three miles to Belmopan. The letter was too important to trust to the Belizean postal service. She delivered it to the prime minister's office herself.

Eleven days later she received a reply. "Dear Ms. Matola: Thank you very much for your letter," wrote the prime minister's secretary. He assured Sharon that her comments had been passed along to the dam's planners, and they would certainly take them into consideration.

"A form letter!" Sharon exclaimed. "They sent me a form letter. Musa probably never even saw my note."

At this point most people would have dropped the issue. Years later Sharon wondered if this was when she should have let the whole thing go. She'd never gone against the government. She'd never even expressed a preference for either party. In her position, politics didn't pay. She kept the zoo afloat with private donations from both sides of the aisle. But there was something about the Macal River valley that drove her to cross that line. All across Central America, megafauna superstars—jaguars, tapirs, monkeys, macaws—were being driven off their land, captured as pets, or killed for their meat. Back in the remote viny jungle where the Raspaculo flowed into the Macal, Sharon had discovered the region's Helm's Deep, a secret refuge flourishing with life, raw and exuberant and wild. To the rest of the country it was just a few acres of bush. If she didn't speak for the river, nobody would.

When Aldous Huxley passed through Belize in 1933, the novelist came away singularly unimpressed. "If the world had any ends," he concluded, "British Honduras would certainly be one of them." Belizeans hate that quote. The problem is twofold. First, there's

the fact that Huxley's observation rings as true today as it did seventy-five years ago. Second, because so little is written about Belize, its citizens possess an extreme sensitivity to the few notices
that appear. The slightest mention in an overseas paper occasions
headlines at home. A few years ago when U.S. congressman
Charles Rangel offered some polite words during a courtesy call
from the Belizean ambassador, the PUP-owned *Belize Times* bannered it on the front page: "U.S. CONGRESSMAN BIGS UP BELIZE."
Conversely, those who act the fool in Washington or London
shame the entire nation. Not long ago Belize's solicitor general
enjoyed one too many cocktails on an American Airlines flight to
Washington. As the plane descended into Reagan National Airport, the cabin attendants asked the man to sit down and buckle
up. He refused. Sorry, sir, the attendants said, it's the law. "Do you
know who I am?" the swaying solicitor demanded. The attendants
did not. "I am the solicitor general of Belize!" The phrase did not
have its intended effect. By the time the plane taxied off the runway, U.S. federal marshals were waiting at the gate. American papers took no notice, but in Belize the incident made headlines for
days.

"I know it sounds crazy, but in a country of two hundred and
seventy-five thousand people, you really do get to know everybody," Lucy Fleming once told me. A brassy New Jersey native,
Fleming came to Belize as a back-to-the-land hippie in the late
seventies. Her husband, Mick, is a robust Englishman with hands
the size of sofa cushions. With sheer pluck and a dose of Swiss
Family Robinson ingenuity, the Flemings turned an abandoned
cattle ranch into Chaa Creek Resort, the country's premier ecotourist retreat.

Lucy Fleming was right. The more time I spent in Belize the
less crazy it sounded. One-quarter of the country's population
lives in Belize City. The other three-quarters are perpetually
going to Belize City or heading home. A ruling elite of perhaps a
thousand educated Belizeans runs the country. Of necessity,
members of the local nobility wear many hats. Prime Minister
Musa's son Yasser is an artist, a writer, an art dealer, a bookstore

owner, the government's culture czar, and his father's public relations adviser. One of Yasser's friends runs Belize's only publishing house and recording studio out of a border-town bungalow. Meb Cutlack practices investigative journalism and moonlights as an innkeeper. The same names show up again and again on the boards of different companies and institutions. In business this sort of arrangement is known as an interlocking directorate. In politics it's an oligarchy. Belize's situation could be more accurately described as a cronigopoly—a tiny state run by a few powerful men and their friends. To be fair, it must be remembered that Belize is one of the least populated countries in the world. There are only so many people to go around. Conflicts of interest are a condition of existence.

"You know everybody and everybody knows you. That's the great thing about Belize," Tony Garel once told me. "It's also one of the worst things about Belize. Everybody knows your business. You have a reputation to live up to, or live down. You show up at a nightclub without your wife, run into the wrong person, uh-oh . . ." Garel was one of Sharon's links to the Belize that existed beyond the reach of outsiders. As a native Belizean he possessed local knowledge of the scuttlebutt, confidences, and social cues from which foreign-born Belizeans were excluded. Garel seemed to be no more than two degrees of separation from anyone worth knowing. I once asked him about one of the cabinet ministers pushing the Chalillo Dam. "Oh, yeah," he said. "I went to school with him." Likewise a Belizean rap musician: "I remember him, little kid growing up down the street." That "ROTTING CORPSE IN A COUNTRYSIDE LATRINE"? It was rotting in Tony Garel's neighbor's latrine. "Some guy get chopped, they dump him down the well. So much for that water."

Sharon's other link to the hidden Belize was Claudia Duenas, the zoo's business manager. A cheerful woman of Spanish descent, Duenas possessed the kind of hypercompetence that goes unrewarded in most offices. Garel and Duenas were the people Sharon relied on to tell her when she was wrong. "Can't do that Sharon," Garel would say. "Sharon," Duenas would instruct her, "you gotta call this man and talk to him. And you gotta be nice." Over the years Garel and Duenas had impressed upon Sharon the value of personal contact in Belize. If you had a problem with the government, you went to see the minister directly. You showed up with a smile and a handshake and a how's-your-sister. Belizeans preferred to keep conflict private. The country ran on family ties, and a proper family kept its dirty laundry indoors.

So the Zoo Lady reined in her impulse to come out firing, angry and loud, against the dam. She decided to give persuasion a try. A few discreet inquiries led her to Joseph Sukhnandan, a senior official with Belize Electricity Limited, the nation's power company. Sukhnandan was a senior engineer in charge of planning the dam. He was the man to see. Politely, she scheduled a meeting. "I figured there was a chance he didn't know what he was about to drown," Sharon later told me, her eyebrows raised in bitter arcs.

The headquarters of Belize Electricity Limited (BEL) sits just off the Northern Highway on the outskirts of Belize City. The modern three-story building radiates an aura of professionalism. In a country where the prime minister's formal dress consists of a white guayabera and slacks, the culture at BEL is unusually formal. Women wear business suits and heels. Junior engineers pace the halls in button-down shirts and ties, wrapped in the ambient hiss of air conditioners. BEL has a reputation for hiring Belize's best and brightest. CEO Lynn Young is the tall, studious son of Sir Colville Young, a respected scholar who serves as Queen Elizabeth's official representative in Belize. Like his father, Lynn Young keeps himself above party politics. Other utilities were notorious patronage mills, bloated with layabouts and party hacks, but BEL kept its payroll trim. The company's communications director, Dawn Sampson, was a former TV anchor and Miss Belize runner-up. Joseph Sukhnandan, the Cambridge-educated executive heading up the Chalillo project, was one of the nation's brightest engineers. Sukhnandan's in-house rival, Ambrose Tillett, boasted degrees in both electrical engineering and environmental science. Michael Polonio, head of customer service, was also president of the National Garifuna Council, one of Belize's most prominent ethnic cultural organizations.*

Not long after my first trip to the Macal River with Sharon, I stopped by BEL headquarters and asked Joseph Sukhnandan to explain the country's energy situation.

"Our task here at BEL is to meet the demand for electricity," Sukhnandan told me. At peak demand—usually around 6 P.M., when Belizeans got home from work and turned on lights, TV sets, and radios—BEL's system could deliver about 59 megawatts. One megawatt (MW) will run about a thousand American homes. In global terms, 59 megawatts is nothing. At peak capacity, the Grand Coulee Dam produces around 6,800 megawatts. "That demand grows ten to fifteen percent every year," Sukhnandan said. The worldwide average is about 2 to 3 percent. "We've got a lot of new houses going up. More tourists come every year. People add air conditioners and computers. That additional power has to come from somewhere.

"In the past few years we've purchased power from Mexico. But that's a limited contract. Mexico won't deliver more than 25 megawatts to us. And their price goes up in the evening, just when we need the power. Beyond that, our resources are limited. Belize has no coal, oil, or natural gas. Wind and solar power are not very economical. The one thing we have is the river. So we developed the Mollejon hydro plant, 25 megawatts. But the water at Mollejon runs out during the dry season, the peak tourist time. So we are planning Chalillo primarily as a dam that will store water to run both its own powerhouse and keep Mollejon generating electricity all year 'round."

The way electricity is generated has remained essentially unchanged for the past 125 years. Some primary force spins the blades of a turbine—a variation on the ancient windmill—which cranks a generator. The generator works on the principle discov-

* The Garifuna are descendants of escaped African slaves and the Carib peoples of the Lesser Antilles. Belize's only ethnic holiday—Garifuna Settlement Day, November 19—celebrates the arrival of the Garifuna in southern Belize in 1802.

ered in 1831 by Michael Faraday, which is that a disrupted mag-
netic field will produce electricity. They do this in my daughter's
elementary school by spinning a loop of wire between two ends of
a horseshoe magnet. A power plant's generator is the magnet/wire
writ large, using enormous iron cores and wire coils and a powerful turbine to spin the whole works.

Magnets and wires are the easy parts. The force that spins the
turbine—that's the stuff of fortune, bloodshed, swindle, and war.
Thomas Edison used coal-fired steam to turn the world's first
electric generator in 1880. We still do that today. The range of
fuels has expanded—we now burn coal, diesel, natural gas, and
biomass—but the basic operation remains the same: Heat water
into high-pressure steam and direct the steam against turbine
blades to crank the generator. Wind power uses the natural
airstream to spin the turbine. Hydroelectric dams force water
through the blades, like aiming a garden hose at a pinwheel. For all
its complexity, nuclear power represents nothing more than a
high-tech horse harnessed to the same Edison-era cart. Nuclear
fission heats water to steam, which spins the turbine, and so on.

There is a way to produce electricity without a generator, and
that's with the photovoltaic (PV) cells that make up a solar energy
system. PV cells contain silicon, which, because of its unique
crystalline structure, tosses off electrons when struck by sunlight.
When sunlight hits the cell, metal contacts draw the freed electrons into a current, which becomes electricity. If you're like me
you're thinking, Central America? Caribbean coast? Perfect spot
for solar energy! But there are drawbacks. It takes a massive number of expensive PV cells to generate a small amount of electricity.
As late as 2005, the world's largest solar power plant, the Shell
Solar facility in Pocking, Germany, could generate only 10
megawatts of electricity. The Pocking facility cost $50 million to
build. That's $5 million per megawatt, the same cost per output as
the Chalillo Dam. The difference is that the solar park can't produce power at night, whereas BEL could run water through the
turbines at Chalillo and Mollejon twenty-four hours a day. (Wind
energy—which BEL is actively investigating—has similar downsides: high setup costs and finicky breezes.)

The challenges Joseph Sukhnandan faced in powering Belize's 59-megawatt grid were a microcosm of the dilemmas vexing the worldwide energy industry at the end of the twentieth century— and still today. The root of the problem was simple: Electricity moves. If the current of free electrons doesn't flow, electricity doesn't exist. Because it moves, it can't be stored. Power companies have to generate it exactly when customers use it. Utility engineers routinely anticipate demand surges in order not to get caught short. One of the most famous examples of this occurred during the 1990 World Cup soccer semifinal between England and Germany. Grid managers in England readied their coal-fired, nuclear, and natural gas plants for the inevitable surge at the end of the match. Germany won 4–3 in a penalty shootout. A couple of minutes later the entire nation fired up its teakettles and produced the greatest power surge—2,800 megawatts—ever recorded up to that time. The century-long struggle to invent a battery big enough and efficient enough to store the power spun off by, say, a tiny 28-megawatt dam has been futile. What power companies use now is only a little better than a stack of car batteries.

If he had a better battery, Joseph Sukhnandan could rev the turbines at the Mollejon Dam when the river ran high and store the energy for use during the dry season. He could draw power from solar panels during the day and dispatch it at night. BEL's deal with Mexico allowed the Belizeans to buy as much power as they wanted during off-peak hours—cheap, too. But BEL didn't need it during off-peak hours. It needed electricity from 6 to 10 P.M., the same time the Mexicans needed it. During those hours, Mexico limited BEL to 25 megawatts at five times the off-peak price.

In Sukhnandan's eyes, the beauty of Chalillo was its ability to store energy. The water backed up behind the dam was pure potential energy, the equivalent of a tank full of oil. When demand rose, BEL engineers only had to open the penstock and send water through the turbines.

"So these are our choices," Sukhnandan told me. "We can buy more from Mexico, if they allow it. We can burn more diesel, which nobody wants to do. We can burn sugar cane. Or we can develop hydro. The truth is, we'll probably have to do all of these things.

"If you knew anything about the Mexican electricity system," he continued, "you'd know that they are in serious trouble right now trying to meet their own needs. And there's the problem of getting that Mexican power all the way to southern Belize. Power moves along wires like water down a leaky hose. The further you get from the source, the more power you lose along the way."

"Our other option is bagasse," Sukhnandan went on. *Bagasse* is a French term for the fiber left over from processed sugar cane. As a fuel it's surprisingly good—pound for pound it puts out more energy than low-grade coal. Most of Belize's sugar crop gets trucked to a single refinery in Orange Walk, a farm town about fifty miles north of Belize City. For years BEL has been in talks with the refinery owner about building a cogeneration plant that would produce electricity by burning bagasse during the six-month harvest season. The harvest coincided with Belize's dry season, when the rivers ran low and the Mollejon powerhouse ground to a halt. Some of the power would run the refinery. The rest would be fed into BEL's grid. So far those talks had come to nothing.

"We've studied it and found that the physical limit of bagasse is about one-third of our energy need," said Sukhnandan. "That's all. It cannot give more. There's only so much sugar. If you burn every scrap of bagasse in Belize you still have to have something else!"

Pointing to a map of Belize on his wall, I asked, "If Mexico is maxed out, why can't you buy from Guatemala?"

Suddenly an elephant appeared in the room. Guatemala. Sukhnandan's face tightened. "They are building a huge plant in Guatemala, in fact right near the bottom of Belize. Two hundred megawatts. The problem with buying from Guatemala is that we don't have a line to Guatemala, not even a road." BEL would have to acquire the right-of-way and sink a ton of money into poles and wires. "We've already invested in the hydro line and the Mexico line," said Michael Polonio, BEL's head of customer service, who had joined the discussion. A pall fell over the room. Polonio glanced at Sukhnandan. Neither man dared go any further on the subject. Too high a cost. No infrastructure. Best to leave it at that.

Neither man would admit the real reason: Belize hated and feared Guatemala. While Sukhnandan and his colleagues tried to sell the Chalillo Dam as the lowest-cost option for generating power, there were deeper underlying forces driving the dam. One of the strongest was Belize's struggle for sovereignty and national security.

Belize's loathing of Guatemala dates back to 1859, the year Guatemala signed a treaty with the British that set the national boundaries that exist today. That treaty called on the British to build a road between Guatemala City and Belize City. The British, of course, had no interest in laying tarmac for Belizeans, much less for Guatemalans, and the road was never built.

Central American colonialism was supposed to have ended in 1823 when the five old Spanish provinces—now Guatemala, Honduras, El Salvador, Nicaragua, and Costa Rica—declared their independence from Spain. Yet the British remained, posting soldiers and pulling timber from territory that Guatemala considered its natural eastern province. The name itself was an indignity. British Honduras: You couldn't speak of the place without acknowledging its foreign ownership. Successive generations of Guatemalan rulers capitalized on the political value of their neighbor to the east. By fostering the idea that the British had stolen Guatemala's rightful land, they whipped voters into a nationalistic fervor to divert attention from trouble at home.

Relations deteriorated when Guatemala drew up a new constitution in 1945. That document included a clause declaring Belize the rightful territory of Guatemala. The claim was dubious at best. Guatemala held that the road promised in the treaty of 1859 was intended as compensation for the loss of Belize. The road was never built, the contract never fulfilled. Therefore, Guatemala claimed, the treaty was null and void.

By all rights Belize should have gained its sovereignty soon after World War II. The rest of the British Empire was going independent. England had little incentive to keep its Central

American toehold. Decades passed and independence didn't
come—all because of, as one Belizean put it, "those bloody Guats."
The generals in Guatemala City made it clear that they expected
to enjoy high tea in Belize City the day after the last British soldier
left the country. "Guatemala will not accept the independence of
Belize even if it costs Guatemalan lives," a Guatemalan minister
once declared.

The dispute culminated in 1975, when Guatemala almost
sparked what might have been one of the fastest, strangest wars of
the seventies. It started with an offhand comment by British
prime minister Harold Wilson at a meeting of Commonwealth
heads of government. Wilson was asked if he would send the
British Navy to defend Belize in the event of a Guatemalan invasion. The prime minister responded by quoting from Rudyard
Kipling's "Recessional":

> Far-call'd, our navies melt away;
> On dune and headland sinks the fire:
> Lo, all our pomp of yesterday
> Is one with Nineveh and Tyre!

In other words, no.

Wilson must have thought himself quite the clever chap. Quoting the empire's bard in the service of dismantling the empire—
what cheek! Unfortunately, the message received in Guatemala
City was not *What a witty fellow* but rather *Please invade immediately.*
The next day's *Times* of London headline made it explicit: "FORCE
TO DEFEND BELIZE RULED OUT." Six months later, Guatemala
massed its twelve-thousand-man army at the border in prepara-
tion for an all-out assault.

This time Wilson's response didn't come wrapped in a Kipling
stanza. Overnight, England dispatched an infantry battalion, a
Royal Navy frigate, and a squadron of Harrier jets to Belize.
"What we are hoping," the British governor of Belize said when
the reinforcements arrived, "is that we have frightened them by
this show of strength into not doing anything." Some of the
British soldiers sent over on that mission liked Belize so much

they never left. Zookeeper John Foster was one of them. "It was the Harriers that stopped the Guatemalans," he told me. Back then the vertical-takeoff fighters were an exotic, fearsome new weapon. "I tell you, you see a Harrier roaring up from behind a little rise in the roadway, its guns aimed straight at you, it'll send you running for the jungle right quick, mate."

Belize's Central American neighbors lined up behind Guatemala. The only countries that backed Belize were its Caribbean island trading partners, who worked the only leverage they had: votes in the United Nations.

The two armies eyeballed each other across the border for weeks, fingers on triggers. Guatemalan strongmen harangued Harold Wilson and his imperialist dogs. British colonels hunkered down in the jungle, itching for the chance to unleash a little British steel on their opponents. And then something extraordinary happened. In the predawn darkness of a winter morning, the Caribbean and North American plates slipped past each other and triggered one of the deadliest earthquakes in Central American history. In less than a minute, one-third of Guatemala City was destroyed. Twenty-three thousand people died. The war ended that day. Guatemala recalled its troops to the capital to deal with rioters and rotting corpses, and the Belizean question was all but forgotten.

Forgotten by Guatemalans, that is. In the minds of most Belizeans, Guatemala remains an ancient rival and ever-present threat. Because of Guatemala, Belize didn't gain its independence until 1981, one of the last jewels to drop off the crown. Because of Guatemala—which refused to recognize the new nation until 1992, and continues to press its claim even today—Belize must suffer the indignity of having British troops as protectors. (About fifteen hundred British soldiers—an infantry battalion—are stationed at a base outside Belize City.) Belizeans view their neighbors to the west as lawless, violent, and untrustworthy. The historical record offers little comfort on that score. Guatemala's civil war, which raged from 1960 to 1996, was one of the bloodiest conflicts in the Western Hemisphere. More than two hundred thousand people were killed. More than fifty thousand "disappeared." For thirty-six years torture, mass graves, and mutilated bodies were commonplace. In Belize a government critic might lose his job or suffer a beating at the hands of party thugs. In Guatemala his whole family would disappear.

Belizeans had no reason to think things would be any different in a Guatemalan-administered Belize. In fact they'd probably be worse. In 1971, Guatemala cut a secret deal with El Salvador. In exchange for El Salvador's cooperation in the planned invasion of Belize, Guatemala agreed to let half a million Salvadoran peasants settle in the future province of "Belice." Whose land they took, and how they took it, wasn't a concern of the Guatemalans. As Guatemalan vice president Sandoval Alarcón said, his country claimed the territory of Belize but not the people, who were free to leave if they didn't want to be Guatemalans.

So when BEL decided to build the Chalillo Dam, there were reasons that the company didn't turn to Guatemala for its electricity. BEL didn't want to pull more power from Mexico and it didn't want to plug into the Central American grid. It didn't want to join the grid because it didn't want to join Central America. If history had taught Belizeans anything, it was that Central America was the enemy of Belize.

Cultural memories of interrupted power and oil shortages also weighed heavily on the men pushing to build Chalillo. In an interview long after my talk with Sukhnandan and Polonio, CEO Lynn Young told me about the old days when electricity came and went like rain. "They would post the rolling blackout schedule in the newspaper," he told me. "Certain neighborhoods in Belize City would get power on certain nights. I was a student then and at night I would have to call around to see whose lights were on. Whoever had power that night, that's where we would study."

Clearly, Belize needed more electricity.

Sharon tried to go through official channels. She met with Joseph Sukhnandan and aired her concerns. Sukhnandan heard her out, then lectured her on how much she didn't know about electrical generation. "To him I was just one more white person telling him what to do," she told me. "Even worse—I was a woman."

That night, after feeding the dogs, she switched on her computer. The machine was one of the few devices in her house that required electricity. Sharon lives in a small bungalow with a simple wooden table and no refrigerator. The décor is jungle kitsch—faux-leopard chairs, a fish tank, animal skulls on bookshelves. While the computer booted, she unsleeved a Rolling Stones album and turned up the volume. She let the opening bars of "Gimme Shelter" bounce off the concrete floor and run into the darkening night. Then she sat and she wrote.

> People from all over the world visit Belize to experience the bountiful natural resources found here. Finances coming into the country from ecotourism now make up the largest part of the nation's GNP, and more and more Belizeans are seeing their livelihoods empowered from this growing industry. However, this will abruptly change if plans to build a dam, known as "the Chalillo scheme," are realized.

She outlined the same problems she'd presented to Sukhnandan. Macaws imperiled. Tapirs and jaguars driven away. And for what? So little power at such a high price. Build this dam, she wrote, and we will kill the ecotourism industry. Near the end of her cri de coeur she paused to find the final note. The snarling turmoil of the Stones washed over her. Finally it came to her.

"This," she wrote, "is an environmental crime of the highest degree."

Sharon sent the piece to every newspaper in Belize. The *Belize Times* refused it. So did *The Guardian* and *The Reporter*. *Amandala* wouldn't touch it. Only the *Cayo Trader*, a struggling broadsheet published out of the western farm town of San Ignacio, agreed to run the article. The *Trader* went out to a few hundred farmers and shopkeepers in Belize's rural west. Those who read the piece did not rise up in protest. No petitions were circulated, no outraged letters written. The *Trader* editor didn't even call back for a follow-up. That is where things might have ended were it not for the unwitting assistance of Norris Hall, a government spokesman who worked closely with Ralph Fonseca.

What irked Hall wasn't so much the *Cayo Trader* piece as the fact that Sharon had e-mailed copies of her protest to friends in the international wildlife community. Here was a woman whom Belize had embraced, whose zoo the government had supported for nearly twenty years, suddenly turning a traitorous finger on her countrymen. That he would not let stand.

Hall composed his own press release. He accused the Zoo Lady of printing distortions, exaggerations, and half-truths. "Ms. Matola's press release does not indicate a desire for meaningful consultation on the issues," he wrote. "As committed as we are to full consultations and transparency on the Macal River Chalillo Project, we ponder Ms. Matola's hidden agenda, and would welcome her transparency."

Amandala, the *Belize Times,* and *The Reporter* each devoted a full page to Hall's statement. The headline read, "A REPLY TO SHARON MATOLA'S ARTICLE." Sharon had struck a match. Norris Hall doused it with gasoline.

Overnight, the Zoo Lady and the dam became the talk of Belize. On Love FM's popular morning show, a call-in cracker barrel around which the country gossiped about everything from pensions to potholes, Sharon defended the river against government officials questioning her patriotism. One of the hosts noted that he'd recently broadcast a canoe race on the Macal River. "I saw plenty of birds," he said.

Sharon explained that there were no more than two hundred scarlet macaws left in Belize and they were alive because the dam hadn't yet been built. "Of course the dam won't drown *them,*" she said. "It'll drown their nests. The adults will survive and eventually die natural deaths. With their nesting trees under water, though, there won't be enough chicks hatched to replace them. And after a few years that'll be the end of them."

Later that day she got a call from the head of Belize's forestry department, a friend with whom she'd worked on a number of conservation projects. He was wise to the ways of Belizean politics. "Sharon," he told her, "I hope you own a pair of asbestos underpants."

Sharon and Norris Hall traded barbs for a couple more weeks until Meb Cutlack stepped in. "Come! Come! Sharon and Norris!" he wrote in *The Reporter*. "Let's all be calm about this!" Like a priest stepping into a street fight, Cutlack recited the environmental bona fides of each to the other. "Sharon's 'hidden agenda' is a true and absolute love of Belize, her people, the country's wildlife and its environment," he wrote. "Norris has written for years in defence of Belize's environment—and often when few others were prepared to stand up and be counted." It was as if to say, Can't you see you're both on the same side?

But they weren't.

Sharon took her show on the road. She gave slide presentations about Chalillo and the Macal River valley in local villages and gathering spots. In doing so she ripped an old page out of the conservation playbook. If you want people to save something, you have to show them what's worth saving. In 1871, landscape artist Thomas Moran and photographer William Henry Jackson accompanied the legendary Hayden Expedition to the Yellowstone area of modern-day Wyoming. The next year, Congress, moved by the splendor of Moran's portraits and Jackson's photos, created Yellowstone National Park, the world's first national conservation preserve. In the early 1950s, David Brower and the Sierra Club saved Dinosaur National Monument in Utah from inundation by publishing what they called "coffee table propaganda"—a large-format photo book showcasing the monument at its most dramatic. Brower delivered a copy to every legislator on Capitol Hill, and the evidence before their eyes convinced Congress to withdraw funding for the Echo Park dam.

One night Sharon booked the banquet room at the San Ignacio Resort Hotel. A weathered roadhouse overlooking the Macal River and the steel lattice of the Hawkesworth Bridge, the hotel's dining room and bar often served as San Ignacio's unofficial meeting hall. Sharon expected only a handful of locals to show up, but by the time 7:30 rolled around every chair was taken. Dusty trucks and dented sedans filled the parking lot.

"I want to thank you all for coming out tonight," Sharon told the crowd. She spotted a number of familiar faces in the crowd. Meb Cutlack scribbled in his notepad. Mick Fleming, the big Englishman, sat with his arms folded. Godsman Ellis, one of the most respected elders in Cayo, sat quietly with an African kufu cap perched on his head. Norris Hall scowled at Sharon from the back of the room.

Her presentation took twenty minutes. When it was over, Norris Hall asked if he might say a few words. "Of course," Sharon said. A seasoned communicator, Hall kept his points brief. First, he said, seventy-five thousand Belizeans live below the poverty line. The electricity from this dam, he said, would be an economic benefit to them. BEL has already spent $400,000 carrying out studies on the dam, he added, and no decision about building it would be made without proper consultation. "There will be the utmost transparency regarding the Chalillo project," he promised.

Mick Fleming approached Sharon after the meeting. "Wonderful presentation," he said. "Just great. You know you've not got a chance of changing Norris's mind on this. But he doesn't matter. If you really want to stop the dam you've got to convince one man. You know who I'm talking about."

Ralph Fonseca wasn't at the San Ignacio Resort Hotel that night. Neither was Prime Minister Said Musa. But Musa had an excuse. He was in the United States attending a conference on combating corruption in developing countries.

Fleming's comment got Sharon thinking. Why not give Fonseca a try? It was a long shot, but he was the only man in Belize who could stop the dam with a snap of his fingers. And so she wrote him a letter. "Please know that I respect you and the Government a great deal," she wrote, before reiterating her opposition to the dam and inviting Fonseca to join her on an upcoming field study on the Macal. "It would be an honour to have you join us," she wrote.

She received no reply.

Other efforts, though, started to pay off. A local coalition known as Bacongo began to openly question the building of Chalillo. Bacongo, an acronym for the Belize Alliance of Conservation NGOs, was the country's most powerful environmental organization. The group's backing gave Sharon some much-needed support.

She kept digging into BEL and the powers behind the dam. The more she dug, the more confusing things became. Though BEL acted as if it was building the dam, in truth the rights to the Chalillo site belonged to Duke Energy, an American power company based in North Carolina. Duke had only recently purchased those rights, along with ownership of the Mollejon Dam, from Dominion Resources, another American energy company. It was tough to get a handle on who owned what, and for good reason. The power industry was at the height of the crazed go-go nineties. A decade of widespread deregulation and privatization had turned the once-sleepy sector of electric utilities into capitalism's Wild West. Companies like Dominion, Duke, and Enron were buying and selling power utilities like penny stocks and reaping record profits. By the end of the year, BEL itself would no longer control its own destiny. In November 1999 the government of Belize, eager to cash in on the privatization boom, sold majority ownership of BEL for $25 million to a little-known Canadian company called Fortis.

Meanwhile, as the companies behind the dam were bought and sold, planning for Chalillo continued apace. Three geological engineers loaded a truck with drilling and seismic equipment and drove deep into the backcountry of the Maya Mountains. When the road gave out they stopped the truck and hiked overland to a spot in the valley where the Macal River spilled over exposed bedrock in cool white tendrils. They checked their GPS units to confirm the location. After dropping their packs they returned to the truck for the rest of the gear. As the sun marked noon, the three men began taking core samples of the rock at Chalillo.

Chapter 6

A FEW MONTHS AFTER my first trip to Belize, I found myself messing around in a creek with my four-year-old daughter, Lucy. We were camping at Lake Crescent in the Olympic Mountains, west of Seattle. Walking in the forest, Lucy and I came upon a stream and began following it like explorers. We hopped fallen logs and waded in ankle-deep pools and collected interesting scratches on our legs. At the edge of the woods, the creek burst into the sunshine and ran across a gravel spit before vanishing into the lake. We sat on the spit in the afternoon sun and let the water rush over our feet. I worked my feet into the ground and enjoyed the gentle grind of pebbles on my heels. Lucy started to rearrange some rocks in the creek, and I joined her. We each gathered stones from the main channel and piled them on the side. There seemed to be an unspoken size-minimum rule: Move nothing smaller than your fist. With a strong levee raised, we started channeling the water. Soon we had it pouring into the lake in a fat ripply tongue. There was only one thing left to do. We lugged over the biggest rocks we could carry and blocked the flow completely. Slowly the stream rose into a pool. We hopped around patching holes and raising walls. It was challenging. It was exciting. It was fun. The pool backed up into the forest. Lucy splashed proudly in the bath we had made. I stood back to assess our work, and I realized what we had done. We'd built a dam.

Nobody knows who built the first dam. The oldest one for which evidence remains is the Sadd el-Kafara ("Dam of the Pagans"), a thirty-seven-foot-high structure about twenty miles south of Cairo. Built around 2600 B.C., about the time the Egyptians were raising the first pyramids, the dam was an impressive structure. The upstream and downstream faces, seventy-eight feet wide and built of masonry, were set like bookends against a central core filled with sixty thousand tons of gravel. The bookends began wide at the base and staircased to the top like a pyramid. It was a sound design—for a while. The dam blocked its river long enough for silt to collect behind the dam, which raised the level of the reservoir. A flash flood resulted, overtopping and ultimately destroying the dam. Engineering historians bicker about the significance of Sadd el-Kafara—after its failure, Egypt didn't raise another dam for thousands of years—but the lesson it offers is clear. After 4,500 years, the left bank of the dam still exists. You can touch its masonry steps. That's how well it was built. And yet the main section couldn't survive more than a few years in the river. Running water is powerful. Stopping it is really, really hard.

That didn't keep others from trying. Along the Tigris and Euphrates rivers, ancient engineers built diversion dams to irrigate Mesopotamian crops. The structures were so common during the time of King Hammurabi, about 1800 B.C., that the Babylonian ruler included a rule specifically addressing the legal liability of dam owners in his famous code. "If anyone be too lazy to keep his dam in proper condition," reads Section 53 of the code, "and does not keep it so, if then the dam breaks and all the fields are flooded, then shall he in whose dam the break occurred be sold for money and the money shall replace the corn which he has caused to be ruined." That's worth a second glance. Notice that the dam owner's *assets* wouldn't be sold to pay for the flood damage. The dam *owner* would be sold.

The Romans, best known for their roads and aqueducts, built plenty of dams too. By turning the Roman arch on its side, they effectively invented the arch dam, which transfers the water's force into the dam's abutments (the natural valley walls) and makes for a much stronger structure. The Romans weren't pioneers only in design. When Nero established a villa for himself on the banks of the Aniene River, a tributary of the Tiber, he ordered architects to dam the river and create three artificial lakes for his pleasure. They were the first dams built purely for recreation.

Today we think of hydropower in terms of electricity, but humans pulled power from rivers long before Michael Faraday started tinkering with magnets. In fact the most critical step in the

development of hydroelectric dams wasn't electricity at all. It was
the water wheel. Invented sometime in the first century B.C., the
water wheel was a large wheel studded with flat blades that turned
as water flowed against the blades. In terms of its influence on the
development of civilization, the water wheel was right up there
with the spear and the plow. By converting the force of a flowing
river into mechanical energy (as the wheel spun a radial shaft), for
the first time humanity drew power from something other than
the muscle of man or beast. Water wheels eased the toil of daily
life and increased food and tool productivity. Historian Terry
Reynolds calculates that a small two- to three-horsepower vertical
water wheel could free as many as thirty to sixty men from the task
of grinding grain.

It took nearly a thousand years for water power to spread
across Europe. By the dawn of the medieval age, water wheels had
become the world's primary energy source. The Domesday Book,
William the Conqueror's census of 1086, recorded 5,624 water-
wheel-powered mills operating across England, an average of one
for every fifty households. Water wheels had to be anchored to
riverbanks, which led to frustration, as the rivers' rise and fall
played havoc with the power supply. Medieval engineers tried to
solve the problem by building floating mills chained to bridges
and boats. Finally, somebody noticed an old irrigation dam divert-
ing water into a farmer's field and put two and two together.
What if, instead of adapting the mill to the river, he thought, we
adapted the river to the mill? Thus the mill dam was born. Mill
dams were small but efficient—so cheap and effective, in fact, that
as late as 1838, forty years after the perfection of the steam engine,
more than one-quarter of all British textile mills still operated on
water power.

By the time commercially produced electricity came along in
the 1880s, a simple two-step process led to the hydroelectric dam.
The first step had been taken in the early 1830s when French engineer Benoit Fourneyron invented the water turbine, putting the
water wheel's power into a package altogether smaller, more efficient, and ten times cheaper. The second step involved modern
electrical infrastructure: transformers, insulated wiring, light-

bulbs. In 1882 a paper manufacturer built the world's first hydro-electric dam on the Fox River in Appleton, Wisconsin. It was small and crude, generating enough direct current to power 250 lightbulbs. Over the next fifty years, hundreds of small hydroelec-tric projects went up in rivers around the world, each improving the technology another half step. Then in 1931, amid the worst economic depression the industrialized world had ever seen, the hydroelectric dam made its greatest leap forward. Construction began on the Hoover Dam.

The idea of damming the Colorado River, the fourteen-hundred-mile artery that drains much of the western slope of the Rocky Mountains, had been kicking around since the late 1800s. The Colorado was a notoriously unruly beast. It dried up in the summer and left southwestern farmers without irrigation when they needed it most. Like the majority of western rivers, it deliv-ered most of its water when the high mountains melted out in spring, sending down massive floods that rolled havoc over the land. Floyd Dominy, director of the U.S. Bureau of Reclamation during its midcentury dam building heyday, once recalled the wild river without fondness. "The unregulated Colorado was a son of a bitch," he said in Marc Reisner's *Cadillac Desert.* "It wasn't any good. It was either in flood or in trickle." In 1931 the S.O.B. finally came under control. In April of that year, men armed with dynamite began blasting pathways out of Boulder Canyon, a tight blackrock ravine that narrowed the river where the southern shard of Nevada cuts into Arizona. At the time, the $55 million project represented the biggest construction contract in the history of the world. The government got its money's worth. Stopping the Col-orado was said to be the biggest engineering challenge since the raising of the pyramids, and it was done with remarkable speed. In a little more than four years—two years ahead of schedule—five thousand men raised a structure nearly three hundred feet higher than any dam in North America, the heaviest, most beautiful lump of concrete anywhere on earth. When Franklin Roosevelt stood before the finished dam, he expressed his awe in the famous quote, "I came, I saw, I was conquered." A less remembered but more telling comment, given the dam's legacy, came from Harold

Ickes, Roosevelt's interior secretary, whose Bureau of Reclamation oversaw the dam's development. Standing on the river's northern bank, looking down on the dam's quarter-moon arc reaching south for Arizona, Ickes stepped to the microphone and said: "Pridefully, man acclaims his conquest of nature."

Technological leaps rarely spring fully formed from the mind of a Leonardo or an Edison. More often a lesser mortal looks at a Roman arch and wonders, What if we turned it on its side? In the case of Hoover Dam, the great leap involved that humble building block of modern life, concrete. Prior to Hoover, the size of concrete structures had been limited by the chemical heat generated by concrete as it cured. Concrete is a mix of gravel, sand, air, water, and cement. It cures, or hardens, as a result of a chemical reaction between the water and cement. Bureau of Reclamation engineers calculated that the massive volume of concrete needed to stop the Colorado River would, if laid in one continuous pour, generate heat sufficient to fracture the entire body. The dam would cook itself to pieces. Ingeniously, Hoover's engineers laid the concrete in five-foot-thick sections separated by pipes carrying refrigerated water. The dam appears to be a seamless slab of concrete, but it's actually made up of interlocking blocks and columns like a Lego set.

Inspired by the triumph at Boulder Canyon and armed with the new concrete technique, the Bureau of Reclamation and its rival, the U.S. Army Corps of Engineers, set off on a forty-year crusade to harness every drop of river water in America. Hoover wasn't finished before work began on the Grand Coulee Dam, tamer of the mighty Columbia River, the first man-made structure to exceed the volume of the Great Pyramid of Cheops. After Coulee there was no stopping the bureau and the corps. American engineering cut the Missouri River in half with the Fort Peck Dam. We turned the Tennessee and the Snake from continental arteries into still bathtubs. We dammed the Clearwater, the Boise, the Santiam, the Deschutes, the Skagit, the Willamette, and the McKenzie. We dammed the North Platte and the North Yuba, the South Platte and the South Yuba. We dammed the Blue, the

Green, the White, and the Little Red River as well. We dammed Basher Kill and Schuylkill. We dammed Salt River and Sugar Creek. We dammed Crystal River and Muddy Creek, the Little River and the Rio Grande. We dammed the Minnewawa, the Minnesota, and the Kalamazoo. We dammed the Swift and we dammed the Dead.

When we finally shut down the earth movers and parked the backhoes, we looked across America and saw 75,000 dams impounding half a million miles of river. In 1980, the National Park Service inventoried all the rivers in the contiguous United States. They found more than 3,000 distinct rivers totaling more than 3,231,000 miles of running water. Of that total, only forty-two sizeable rivers (longer than 125 miles) remained free-flowing and undammed. The number of major rivers (longer than 620 miles) left untouched by the twentieth century's great damming frenzy was exactly one: the Yellowstone.

Where I come from, dams are revered as icons of progress. The Pacific Northwest draws most of its power from a vast network of hydroelectric dams. On the main stem of the Columbia, fourteen dams pen the nation's second largest river into a series of sluggish reservoirs. Water from those reservoirs turned the state's eastern scrubland into golden wheatfields. Electricity from those dams powered the Boeing factories that built the airplanes that won World War II. Our dams stand as physical manifestations of the westerner's will to carve civilization out of the wilderness.

Dams are part of my family's heritage. My grandfather raised Ross Dam in the North Cascades in the 1940s. He built the refrigeration system that chilled the water that cooled the concrete. He loves to spin tales about riding the skip, an open-air construction elevator, to the top of the dam. "Wildest roller coaster ever made," he says. His dam stories are his war stories. My wife, Claire, learned the dam-praising songs of Woody Guthrie in grade school, and she insists on singing "Roll On, Columbia" every time we cross the river. *Your power is turning our darkness to dawn / So roll on*

Columbia, roll on! It's become one of our most cherished family traditions. I like to think that the children of our children will sing the same paean to hydropower long after we're gone.

At the same time, I've seen those dams slowly destroy our rivers. Salmon were once as plentiful here as cod on the Grand Banks. Now only a few survivors make their way upriver to spawn. The U.S. government spends billions of dollars to keep fading runs of chinook and sockeye from vanishing altogether. Nisqually Tribe leader Billy Frank, Jr., lives with the trade-off every day. "They talk about cheap electricity," he once said. "Hydropower. It's not cheap. It's all been paid for by the salmon. Every time those lights come on, a salmon comes flying out." We know things about dams now that we didn't know in the sixties. We know that a river isn't just a water pipe. Historian Richard White once offered a more elegant metaphor: he described a river as an organic machine. Like the wind and the tides, a river's rushing water acts as a self-sustaining engine of change. Its swift-flowing current moves nutrients from the mountains to the sea and from the forest floor to the flesh of fish, salamanders, and snails. Those creatures in turn push nutrients back upstream. Otters and eagles snatch fish from bankside eddies and leave half-eaten carcasses. Trees thrive on the nitrogen provided by the rotting meat. Seasonal floods replenish the valley floor with sediment, the rich organic muck that blends life and death and decay into nature's own fertilizer. Ecologists often speak of rivers as energy systems, and I find it helpful when thinking about rivers to remember that food is a form of energy. A river mixes the food. If you were to track the motion of water in a free-flowing river you'd draw an endless chain of circular arrows. A wild river moves energy in a million tumbling circles.

To do that, a river has to run. When a dam stops the flow, the organic machine goes haywire. All the energy that moved through the system stops at the dam. It takes a while to get it started again. Flowing water entrains sediment—it traps fine grains and transports them downstream. When the flow hits the dam and stops, sediment falls to the bottom. It's a problem that doomed the Dam of the Pagans four and a half millennia ago, and it's still a problem today. Many dams will stand for centuries, but they won't necessarily function for centuries. Their reservoirs are slowly filling with sediment. Dam engineers in North America and Europe have devised ways to alleviate the problem, but in developing countries like Belize, where corners are often cut, sediment can take decades off a dam's productive lifespan. In Colombia, the reservoir behind that country's Anchicaya Dam silted up within ten years of the project's completion. Nepal's 92-megawatt Kulekhani project, completed in 1981, shut down in 1996 after more than thirteen million cubic yards of sediment filled its reservoir's almost sixteen million cubic yards of dead storage. (Water above the level of a dam's lowest outlet is referred to as live storage; water below it is dead storage.) It cost $40 million to get the Kulekhani Dam up and working again.

A river robbed of its sediment load is often described as "hungry." Rivers are always picking up sediment and moving it downstream, but they're usually depositing sediment as they do it. It's a never-ending process of leave some, take some. Downstream of a dam, though, a river doesn't have any sediment to deposit. So the rushing water scours its bed and banks, leaving the channel as clean as a swept porch. In one stretch of the Colorado River below the Glen Canyon Dam, the outflow from Lake Powell stripped thirteen million cubic yards of sediment from the riverbed, leaving little of the sand, gravel, and muck that nourish plants and insects and serve as spawning grounds for fish.

The most visible canaries in this coal mine are the fish. In a dam reservoir, warm stillwater species like carp and catfish flourish while those adapted to colder, faster rushes, like trout and salmon, dwindle and die. A typical dam will eliminate one-quarter to three-quarters of the fish species in a river. The problem isn't limited to fish. Everything living in the river downstream of a new dam struggles to survive in its unhealthy water. The problem starts when a new dam floods its basin. If the basin hasn't been cleared of vegetation—a step often skipped to boost the contractor's profit—then the drowned trees, roots, leaves, and soil decompose and produce a host of noxious gases, including hydrogen sulfide, methane, and carbon dioxide. The problem is most acute in subtropical reservoirs like the one planned at Chalillo. Deeper reservoirs in colder climates entomb vegetation. Cold anoxic (oxygen-depleted) water holds the organic matter in stasis, much like ancient wooden ships that remain intact centuries after sinking. But vegetation decays quickly in warm reservoirs. At the Brokopondo Dam in Suriname, French Guiana's western neighbor, the rotten-egg stink of hydrogen sulfide produced by its reservoir was so bad that dam workers had to wear gas masks for two years after the dam's closure. The water turned so acidic that it ate away the dam's cooling system.

As it turns out, hydrogen sulfide is the least of a reservoir's problems. Dam proponents often tout hydro as a clean alternative to coal. After all, dams produce electricity without soot-spewing smokestacks. Dams are supposed to produce neither carbon dioxide nor mercury. In our age of global warming and mercury-loaded seafood, those benefits can't be dismissed lightly. In fact they bear directly on the benefit-loss balance of Chalillo, which would displace energy otherwise produced by Mexico's natural gas plants, BEL's diesel generators, or a sugar cane cogeneration plant in Orange Walk. But here's the rub. The more researchers find out about dams, the more suspect those clean-green claims become. Ten years ago we assumed that dam reservoirs produced negligible amounts of carbon dioxide, the greenhouse gas most responsible for global warming. Now researchers aren't so sure. Water in a reservoir tends to stratify like a layer cake. At the bottom of warm subtropical reservoirs, vegetation decaying in oxygen-poor water produces methane, a greenhouse gas twenty times as potent as CO_2 at inducing climate change. At the top, plants rotting in oxygen-rich water produce carbon dioxide. Reservoirs hold down those dissolved gases until the water churns through a dam's turbines. Gas release varies from dam to dam, but most reservoirs produce about one-tenth the amount of a coal-fired power plant. That's significant. One of the compelling arguments for China's Three Gorges Dam, scheduled for completion in 2009, is that the 18,200-megawatt project will displace forty million tons of coal that China would otherwise burn every year. Other dams, though, match coal ton for ton. Philip Fearnside, a researcher with Brazil's

National Institute for Research in the Amazon, and one of the world's leading experts on Latin American dams, calculates that Brazil's Balbina Dam produces more greenhouse gases, year after year and megawatt for megawatt, than the diesel and fuel oil burned in an old power plant in the nearby city of Manaus. At the Curua-Una Dam, a structure that wiped out twenty-eight of its river's thirty-six species of fish, Fearnside found that in the dam's early years the greenhouse gas production of its reservoir was more than three and a half times what would have been produced by generating the same amount of electricity from oil.

I don't want to overstate the problem. Rotting plants in dam reservoirs are not a major cause of global warming. But they're not helping things, either. In 2006, the U.N. Intergovernmental Panel on Climate Change for the first time considered emissions from dam reservoirs in its proposed national greenhouse gas inventory program, which calculates each nation's carbon budget.

Dams also play a role in the formation of other toxins, including mercury. Trace amounts of inorganic mercury occur naturally in the soil. It's harmless. When a reservoir floods a forest, however, bacteria feed on the decaying plants and transform inorganic mercury into organic methyl mercury, which is a harmful neurotoxin. Plankton ingest the methyl mercury, small fish eat the plankton, and the mercury moves up the food chain. Fish can't flush mercury from their system, so it concentrates in the biggest fish—the ones that end up on our dinner tables.

The damage doesn't stop there. Flowing rivers are oxygen-rich environments. All that crashing and tumbling entrains a lot of air. Stopping a river in a reservoir is like pinching off an aquarium's aerator. Decaying plants further deplete the water's dissolved oxygen by stealing it to make carbon dioxide. Increased human activity around the reservoir—everything from vacationing families to ranchers watering their cattle—loads the water with nutrients like phosphorus, which encourages algae outbreaks, which sucks more oxygen out of the water. Those factors produce water with asphyxiating levels of oxygen. In mountaineering, experienced climbers have a phrase for the terrain above twenty-seven thou-

sand feet, where the oxygen grows so thin that mountaineers'
bodies waste away no matter how much food they eat. They call it
the Death Zone. Downstream of a dam, we call it a river.

History places certain demands upon us. One is that we learn
from the experience of others. Forty years ago, we didn't know
that dams kill rivers. Now we do. Some of our previously accepted
customs are now understood as morally indefensible: slavery,
racial segregation, anti-Semitism. Other practices exist in a more
complicated realm where no bright line separates right from
wrong. Damming a river now resides in this unsettled limbo.
River power has never come without a certain cost, but the men
who built the dams of the past century lived in an age of abundance. My grandfather didn't worry about environmental damage.
"We knew the dams were no good for salmon," he once told me.
"But heck, we didn't care about the salmon. We wanted the
power!" Back then salmon were so common they were known as
the poor man's steak. When the Skagit River flooded its banks, my
grandfather and his buddies would use pitchforks to spear
twenty-pound chinook and coho out of roadside ditches.

In the age of abundance, there would be no question about
Chalillo. In an age of limits, it's something else entirely. The
planet is running out of wild rivers. There aren't two hundred
thousand scarlet macaws in Belize. There aren't even two thousand. There are less than two hundred. And in 1999, they all
nested in a place that the power company and the government
wanted to put under water.

CHAPTER 7

SHARON'S CRUSADE BEGAN attracting converts in the late spring of 1999, about the time the first squalls rolled in from the coast and broke the back of Belize's dry season. One by one people started questioning the dam.

Meb Cutlack came aboard first. The *Reporter* columnist had been an early supporter of Prime Minister Musa and the Chalillo scheme, but Norris Hall's over-the-top attacks didn't sit right with him. His newsman's experience told him that when a government flack went ballistic, there had to be more to the story. Cutlack smelled something crooked hiding behind Hall's response.

Something else played on his mind. Back in the mid-1990s, during the construction of the Mollejon Dam, Cutlack killed a pack of smokes and a bottle of booze with an old geologist named Charles Wright. A British government surveyor, Wright came to Belize in the 1950s to map the colony and never went home. After writing *Land Use in British Honduras,* the definitive work of Belizean natural history, Wright retired to a bungalow in Punta Gorda and lived out his days sipping rum in the shade of a wooden porch. It was rumored that he had discovered a secret vein of gold somewhere in the Maya Mountains.

Wright told Cutlack that the Macal River was the worst place he could think of to build a dam. He'd surveyed the area in the sixties. "The rock there is no good," he said to Cutlack. "It's sandstone. Shale. Weak material. For a dam you want good strong granite. I've been up and down that river. There is no granite there."

Cutlack asked if he could see a copy of Wright's report. "I don't have one," Wright told him. "But there are at least two out there.

BEL's got one and there's one in the government archive at Belmopan."

Cutlack let the subject drop. At the time, the Mollejon Dam wasn't considered a big deal. But now that Sharon was raising a fuss about Chalillo it seemed like a good idea to check out Wright's report. Unfortunately, the old geologist was no longer around. He died in 1998 a few months before Musa and Fonseca greenlighted the new dam.

There are at least two out there. Cutlack tried Charles Gibson at the national archive. Gibson is one of those quietly heroic civil servants who make sure the government opens at nine and closes at five. He runs a tidy archive in a cinder-block building in a quiet residential neighborhood in Belmopan.

Gibson told Cutlack he recalled Charles Wright's report. A search of the files turned up nothing, though. "That's all right," Cutlack told him. "I'll try BEL."

He got nowhere at BEL. Officials at the power company told him they knew nothing about Wright's report. Cutlack's nose twitched. Somebody was hiding something.

He called Said Musa. "Look, I know there was a copy of the report in the archives, and now it's gone," Cutlack told the prime minister. "The only other copy I know of is with BEL."

Musa considered the reporter's request. Cutlack was friendly to the young PUP government. The influential columnist had thrown his support to Musa during the 1998 campaign, mostly out of disgust with the incompetence of the UDP government. "I will tell BEL to open their paperwork to you," the prime minister said.

The next day Cutlack called BEL. Yes, they'd heard from Prime Minister Musa. Come in next Tuesday, they told the reporter.

On the appointed day, Cutlack parked his Geo in the BEL parking lot and found a phalanx of officials waiting for him. Joseph Sukhnandan was there, along with CEO Lynn Young and BEL board chairman and PUP party boss Robert Usher. "The PM said I was to go through BEL's paperwork on Chalillo," Cutlack told them. "Charles Wright's report in particular. Could I see it?"

Sukhnandan disappeared. He came back a few minutes later

with a single sheet of paper summarizing Wright's findings. It looked as though somebody had typed it up the previous day.

Cutlack exploded. "Christ!" he said. "This is what I suspected! This mocks the whole idea of transparency!"

Meanwhile, Mick Fleming, owner of the Chaa Creek Resort, was running his own investigation. Fleming's resort sprawls over 330 acres of riverside jungle a few miles east of the Guatemalan border and directly downriver of the Chalillo site. Bird watchers and wildlife enthusiasts from all over the world journeyed to their spot on the Macal River—and paid $300 a night—to cross keel-billed toucans and crested guans off their life lists. Howler monkeys serenaded Chaa Creek's guests as the visitors paddled downstream past oropendola nests and sunbathing crocodiles. Business and the environment were never at odds to Fleming. The environment was his business.

At the heart of that business was the river. If Chalillo was going to screw up the Macal, Mick Fleming wanted to know about it. After listening to Sharon's presentation in San Ignacio, he called an old family friend named Kimo Jolly. An athletic man with enormous teeth, Jolly was an environmental engineer who taught science at Sacred Heart Junior College in San Ignacio. "I want to know what this thing will do to the river," Fleming told Jolly. "Do you have any sense of it?"

Jolly couldn't say how this particular dam would impact the Macal. "It's fairly well known that dams tear up a river," he said. "They disconnect the headwaters. They don't allow the migration of organisms so they stop the flow of nutrients up and down the river. It's an open-and-shut case that they're no good for rivers. Unless it's a run-of-the-river dam."

"This is no run-of-the-river dam," Fleming said. "They're talking about a fifty-meter wall."

Without scientific studies, Jolly couldn't say what would happen. "Sharon's already raising hell about how it's going to kill her parrots and all that," he told Fleming. "But I tell you, man, we ought to take a look at the economics. People here, what they really care about is how it's going to affect their pocket. They're not too concerned about a piece of bush way up the river."

Over the next few days Fleming made discreet inquiries up and down the river. Other resort owners were also worried about the dam. Fleming persuaded a few of them to chip in to hire Kimo Jolly to study the project. A few weeks later Jolly returned with his summary.

"It's worse than you think," he told Fleming.

"How so?"

"I read the company's feasibility study," Jolly said. "Or at least what I could get my hands on. Five of the eight sections are missing. BEL is withholding the rest. What's there is revealing, though. They admit the dam can't make electricity costs go down. It can never be competitive with the price of Mexican power. They don't have enough hydrological data to know with any certainty how much electricity they can generate. But they do know that both dams, combined, have the potential to shut off seventy percent of the flow of the Macal."

"That's what your report says?"

"That's what their own study says," Jolly said. "I just pointed out the passages and footnoted it all." The power company justified the dam with a study it commissioned from General Electric, he said. GE's consultants came down to Belize, studied the country's power options, and concluded that Chalillo would provide the most power for the least cost. At least that's what BEL said the study concluded. The company wouldn't let anybody actually see the GE report.

Fleming went quiet as he thumbed through Jolly's notes.

"We've got to publicize this," he said.

Jolly blanched. "What *we?*" he said. "You guys commissioned this report. You present it." Recalling this conversation years later, Kimo Jolly said that this was a moment he feared might come. You watch yourself, Kimo, his friends told him. Bwah, them gringos usin' you. They gon' mess you up. Jolly occupied an awkward niche in Belizean society. Born in Puerto Rico and raised in Belize, he wasn't fully Belizean, but he wasn't a white foreigner either.

"We're not as well versed in the issues as you are," Fleming said.

"Plus, you're a Belizean. If we present this they'll just write it off as a bunch of foreign gibberish."

Jolly thought it over. Speaking out against the dam was nothing but trouble. He surely didn't want to make an enemy of Norris Hall—to say nothing of Hall's boss. But then he thought about the river. He spent his teenage years playing in the Macal. He drank its water. He bathed in it. He cooked with it. It was a part of him whether he wanted it or not. He felt the gringos were pushing him to the front of the line because they didn't want to stick their own necks out. But in the end he figured he owed it to the river.

Jolly presented his findings at a meeting of the Belize Audubon Society. The next day's *Reporter* splashed him across the front page. "ENGINEER BASHES CHALILLO," the headline said.

Bwah, Jolly thought, you're in for it now.

For the next two weeks Kimo Jolly was the talk of Belize. The radio call-in shows on Love FM and KREM became Kimo debates. He faced down Norris Hall and BEL engineer Joseph Sukhnandan on *One on One*, Belize's political television talk show. Politicians attacked him. Friends and neighbors defended him. Mick Fleming called him up during the height of the storm. "Don't worry about it, Kimo," he said. "They're not going to do anything."

That was easy for Fleming to say. Jolly wasn't so sure. He talked to an old friend named Maggie Cho one night. Maggie was the widow of Julian Cho, a Maya activist who fought to stop a Malaysian logging company from clear-cutting ancestral Mayan land in southern Belize. Six months before Jolly presented his report, Julian Cho had been found dead at the bottom of a staircase in his own house. The police called it an accident. Maggie Cho believed her husband was murdered.

"Kimo, you watch out. They gonna kill you," she said. "This dam is bigger than any of what Julian was into."

Recruiting Meb Cutlack and Mick Fleming was one thing. Bringing a government minister aboard her campaign was something else entirely. Undeterred by Ralph Fonseca's brush-off, Sharon pressed John Briceño, Belize's deputy prime minister, to join her on a trip up the Macal and Raspaculo. To her surprise, he agreed.

Briceño was Sharon's one solid contact in the Musa cabinet. As minister of natural resources, he often worked with her on conservation and education projects. Briceño was a reasonable man and a powerful ally. In the "royal family" of the PUP, the fifty-something politician was considered a prime minister in training, one of the men expected to take over when Musa and Fonseca retired.

Flush with optimism, Sharon went to town planning his visit. "I figured if I could get at least one minister out there to see what they're about to destroy, the land itself might change his mind," she later told me. Calling in favors with her British military friends, she arranged to have a British Forces helicopter drop her, Briceño, and Maya guide Greg Sho into the bush upriver from Chalillo.

Briceño seemed at ease in the backcountry. He and Sharon chatted amiably about the cycle of the river and its lifegiving floods. They stopped and watched macaws dart overhead and chatter in the ceiba trees. They gathered around a small campfire that night.

"I had no idea this was here," Briceño said.

"That's the problem," Sharon said. "Most people don't."

A few weeks later Sharon dropped in on Minister Briceño at his office in Belmopan. He thanked her for the river trip. "Best vacation I ever had," he said.

Sharon asked if he sensed any movement in the government's position on Chalillo.

He shook his head. "My hands are tied, Sharon."

"Oh, John, don't give me that," she said.

"We understand your concerns," he said. "But government has decided to go ahead anyway."

Her body sagged. *We understand your concerns.* Briceño was giving her form-letter bullshit.

"You know what, John?" she said. "I'm going to tell you something. If that's your final answer, I'm going to get on my computer and start calling, e-mailing, and faxing everyone I know. I will tell the world what you're doing."

Briceño had no answer for her.

Belizeans are masters at the art of parting foreigners from their money. "This place is a millionaire's graveyard," a Belizean businessman once told me. "People come in with big ideas about how they're going to print money down here and they go home with lint in their pockets." There's an old joke that locals tell. What's the best way to leave Belize with a million dollars? they say. Arrive with two!

Is Belize corrupt? Sure. Proof is well-nigh impossible, but talk of ministers with Cayman Island bank accounts, silent Salvadoran partnerships, drug payoffs, and yachts with names like *It Wasn't Me* float casually on the country's conversational breeze. Is Belize as corrupt as Nigeria? Not by a long shot. Transparency International's 2005 ranking of the most corrupt countries lists Belize in the middle of the pack, between Colombia and Mexico. In Belize, robbery is carried out by pen, not pistol. Few other countries are as adept in the art of laundering development money into the pockets of ministers and their well-connected friends. In 1998, Said Musa's government swept into power with a promise of immediate ramped-up development. "We will build ten thousand new houses!" They actually said that. And they did build some new houses. But early in the Musa era, huge development loans began finding their way to good friends of the PUP. It took a curiously long time to get those houses built—not ten thousand and not one thousand but a few hundred—on land owned by a friend of the party hierarchy. The government paid the crony $3.5 million for land he had earlier purchased from the government for $500,000. Other cronies took out development loans that were never repaid. Musa and his finance minister, Ralph Fonseca, kept returning to the international bond market to float more and more Belizean notes. Where that bond money got to, nobody was really quite sure. In 1999 and 2000 there were whispers about "a

certain minister" and the power he had amassed. *A certain minister* is
behind the money problems in Belmopan, the newspapers said.
Nobody had the temerity to call him out by name.

Belizeans are poor, but they aren't as destitute as their
Guatemalan neighbors. What Belize lacks is infrastructure. When
Belizeans need a modern hospital, they drive to Guatemala.
When they want to visit a well-stocked library, they catch a bus to
Mexico. While hospitals and libraries go unbuilt, good friends of
government ministers somehow find the money to raise elaborate
oceanside mansions. As Belizean politicians have mastered the art
of subtle thievery, Belizean citizens have mastered the art of ignoring the theft. When they referred to their elected leaders, Belizeans didn't say "the government." They said "government,"
dropping the definite article and coating the word in a warm fa-
miliarity. Government gonna sell off the port. Government cuttin'
deals with the cruise ships. Government gonna build Chalillo. It
was as if the government was an incorrigible rich uncle forever
pulling half-baked scams and jetting off to Vegas with floozies. He
couldn't be saved from himself. Best thing was to stay out of his
way. Government gonna do what government wanna do.

In Belize you took the good with the bad. The bad was the corruption, the good was the lack of political violence. Even compared to its Caribbean neighbors, Belize was an innocent when it
came to political mayhem. During every run-up to national elections in Jamaica, criminal gangs often roamed the streets beating
and killing opposition supporters. During the run-up to national
elections in Belize, politicians doled out hams, washing machines,
and fistfuls of cash to their constituents.

That tradition of peaceful elections grew out of the nation's
precarious position in world affairs. Because of the ever-present
threat of Guatemalan invasion, Belize's break from Great Britain
required years of artful diplomacy. A quick revolt might have
gained Belize five hours of independence and fifty years of
Guatemalan rule. By the 1950s, though, Belizeans were tired of
approaching the queen on their knees. Philip Goldson, the man
for whom Belize's airport is named, captured the essence of Belize's worn patience in an essay written in 1951. "Historically, inde-

pendence has come through one of two paths: evolution and revolution," he warned the British. "We are currently trying evolution."

George Price guided much of that evolution. A thin mestizo
with a taste for guayabera shirts and Buddy Holly eyeglasses, the
PUP founder was an old-school politician in the style of Chicago
mayor Richard J. Daley. Price knew the name of practically every
Belizean alive. He drove himself around the country in an old
Land Rover painted PUP blue. When it came to nudging and
prodding the British, nobody was better than George Price. In
1958 he gave a speech in Belize City after returning from New
York, where he'd witnessed a ticker-tape parade given in honor of
young Queen Elizabeth II. Price wryly noted that when New
Yorkers ran out of ticker tape they threw streamers of toilet paper.
"Now, you know what toilet paper is used for, don't you?" he said.
In response, the British authorities threw him in jail and tried him
for sedition. After a jury acquitted him, Belize City erupted in cel-
ebration. Legend has it the streets ran white with toilet paper.

Not long into her crusade, Sharon went to lunch with Carolyn
Curiel, the United States ambassador to Belize. Sharon was often
friendly with the American ambassadors, but it rarely went beyond a cordial acquaintance. The post of Belizean ambassador
wasn't a prestige position. It usually went to a campaign contribu-
tor from a cold northern state, a bland man practiced in the trade
of smiling and waving. Curiel was different. A former journalist
and speechwriter for Bill Clinton, Curiel was a sharp, tough diplomat. Sharon and the ambassador struck up a friendship from the
moment they met. Both were American women who came of age
in the late sixties and seventies, a time when young women were
told they could do anything and be anything. Now Sharon and the
ambassador *were* doing and being anything they wanted. But it was
a little strange. They were leading successful lives in a country
with old-fashioned ideas about women. As Sharon once put it to
me, "Some Belizean men can't stand a woman who's got any
power. They'll put up with it. But they don't like it."

Over lunch at a seafood restaurant in Belize City, Sharon asked Curiel what she knew about the dam.

"Not much," Curiel told her. "I hear the government is behind it, and they say it's a done deal."

"Is it built yet?" Sharon said.

"No."

"Then it's not a done deal, is it?"

Sharon asked for advice about fighting the dam. The ambassador remained neutral on the project—as any diplomat would—but she offered Sharon a suggestion. "Raise your profile," Sharon recalls her saying. "It'll make it more difficult for them to retaliate against you." (Curiel remembers talking with Sharon about her safety, but doesn't recall giving that advice.)

While political violence was rare, political retribution was common. This was one of the less discussed aspects of George Price's rule. Price placed a high value on loyalty, and those who crossed him suffered the consequences. Land grants were denied. Jobs disappeared. Scholarships went to other people's children. Partisan reprisals became an everyday part of life in Belize.

Sharon took Curiel's advice to heart. She redoubled her efforts to spread the word about Chalillo to her international contacts. She e-mailed and faxed green groups in the United States, England, and Mexico. She sent pleas to newspapers abroad. Her actions only stoked the fury against her in Belmopan, where her efforts were seen as an attempt to embarrass Belize in the court of world opinion.

While Sharon worked the international angle, Bacongo, the Belizean environmental group, hired John Reid, an economist with the California-based Conservation Strategy Fund, to look into the hard data behind the dam. "Environmental costs aside," he found, "the economics of further development of the Macal River are very dubious." BEL claimed that Chalillo would keep Belizean power prices low. Reid found just the opposite. Building the dam, he wrote, would actually maximize economic losses to Belize and BEL's customers. "Each dollar spent on Chalillo," he concluded, "would buy $0.85 worth of electricity."

Not long after her lunch with the ambassador, Sharon received an unexpected visitor at the zoo. "Sharon, you better come to the front gate," the booth attendant called over the radio. "Mistah Barry Bowen is here."

Barry Bowen was second only to the government in the amount of Belizean acreage under his control. His empire stretched back to 1750, when the first Bowen climbed off a British ship and joined the rowdy encampment of Baymen at the mouth of the Belize River. Bowen's father had been the last colonial-era owner of the Belize Estate Company, which was to Belize what the Hudson's Bay Company was to Canada. After independence in 1981, Bowen diversified the company, and by the late 1990s his empire encompassed everything from breweries to shrimp farms. His close ties to the PUP were an integral part of his business. Bowen cut enormous campaign checks during election time, which the PUP used to finance its "blue bills" largesse (hams, washing machines). In turn, the PUP rewarded Bowen with tax breaks and monopoly concessions. Government regulations effectively banned competition in certain markets like beer and bottled water. If you wanted a Coca-Cola, you paid Barry Bowen. If you wanted a bottle of Belikin Beer, you paid Barry Bowen. If you wanted a new Ford truck, you paid Barry Bowen.

Bowen may have been a sharp businessman, but he wasn't a bad guy. Like Mick Fleming, he had an entrepreneur's head and a conservationist's heart. In the late 1980s he sold and donated huge swaths of Belize Estate land for the establishment of the Rio Bravo Conservation Area, an enormous nature preserve in northwestern Belize. Bowen's shrimp farms were models of responsible stewardship. He donated money to the zoo.

"Well, look who's here," Sharon said, greeting Bowen with a hug. "I'm just feeding the jaguarundis. Why don't you come back with me?"

As they walked, Bowen came to the point.

"Sharon, look. I came here as a friend to ask you to stop what you're doing with Chalillo," he said. "It's going to happen whether you want it or not."

"It's a done deal, is it?" she said. "I've heard that one before."

In Sharon's office, Bowen got out a pen and drew a sketch of the dam. He explained how it would work, what it would cost, why it was a good deal for Belize. "How much land are we talking about, really?" he said. "Three-fiftieths of one percent of the area of Belize. That's point-zero-zero-zero-six percent! I'll trade that for energy independence any day."

"Oh, come on, Barry," Sharon said. "It's not about the acreage, it's about what's there."

Bowen tried other arguments. He pointed out that buying electricity from Mexico took American dollars out of Belize. "Hydropower is *ours*," he said. "It doesn't require a constant drain of hard currency."

Sharon heard Bowen out and then walked him to his car. Before driving off, he offered her a warning.

"You wouldn't believe what they're saying about you in Belmopan," he said. He spoke from firsthand experience. When he wasn't running his business, Bowen held a seat in the national senate. "I don't want you to get hurt because of all this."

"I can take care of myself," Sharon said.

Later that summer a fax arrived at the zoo.

"Sharon, I think you should see this," said Tony Garel. He slid the paper across her desk. Sharon scanned the page. It was an announcement from the Department of the Environment. After a long and thorough search, the Belizean government had chosen a site for its new national garbage dump: Mile 27 on the Western Highway, right next to the Belize Zoo.

"Oh. My. God," Sharon said. "This would put us out of business."

An image of Belize's existing dump flashed in Garel's mind. The Mile Three Landfill, so called because it sat three miles out of Belize City on the Western Highway, was an environmental catastrophe. Every day garbage trucks dumped tons of chicken bones, candy wrappers, oil cans, and soiled diapers onto a fetid, rotting field the size of ten soccer pitches. Cockroaches and rats scuttled over the fifty-foot mounds, competing with raccoons, vultures, and destitute men to find edible morsels hidden within the rubbish.

"They got all kinda predators at the Mile Three Dump," Garel said. "We couldn't keep them out."

"To say nothing of the stench," said Sharon. "Can you imagine? You know what this is, don't you?" she told Garel. "This is payback."

Garel heard her but said nothing.

"They've got thousands of square miles to choose from and they choose the spot right next to us," she said. Sharon took out a fat black marker. "Here," she said. "Send this back to them."

Garel read what she'd scrawled on the fax: "SCREW YOU! MOVE IT!"

"We've got a lot of work ahead of us," she said, and stormed out of the room.

Garel never sent Sharon's response. He knew better.

Tony Garel made himself into a garbage expert that summer. The more he learned, the worse the proposed dump looked for both the zoo and the surrounding villages. The "sanitary landfill," as it was officially known, would concentrate the refuse of a hundred thousand Belizeans on a 250-acre site at Mile 27. The zoo's entrance is at Mile 29, but its grounds and research facility, known as the Tropical Education Center, extend to Mile 28, adjacent to the proposed landfill.

At that landfill, trucks would dump the trash into large pits called cells. Each cell would be lined with naturally occurring clay to prevent leachate, the toxic garbage juice that forms when you add rainwater to trash, from leaking into the nearby Sibun River, one of Belize's major waterways. The landfill designers claimed the cells could withstand hours of heavy rainfall without overflowing. Problem was, during the rainy season in Belize heavy rain fell not for hours but for days. Two downstream villages drew their drinking water directly from the river.

Garel and Sharon divided duties. She concentrated on the dam and he fought the dump. Garel persuaded a local watershed group to join the battle, and he began talking in a low-key way to villagers along the river. As summer turned to fall, Garel geared up to present his case to the National Environmental Appraisal Committee (NEAC). One of Belize's few environmental safeguards, NEAC was made up of ten federal department heads and two NGO representatives. It existed to ensure that development projects didn't ruin the country's natural resources. NEAC members took their duty seriously, but like any government employees they were susceptible to political pressure. Jobs could be lost and budgets slashed if NEAC held up a minister's favorite project.

As the NEAC meeting neared, Garel picked up word that a few committee members were hardening their stance against the zoo. The problem, apparently, wasn't Garel's door-to-door campaigning. The problem was Sharon.

A few weeks before the meeting, the Zoo Lady sent a letter to Deputy Prime Minister Briceño. "I want to tell you that I will not oppose the proposed Mile 27 dump site," she wrote. "However, should it go forward, I won't have any choice but to close down the zoo." She put a gun to her own head. It was a risky strategy. The threat might have worked if she'd stopped there. But Sharon couldn't help herself. Emboldened by her time spent with Briceño in the bush, she added a chummy coda to the note.

"You asked me about my thoughts on alternative dump sites and I believe I've come up with the perfect solution," she wrote. Since the landfill's proponents hailed its state-of-the-art design as worthy of tourist visits and school field trips, she suggested, why not locate it near Chan Chich, Barry Bowen's luxury ecotourist lodge? "It could be a 'must do' stop on one's vacation itinerary." Sharon concluded with an ill-advised invitation. "Please feel more than welcome to read the above out loud at a Cabinet meeting."

John Briceño didn't reply. That's not to say the letter had no effect. On the appointed day, Tony Garel drove to Belmopan and waited for his turn to speak to the environmental committee. As Garel sat gathering his thoughts, he watched NEAC chairman Ismael Fabro, head of Belize's Department of the Environment, distribute a copy of Sharon's letter. "Before Mr. Garel addresses the committee, let me first say that I am most concerned about the Belize Zoo's ploy to misinform the public about this project,"

Fabro said. "In this letter you will see that zoo director Sharon Matola informs Minister Briceño that she will close the zoo if the 'dumpsite,' as she calls it, is developed. She also recommends that the project be moved to 'Barry World,' an apparent reference to Mr. Barry Bowen."

Garel's eyes narrowed. Brilliant move, Sharon, he thought.

For Garel, the next sixty minutes were excruciating. Each government official took a turn flaying the Zoo Lady. In Sharon's absence, they took their anger out on Garel. Some scolded him for referring to the sanitary landfill as a dump. Others accused him and Sharon of holding back the development of Belize. Evadne Wade, head of the Geology and Petroleum Department, gave him the worst of it.

"Frankly, Mr. Garel, I think this is just a ploy to discredit the project," she said. "If you close the zoo, we the government will take it over!"

When they finished, Garel asked if he could say a final word. He gathered his thoughts. Tony Garel was a proud Belizean. He considered himself a patriot. He believed in his good little country. To be attacked by powerful figures like Ismael Fabro and Evadne Wade shook him to his core. Garel raised his head and spoke slowly. "The truth is, I don't really want to be here," he told the committee. "But the zoo is a place in which I've invested fifteen years of my life. Whatever you may think of Sharon, the zoo has become part of the life of Belize. My job is there. My life is there. And now it's going to close down because out of all the empty stretches of highway in Belize, government wants to put its national dump—excuse me, national landfill—right next to one of the most beloved institutions in our country. It doesn't make sense."

The next day Garel passed Sharon coming out of the zoo commissary.

"How'd it go yesterday?" she asked.

"Not too good," he said, and kept on walking.

CHAPTER 8

S CARLET MACAWS WERE ONCE wildly abundant in
Latin America. The ancient Maya depicted them as in-
carnations of a supernatural bird god, although there's no evidence the Maya worshipped the actual macaws. They also had a
maize god, and that didn't keep them from eating corn. Early
Spanish explorers found the Caribbean and Central America
teeming with macaws. In 1492, Christopher Columbus observed
that "flocks of parrots obscured the heavens" during his first encounter with the New World. The Genoan explorer presented
scarlet macaws to his patrons, Isabella and Ferdinand, upon his return to Spain. Macaws were popular as gifts exchanged among
kings, and the caged birds became status symbols among the aristocracy. The bird's striking beauty, exoticism, and domesticity
made it an ideal pet and a fanciful icon.

That popularity has contributed to the macaw's demise. The
trade in exotic birds from Central America and the Caribbean
stretches back to the sixteenth century, but reliable statistics are
only available from the past hundred years. Between 1900 and
2000, nearly thirty million live birds of all species were imported
to the United States for retail sale. The 1975 implementation of
CITES, the Convention on International Trade in Endangered
Species, reduced the global trade in endangered species so dra-
matically that it's considered one of the most successful environmental treaties ever drafted. Still, even with CITES enforcement,
birds continued to be sold for profit. Wealthy clients in Mexico,
Costa Rica, and other Central American countries paid up to
$1,500 for a live scarlet macaw. In a poor country, the lure of easy
profit is hard to resist. Scarlet macaw researchers often tell the tale
of a Guatemalan macaw expert who watched helplessly, year after
year, as his field assistants scooped up juvenile macaws and smug-

gled them to local markets. "He didn't actually watch the poaching take place," one parrot expert told me. "He'd monitor the macaw nests and gather as much data as he could, knowing that at a certain point all the chicks would mysteriously disappear. They're so valuable that there's no way he could pay his field assistants enough to stop them from poaching. That's the reality of large parrots in Central America."

Between 1982 and 1998, more than 1.8 million parrots were exported from the neotropics, the region encompassing the Caribbean and Central and South America.

The pet trade depressed the macaw population, but the real destroyer was, and continues to be, deforestation. Since 1960 Central America has lost more than 70 percent of its forest cover. Most of that territory was cleared to make way for cattle ranches, sugar cane fields, and coffee plantations. El Salvador was once an unbroken sea of green. Forests now cover a mere 2 percent of the country. Intensive logging has destroyed more than one-third of Honduras's forest land. Between 1990 and 2005 the country lost 10,567 square miles of forest, an area larger than the entire nation of Belize.

As the forests were cleared, macaws lost their traditional nesting grounds. They moved into trees with less protection from four- and two-legged predators. The remaining birds hid out in scattered pockets of habitat. Panama's three hundred scarlet macaws survive in two populations, one of which nests on the island of Coiba. Coiba is home to a high-security prison that allows few visitors, a coincidental arrangement that affords the macaws twenty-four-hour armed guard protection. Mexico has fewer than one hundred wild scarlet macaws, most of them concentrated in the Lacandon forest in eastern Chiapas. Guatemala has a little more than two hundred. It's unclear how many are left in Honduras and Nicaragua. Costa Rica has about one thousand. In El Salvador, scarlet macaws disappeared entirely during the 1980s. The Convention on International Trade in Endangered Species lists species in appendices to the treaty. Animals categorized as Appendix III species come under the lightest protection; the most endangered species appear in Appendix I. In nine years, from 1976 to 1985, the scarlet macaw moved from Appendix III to Appendix II to Appendix I. The bird was disappearing fast.

The only exception to Central America's deforestation trend was Belize, which discouraged the widespread clearing of its jungles and pine forests. Belize retains 72 percent of its forest cover, one of the highest ratios of forestation in the world. Despite the country's more enlightened conservation policies, though, over the past twenty years the sight of scarlet macaws has turned from common to rare. The birds used to be spotted in the Mountain Pine Ridge region, and along the Belize River, and in the coastal pines, and in the upper parts of Stann Creek—but not anymore. In the sixties and seventies, geologist Charles Wright enjoyed watching scarlet macaws fly over his house every April on their way to a stand of pine trees north of the Rio Grande, near Punta Gorda. In 1985 the forest was cleared and the overflights ceased.

Despite the bird's enduring popularity, surprisingly little is known about the life of macaws in the wild. The first study of Belize's macaws didn't occur until 1993, when Sharon and biologist Elizabeth Mallory explored the Upper Raspaculo Valley with the Joint Services Scientific Expedition.

"Elizabeth's theory was that the macaws used the Macal and Raspaculo rivers to nest, but flew long distances to look for food," Sharon told me. "She thought they might be crossing the Maya Mountain divide to feed in the hills above Red Bank." Local villagers in Red Bank reported seeing upwards of forty macaws feeding in the hillside trees. If Mallory's hypothesis was true, Belize had fewer macaws than anybody knew: not two separate populations but one, counted twice. Other research took Mallory away from Belize, so in 1998 Sharon took up the work herself. She built an observation blind thirty feet up a ceiba tree near a nesting site on the Raspaculo. "The birds knew I was there, but after a few days they saw I wasn't a threat and paid no attention to me," she said.

One of the few biologists studying macaws in the 1990s was an

American ornithologist named David Wiedenfeld. In 1994, Wiedenfeld discovered that scarlet macaws living north of Costa Rica differed from their southern kin. The northern birds were slightly larger and had no green band in their wing feathers. The difference was so striking that Wiedenfeld pronounced the northern birds a distinct subspecies, which he named *Ara macao cyanoptera* in a study published in *Ornitología Neotropical,* the leading scientific journal for neotropical birds. Belize's macaws were included in this new subspecies, which Wiedenfeld noted was "already in danger of extinction."

Sharon spent months sitting in her bird blind peering through binoculars and taking notes. With each passing day a little more of the macaw mystery revealed itself. The birds weren't merely a random flock; they were a highly social village. If falcons and eagles were the solitary hunters of the avian world, macaws were the communal gatherers. They did nearly everything together. Because their nest cavities had to be found, not made, they couldn't cluster as tight as twelve-in-a-tree oropendolas, but where you found one macaw cavity you tended to find others nearby.

Parrots are seed eaters, and scarlet macaws will eat just about anything in the category. Researchers have found that the birds will eat the seeds, fruit, pulp, nectar, and leaves from as many as forty different species of tree and vine. Their hard black beaks can crack through just about anything that grows in a forest. The bird grasps a piece of fruit or nut in its beak, then uses its nimble tongue to maneuver the object into optimal cracking position. The macaws of the Macal and Raspaculo ate from salmwood trees, wild atta, mountain trumpet, and polewood, but their favorite delicacy was the fruit, flower, and leaf stems of the quamwood, a graceful tree with long spreading limbs that provide room for the birds to gather.

When they're not eating, macaws preen. Life-mated pairs often nibble each other's feathers suggestively. "They enjoy each other's company," Sharon told me. Arguments and fights are common, but when danger threatens from without, macaws are one for all and all for one. More than once Sharon watched a great black hawk swoop down, talons first, hoping to pick off a parrot. The macaws banded together and fought as a pack, fending off the hawk by turning themselves into an angry cloud of claw and beak.

Macaws often follow a daily routine. The parents of newborn chicks leave the nest early in the morning and return with food around nine. Then they'll leave again and return around noon. "The hours between ten and twelve were free time for me, because the birds were always gone," Sharon recalled. "I could kayak down the river, take a swim, wash my clothes, eat some lunch. Around noon they'd be back. I could judge time by their behavior."

Not every bird would come back at noon. Some would fly away in the morning and return in the late afternoon. Were they commuting to Red Bank? In early 2000, Sharon and Greg Sho shrugged on heavy backpacks and climbed the Maya Mountain divide to find out for themselves.

Weeks earlier Sharon and Elizabeth Mallory had pored over maps of the Maya range and plotted the macaws' most likely route. "Animals aren't in the business of wasting energy," Sharon explained. "Every foot of altitude is a foot a macaw has to earn." Macaws aren't built for soaring. They take two or three vigorous flaps, then draw their wings against their body and bob on the wind like corks in a light chop. The most direct low-altitude route took them up an unnamed tributary of the Raspaculo and over the divide at a 2,400-foot gap due west of Red Bank.

It was rough travel. Sharon and Sho kicked their way up steep ridges, using roots and shrubs for handholds. The constant cutting dulled Sho's machete. At night they ate rice fortified with palm hearts sliced out of nearby trees. They covered twenty-two miles in four days. On the morning of the fifth day they rose early and made the divide around 9 A.M. "We heard them overhead, and the closer we got to the gap the more we began to see them," Sharon recalled. They traveled in small units—some solo, most in pairs or groups of three to four, plump red comets against a brilliant blue sky. "I remember the time exactly," she told me: "9:04 A.M., March 21, 2000. That's when we saw them cross the divide and turn to the southeast." There was only one feature on the map to the southeast: Red Bank. Sharon and Sho stood in their muddy boots, their bodies scraped and stinking, and watched nine years of speculation turn into fact.

Exhilarated, Sharon and Sho descended the eastern slope to Red Bank, where they met with Geronimo Sho, the village alcalde. (Geronimo and Greg aren't related.) Yes, Geronimo told them, a flock of about eighty scarlet macaws had been coming down the Swasey River valley for the past two weeks and feeding in the polewood trees outside of town. They came in the morning and left in the late afternoon, heading back toward the divide.

The macaws brought prosperity to Red Bank, the alcalde said. Tourists drove over from Placencia's resort hotels to see the birds. With eighty birds in the hills, word of mouth spread quickly. Satisfied customers returned to their hotels and broadcast word around the bar, and the next morning twice as many tourists turned up in Red Bank looking to hire a guide.

What Geronimo Sho described was the realized dream of ecotourism. The macaws drew tourists to Red Bank, and the tourists hired local guides, bought local lunches, and purchased local handicrafts. The economic benefits gave villagers a cash-in-hand incentive to protect the macaws and the trees in which the birds fed. It wasn't always thus. In fact, Red Bank's macaw economy developed only after the village nearly wiped out the flock.

About four hundred Mopan and Kekchi Maya live in Red Bank. Poor even by Belizean standards, most live in tiny dirt-floor shacks. In early 1997, a handful of hungry local men looked to the hills and saw what countless generations of hungry men before them had seen: brilliantly colored chickens. In one afternoon they shot twenty scarlet macaws, brought them home, plucked them, and ate them. Twenty years earlier the incident would have passed unnoticed. But because a generation of Belizeans had learned from the Zoo Lady that scarlet macaws weren't bush hens, outrage spread. Killing scarlet macaws is illegal in Belize. But the local police chose not to arrest the poachers. And that's when things got interesting.

One of the challenges of global conservation is the difficulty of monetizing the nonextractive value of natural resources. In other words, how do you make money from a forest without destroying it? Over the course of human history, we've found countless ways to rip out the bounty of the earth and sell it on the open market. We turn forests into stacked lumber. We level mountains to mine coal. We're very, very good at this. Where we struggle is in finding ways to make money from a standing forest. There is value there, though, and economists are just now figuring out how to measure it. In the American West, for instance, a new school of economists have found that protected wilderness acts as a magnet for new businesses and residents. People are willing to pay more to live near wild places.

In developing countries, the problem comes down to a more basic equation: If a Red Bank villager sees a scarlet macaw as food on the table, what can be done to convince him he shouldn't shoot it? Jail time isn't the answer. The poachers would serve light sentences, return to Red Bank, and keep on killing macaws—only next time they'd be sneakier. The solution is clear: Make a live macaw in the bush more valuable than a roasted macaw on the table.

In the months following the macaw massacre, Belizean government officials got together with a local environmental group, Programme for Belize, and nurtured a macaw-based economy in Red Bank. With money from the United Nations Development Program and the Nature Conservancy, Geronimo Sho organized the Red Bank Scarlet Macaw Conservation Project. The project invited naturalists to give public talks about macaws. They hired local men to cut fire breaks and patrol the hills against poachers. A tourist center, including a dining hall, a four-room cabana, and a resource center, was built. Tourists could hire a guide at the center instead of knocking on random doors. Another NGO funded a community corn mill, which allowed local women to grind their corn in five minutes instead of spending an hour per meal on the task.

The program was a success. Rather than letting the slaughter become a stain on Red Bank's name, the village became famous throughout Belize as the home of the scarlet macaws. Resorts in Placencia made the village a regular part of their ecotourism packages. Money came to Red Bank, and the macaws were what brought it.

In July 2000, tropical storms swept across Belize's coastal plain and hammered the Maya Mountains. Rain fell like wrath. The hilly jungle absorbed what it could and sent the rest rushing toward the sea. The Macal River rose ten feet in two days, turning into a fat and greedy beast. It reached out and grabbed everything within reach: twigs, branches, canoes, cars, houses. Uprooted trees as big as boxcars rode the muddy current. They slid under San Ignacio's mighty Hawkesworth Bridge and tumbled over the town's secondary concrete bridge, which the river had swallowed whole. When the full force of the rainy season hit Belize, the country turned into a green pasture shot through with rivers like chocolate veins.

When the rains let up, Sharon and Greg Sho returned to the Macal and Raspaculo to check on the macaws. Four months had passed since their expedition across the divide. Sharon wanted to see whether the flock's four mated pairs had reared any chicks.

As they climbed upstream past the confluence of the Raspaculo, they saw movements in the forest. Two nesting pairs flitted through the canopy with fledglings following behind. The parents *rawwk*ed encouragement and kept an eye out for predators. The fact that they'd made it this far was encouraging. Macaws aren't prolific breeders. A female will lay one to three eggs and incubate them for about a month. The first chick to hatch wins a brutal sweepstakes. The firstborn receives the best food and the most attention; the others survive on whatever's left. When young macaws are ready to fledge, about ten weeks after birth, the eldest chick is often the strongest, most coordinated, and least likely to die. And make no mistake: Fledging season is dying season. Pet-trade poachers try to nab macaw chicks just before they spread their wings, when they're strong enough to survive outside the nest but unable to escape by flight. Kinkajous, pumas, tayras, and jaguars also lurk around the base of a nest tree waiting for the young to emerge.

Two of the nesting pairs remained unaccounted for. Sharon and Sho climbed a cliff to scan the valley and saw no sign of them. On their way back to camp Sharon spotted an adult macaw diving into a riverside bush. Sho crept up to the bank. Sharon followed. A young macaw perched there, alone, clinging to an inga tree branch no higher than a basketball hoop. The bird saw Sharon and Sho but made no effort to flee. It was obvious why. "Look at that wing," Sharon whispered to Sho. The macaw's wing hung from its shoulder as if it had been ripped from the joint. Sho pointed higher on the tree. Two adult macaws stared back at them from separate branches.

Sharon knew she was looking at a young macaw with minutes to live. As a naturalist she held the rule of nonintervention as sacred as a doctor does the Hippocratic oath. Pluck one string in the web of life and you didn't know what havoc the vibrations would cause. Saving this macaw might starve a family of tayras. Let the wild be wild. And yet principle rarely dulls the pain of its practice. It never gets any easier to watch the neighbor's dachshund eat Dolly the mouse.

"Let's not interfere, Greg," she said, and retreated slowly to the river.

That night, Sharon listened for the sound of a kinkajou attacking the young bird. Sho whispered a prayer for the little macaw.

The next morning they rose early and boiled water for coffee. Neither spoke much. Around 7:30, as they prepared to launch upriver for the day's research, a pair of scarlet macaws appeared over their camp. The birds flew unusually low. They spotted Sho and Sharon and circled. Then they landed in a nearby tree and let loose a series of raspy calls, as if they were squawking directly at the humans. Sharon knew they were smart birds. Researchers have shown that macaws, like ravens and crows, can recognize and remember human faces. And she wasn't imagining this. Sho saw it too. He noted the behavior in his field notebook: "They fly in circle 3 times and land and squawk."

"We go check on the little macaw?" Sho asked.

"You got it," Sharon said.

They paddled hard for the nesting tree. An hour later they parted the bush to find the fledgling still clinging to the branch. "Oh my god. It's still alive," Sharon said. A racket broke out up-river. Sharon raised her binoculars. Two adult macaws were dive-bombing an ornate hawk-eagle perched in a ceiba tree a hundred feet away. Seeing the hawk-eagle clarified the issue. Ornates were common throughout Central and South America. Macaws in Belize were down to their last two hundred birds. Sometimes a principle had to be broken.

"Okay, Greg," she said, "we are about to do a rescue."

Sho grabbed an empty five-gallon bucket from the canoe. Sharon pulled her hat down snug and prepared to get bitten. The fledgling would snap at her, and she figured she'd have about six seconds before the parents were on her. Sho grasped the end of the inca branch and bowed it to the ground. Sharon approached holding the bucket above her head. She murmured soothing words. Using a stick, she gently nudged the macaw toward the bucket. The bird seemed to get it. The macaw looked at her, looked at the bucket, and simply hopped in.

They returned to the canoe. Sharon held the bucket while Sho paddled away. "Can you believe this?" she said. "It's like the bird's been doing bucket transfers all its life!"

Sho smiled.

Back at camp, Sharon offered rice to the macaw. The bird leaned forward and accepted it grain by grain. As its fear waned, the macaw hopped to the rim of the bucket and perched there, eyeing Sharon. The Zoo Lady told the macaw she'd been watching it since the day its mother began preparing the nest. "I remember when you first peeked your head out of that hole," she said. Sharon slowly brought her hand to the bird's head. The macaw puffed out its crown feathers, inviting a scratch.

She named the bird Blue, and spent the rest of the day documenting everything in a report for the Belize Forestry Department. Taking a macaw out of the jungle was illegal, even for the Zoo Lady, except in extraordinary circumstances. Forestry officials would want to know exactly where, when, how, and why they had captured the bird. As she downloaded the GPS waypoints, Sharon heard macaws calling from upriver. Blue, still perched on the bucket rim, snapped to attention. The macaws called again. Blue answered. Sharon looked up and spotted Blue's parents circling sixty feet overhead. The birds *rawwk*ed sky to ground, ground to sky. They called and responded for a good long while, until each seemed satisfied with the other's condition. Then the calls ended and Sharon looked up and saw nothing but sky.

That night Sharon fed the bird and sealed the bucket with a vented lid to protect Blue from predators in the night. "We're lucky," she told Sho. "Can you believe our timing? To stumble on a broken-wing macaw about to be eaten?"

Sho sharpened his machete by the fire. "No, Sharon, I don't think that's true," he said. "These parent macaws know us. They have watched us watching them for months. They gave us their injured baby because they knew we would take care of it."

Sharon stared at the flames a long time before answering. "I hope you're right, my friend."

CHAPTER 9

"M Y FAVORITE TIME OF DAY is between four and six-thirty in the morning," Sharon once told me. "Nobody's up, nobody's bothering you. Dark turns to light and the birds come to life. I listen for the forest falcons. They have a haunting cry, and they're usually up before anything else. Then as it gets lighter the clay-colored robins and parakeets come in. The energy level of nature is at its peak in the morning. Everything just dances."

When light came into the sky, Sharon walked to the zoo across savannah grass beaded with dew. The sound of her swish sometimes startled a fox and she watched it scamper into the bush. Although it was her habit to arrive through the visitors' entrance, as the battle over Chalillo intensified she found herself using the back gate more often. It was easier that way. The scarlet macaws were the first animals you saw when you came in the front. Sharon couldn't pass the birds without her stomach clenching. At the commissary she kicked off her sandals and slipped into a pair of rubber boots.

It was amazing to walk the zoo with Sharon in the morning. The animals came running to her. Jaguars leapt down from high branches. Pumas scampered over dead leaves. One morning, as we approached a cloudy pond that held crocodiles, turtles, and pancake-size fish known as cychlids, I watched in astonishment as a rippling flotilla came toward her at full charge. "What's going on?" I asked. "Those fish can't see over here. They don't know it's you."

"It's my footfall," she said. "Each of us has our own way of walking. It's as distinctive as your fingerprint. Your stride, your pace, your weight, whether you shuffle. The animals pick up on that. Gravel is especially good at carrying the sound. The fish pick up the vibrations."

It wasn't Sharon's personality drawing the animals. "They equate me with food," she explained as she tossed a handful of raw chicken into the pond. "That's the main thing that drives animals, you know: food. Food and mating. But mostly food. If you spot an animal out in the wild and want to know why it's there, look around and see what it's eating."

"And why are you here?" I asked.

"This is where the animals are," she said.

On some mornings she drove into the British Forces Broadcasting Service (BFBS) station. BFBS broadcasts from the military base near the airport as a service to homesick soldiers. Sharon pulled three shifts a week to bring in some extra money. I dropped her off there one day before borrowing her truck to get some groceries. About a mile from Belize City, Sharon came over my radio. "Let's check out the weather forecast," she said. "It's moist and unstable for the next twenty-four hours. Bet some of you like *that*. Showers and thunderstorms, especially in the south. Here in the studio it is blistering hot and you know why, don't you. We are ninety-nine point one, Belize BFBS." Marilyn Manson's version of "Tainted Love" came on. A smile crossed my face. Sharon's radio persona never failed to crack me up. At the zoo she was Sarge in Charge, the boss lady in rough pants. At BFBS she slipped behind the microphone and became *Shhharon Ma-towwwla,* bawdy rock mama.

At the grocery store I picked up some peanut butter, bread, bottled water, and a copy of *Amandala.* When I got back in the truck Sharon was thanking the British Forces butcher for saving bones for her problem jaguars. "Part of jaguar rehab is getting the cats used to getting close to you, and one of the ways I do that is with boners, I think you guys can understand that." My eyebrows jumped. Did she just say that? "Thank you, guys. Those cats wouldn't be here if it weren't for the stuff you're doing." She stopped talking and the opening chords of "Eye of the Tiger" crashed out of the speakers.

If scarlet macaws were Sharon's first love, jaguars ran a close second. The powerful cats are at once the most loved and the most feared creatures in Belize. Locals know it as *da tígah,* a shadowy nocturnal beast lurking at the forest's fringe. As the jungle's top predator, the jaguar is to Central America what the gray wolf once was to the American West: a mythical malevolent force roaming the countryside. Unfortunately, the jaguar seems doomed to share the gray wolf's fate. In the nineteenth and twentieth centuries, ranchers across the American West shot every wolf within reach of a bullet. By the 1970s, wolves were all but eliminated from the landscape. The gray wolf is now slowly returning to its former habitat, but it's taken twenty years of conservation battles and millions of dollars to do it.

What we learned from that near extinction is that taking top predators out of the food chain doesn't work. It throws the whole biotic system out of whack. The most famous example occurred on Arizona's Kaibab Plateau, the high forested tableland that rims the Grand Canyon. In 1906, President Theodore Roosevelt created the Grand Canyon National Game Preserve and hired local hunters to wipe out cougars, bobcats, coyotes, and wolves. Instead of creating, as Roosevelt hoped, "the finest deer herd in America," he created a disaster. Without predators to cull the herd, the deer population skyrocketed. Land that formerly carried four thousand deer soon saw populations jump to thirty thousand and more. One estimate put the deer population, at its height, near a hundred thousand. The land couldn't support that size herd. The inevitable crash followed. Disease and starvation culled the deer by the tens of thousands. The experience at Kaibab Plateau eventually led Aldo Leopold to write "Thinking Like a Mountain," one of the seminal environmental essays of the twentieth century. Leopold told the story of killing a wolf in 1909, not long after Roosevelt declared open season on the predators. After watching the "fierce green fire" die in the wolf's eyes, Leopold realized the error of his—and T.R.'s—ways. "I was young then, and full of trigger-itch," he wrote; "I thought that because fewer wolves meant more deer, that no wolves would mean hunters' paradise. But after seeing the green fire die, I sensed that neither the wolf nor the mountain agreed with such a view."

Belize's jaguars were lucky. They already had their own Aldo Leopold. In the 1980s, American zoologist Alan Rabinowitz came to the country and spent two years studying jaguars in Belize's Cockscomb Basin, a dense tropical forest in central Belize. Rabinowitz compiled the most comprehensive picture of jaguar life ever produced. He found that, despite the man-eating mythology, jaguars posed little threat to humans. Like bears, jaguars don't hunt humans, but they will attack if surprised, angered, or cornered. Jaguars eat mostly armadillos, deer, peccaries, and opossums. Rabinowitz also discovered that ranchers, loggers, and poachers were killing the cats in alarming numbers. Despite an international ban on the sale of jaguar pelts in the mid-seventies, the population of jaguars in Central and South America continued to plummet. Working with international conservation groups and the government of Prime Minister George Price, Rabinowitz established the Cockscomb Basin Wildlife Sanctuary and Jaguar Preserve, the world's first wild jaguar refuge. Crucially, the preserve was set up in partnership with the local Maya population, which exchanged traditional milpa land for a stipulation that only local Maya would be hired as trail guides and park managers. Tourists started trickling down from Belize City to see the jaguars. The Jaguar Car Company contributed more than $1 million to expand the sanctuary and its research. By the late 1990s the sanctuary had grown to encompass nearly a hundred thousand acres.

Today an estimated six hundred to two thousand jaguars roam throughout Belize. It's hard to know the exact count because jaguars are solitary and shy and roam across vast stretches of territory. Researchers believe that upwards of two hundred jaguars roam in and out of the 150-square-mile Cockscomb preserve, the largest concentration of the cats in the world. Outside the sanctuary, however, a familiar story is playing out. Development is encroaching on the jaguar's habitat. Cane fields and shrimp farms are expanding acre by acre. Village roads are extending into the bakabush. Jaguars hunt over vast stretches of land. A lone male may roam over nearly fifteen square miles. Up to three females might work the same ground. If a jaguar makes his rounds and discovers that what used to be jungle is now a pasture supporting thirty head of cattle, the cat will go after the cattle. The first meal is free. The second will come at the price of a bullet.

"Until recently, sixty jaguars were being killed every year," Sharon told me. "That's more than one a week! And those were official government figures. So you know the real figure was double or triple that." To stop the killing Sharon turned a little-used section of the zoo into a halfway house for problem jaguars. She made a deal with the government: If they'd trap the jaguars, she'd pick them up and bring them to the zoo. She sent flyers to farmers and ranchers across the country asking them to call the jaguar hotline before they reached for their rifles.

Returning the captured cats to the wild was out of the question. "Once they get a taste of cattle or chicken it's almost impossible to get that out of their system," Sharon told me. "They'll keep coming back. It's the ancient driver, man: food." She found an answer in another ancient driver: sex. In the early 1990s, zoo officials in the United States realized they needed to refresh the jaguar gene pool. "We had about a hundred cats in the American population and nobody knew much about their ancestry," Bob Wiese told me. "We didn't know if we were mating first cousins with first cousins." Wiese, the director of animal collections at the Fort Worth Zoo, serves as the jaguar coordinator for the Species Survival Program, a database that tracks the genealogy of animals in American zoos. Without an infusion of fresh DNA, the captive jaguars risked going the way of the old royal houses of Europe, producing a generation of sickly, blind, and stunted cats. The wild jaguars brought to the Belize Zoo represented a commodity highly sought by Sharon's American colleagues. Once word got out, Sharon had a waiting list of zoos in need of cats.

Sharon dipped her hand into a bucket of raw chicken. A spotted cat sauntered up to the fence. "Wild Boy!" she said. "Do I get a paws-up for some food? Do I get a paws-up?" The 140-pound jaguar pressed its paw to the fence. Sharon tossed a piece of meat into its jaws. A second cat watched warily from behind a bush. "That's Zabby," she said. "She's a sheep killer. She won't come out until we're gone. She's been too mistreated." Zabby had gone through the wringer. Sheep ranchers shot her, then trapped her, then beat her in the trap, then let her go. She came back. The ranchers trapped her again and beat her again and let her go. "When they trapped her a third time, they brought her to us," Sharon said. "She's not exactly attuned to people."

Jaguar rehab proceeds in stages. Once they arrive at the zoo, the jags stay for a few weeks in a small concrete cell. The cats can see and hear the other jaguars in open enclosures nearby. By their nature, jaguars are solitary creatures. They live alone except when breeding and raising their young. "We're acclimating them to the presence of other jags and humans," Sharon explained. "After a few weeks they'll come out into their own open enclosure. If they learn to be more at ease with the other cats we'll put them in together."

We circled a concrete bunker that held the latest arrival, a jaguar named Field Master. Sharon shoved a plywood slab into a slot in the wall, and we entered through a short door. The jaguar backed into the corner and hissed. Three layers of chain link separated the cat from the humans. The stench of urine and wet fur enveloped the room. "How's my big boy today?" Sharon said. The cat bared its teeth, or at least what was left of them.

"Field Master lost most of his teeth," she said. "We have to mash up his food. He was a cattle killer. When he came in here he had forty botflies in his coat." The cat rose and paced. Under Field Master's scruffy pelt there still existed strong muscle and bone. Tattered, beaten, and nearly toothless, the jaguar had lost none of its elegant power.

Sharon reached into her guitar case and brought out a rosewood six-string. "This is one I wrote last week for Field Master," she whispered to me. The strum of a G chord perked the jaguar's ears. Sharon began to sing.

> I killed them big and I killed them small,
> I ate them short and I ate them tall.

> *One day I wandered in a trap;*
> *Ranchers jumped for joy, you can bet on that.*

Field Master growled in protest. The jaguar settled near the fence, his growls turning soft and helpless, as if fighting the narcosis of a tranquilizer dart.

> *Jaguar rehab, that's my deal.*
> *This chick can feed me every meal.*
> *She sings to me and she brings me bones.*
> *The hell with cows, I've found a home.*

As a lyricist, Sharon is strictly moon-June. As a guitarist, she is a brilliant lyricist. There's no disputing the power of her performance, however. The savage beast lay before us, soothed.

Sharon fed Field Master a cut of chicken through the fence.

"The song is a repetitive thing," she told me. "He hears his name, he hears the song, and he knows he'll get a treat at the end of it. Sometimes he'll roll on his back when I play, which is a key behavioral trait. It signifies total acceptance." She turned back to the jaguar. "Is it paws up?" she said in a loud upbeat voice. "Paws up!" Field Master lifted his left paw to the fence. "That's my boy."

Simple commands, positive reinforcement, show no fear: More than a quarter century after her apprenticeship with the Romanian tiger tamer, Sharon was still using his tenets to save the last great cats in the Western Hemisphere. I mentioned this to her and she nodded. "Jaguars have the biggest brain-to-body-mass ratio of all the big cats," she said. "They're extremely intelligent, which makes them independent, unpredictable, and dangerous. You'll never see a jaguar tamer in the circus. If you do, buy a ticket, because that'll be a onetime show."

The guitar packed away, we made our way back to the commissary, where zookeeper Humberto Wohlers handed her a bowl of chopped rat. "Fresh for Alvin," he said. Sharon and I ducked into a nearby aviary. She handed me a pair of thick leather gloves, the kind you use for stacking firewood. Alvin, a roadside hawk the size of a Scotch terrier, let out a screech from atop a wooden T-post.

Sharon stood at the enclosure's other end and pinched a piece of rat meat. Alvin lifted himself with two flaps—the wings sent a breeze across the cage—and glided to a perch on Sharon's wrist. "Alvin came to us a few months ago," Sharon said. "I'm trying to train him so we can put on a birds of prey show for the kids that come through."

As she finished feeding Alvin, Sharon caught sight of business manager Claudia Duenas waiting for her outside the aviary. "Hey, Claudia," she said. "What's up?"

Duenas held papers in her hand. She glanced at me. "Gotta talk to you about something, Sharon." A grimace crossed Sharon's face. Duenas wouldn't keep good news private.

The two women huddled out of earshot. Duenas pointed at a couple of sheets and circled something with a pen. A few minutes later Duenas split off and Sharon returned to me. "Our checks are bouncing," she said. "It happens. The rainy season comes, attendance drops off, cash flow dries up. What's annoying is we've got a bunch of invoices waiting for payment from groups that held conferences here months ago. I'm pleading with them, hey, man, put a check in the mail, will you? Because BTL's going to cut off our phone in a few days."

We walked along in silence. Sharon worried the problem.

"How do you keep this place running?" I said. "How did you think it would work in the first place?"

She smiled. "I was dumb enough to give it a try."

The dump weighed heavily on Sharon. "The whole thing is meant to scare me off Chalillo," she said. "And I considered it. With the dump, we're not just talking about the zoo—we're talking about poisoning the drinking water of villages along the Sibun. If that happened, I couldn't live with myself." She wondered if she should just drop Chalillo. Walk into John Briceño's office and cut a deal: She'd go away if the dump went away. Then something happened that changed her mind.

"I was walking through the zoo one afternoon and I passed the otters," she told me. Standing before the sleek mustelids was a mother with her five-year-old son. Sharon stopped to greet them. "Hey, you want to feed a fish to the otter?" she said.

The boy's name was Zeke. His eyes lit up.

She fetched a bucket of mackerel from the commissary and dangled one by its tail. "Hold it like this," she told Zeke.

Zeke followed her instructions. He pushed a fish through the fence. The otters scurried to the food and nipped it from his hand. Zeke squealed with delight.

Sharon went on her way.

Months passed. Chalillo and the dump ate up her days and knotted her nights. "I was having a horrible day," she recalled. "Nothing was going our way. We were losing on both the dam and the dump and I sat there thinking, 'You know what? I don't need this. If they want to screw up this country, who am I to stand in their way?' " For the first time, she considered leaving Belize.

The phone rang. It was the front gate. "Sharon, there's a Mr. and Mrs. Nesbitt here to see you."

"Who?"

"The Nesbitts."

She didn't know any Nesbitts. A flush of frustration came over her. Probably a tourist couple she'd never heard of wanting a personal tour. As she made her way to the front gate, her mind ran down a list of excuses to gently brush them off.

A man and a woman in their late twenties slumped on the wooden bench. The Zoo Lady offered them her hand. "Hi, I'm Sharon," she said. "Can I help you?"

The Nesbitts told her their story. Two weeks earlier Chris Nesbitt, the husband, had taken his five-year-old son out to dinner at a seaside restaurant in Punta Gorda, where they lived. As Chris waited for their order, his son wandered outside to catch crabs along the rocky shore. Fifteen minutes later the boy hadn't returned. Chris called out into the darkness and heard nothing back. He ran up and down the shore in a panic. Locals joined him in the search. Two hours later, the boy's body washed up not far from the restaurant.

"Oh my god, I'm so sorry," Sharon said.

The woman spoke. "His name was Zeke."

Instantly, Sharon recalled the woman's face. And Zeke's.

"We're on our way back from the funeral," the man said. "We just wanted to stop by and thank you for the zoo. It made Zeke so happy. He knew all the animals by name, and his life was so full because of the otters and jaguars he visited here."

Sharon embraced the couple. Then she went back upstairs to the office. Zeke Nesbitt's face wasn't one you'd forget. It burned in her memory. She turned on the computer and began to write—to no one in particular. Just to write.

"Over my dead body," she wrote. "They are not going to take this away. Not the zoo, not the river, not the country." She would stay and fight. But she couldn't do it by herself. She needed help.

CHAPTER 10

*J*ACOB SCHERR IS ONE of the toughest environmental lawyers alive. A handsome man with a shock of thick black hair, he wears tailored suits and carries himself as a gentleman who knows his way around the corridors of power. Shortly after the first Earth Day in 1970, a handful of American environmentalists founded the Natural Resources Defense Council (NRDC) with the idea that a few good lawyers could save the world. Jacob Scherr was one of the lawyers who made it happen.

In the 1970s he fought the Philippine government's plan to build a nuclear reactor in an earthquake zone next to the then-dormant Mount Pinatubo volcano. In the 1980s Scherr was part of an NRDC team that talked the Soviet Union into letting the environmental group install seismic equipment near the Semipalatinsk proving ground to monitor nuclear-treaty compliance. Ronald Reagan's "trust but verify" stance toward the Soviets was possible because of those seismometers. In the 1990s Scherr rose to head the NRDC's international division, where he oversaw campaigns in Canada, Chile, Brazil, Guatemala, and other countries.

In the fall of 1999, Scherr traveled to an environmental conference in Cuernavaca, Mexico. He talked about projects to halt clear-cut logging and destructive oil exploration, but the centerpiece of his speech was the whale nursery. Every year gray whales from as far north as the Bering Sea migrated south to give birth in the warm waters of Laguna San Ignacio, a sheltered lagoon midway down the Baja Peninsula. In the mid-nineties, Japan's Mitsubishi Corporation announced plans to turn the calving ground into the world's largest industrial salt factory. The NRDC teamed up with local Mexican environmentalists to fight the plan, and by the end of the decade the whales of Baja had garnered support from scientists and citizens around the world.

As people clustered around Scherr after his speech, a petite woman clutching a sheaf of documents stood off to the side. When the crowd thinned, she approached.

"Jacob, my name is Candy Gonzalez," the woman said. "I'm from Belize. I have an issue that might interest you."

Scherr heard a lot of pleas for help in his line of work. There were thousands of environmental groups all over the world and none of them had much money. The NRDC was a rare exception. The organization boasted a $26 million budget and a database of 450,000 members. When Jacob Scherr went to battle, he came loaded for bear: battle-hardened lawyers, Hollywood celebrities (Leonardo DiCaprio! Pierce Brosnan! Cameron Diaz!), full-page ads in *The New York Times,* and political clout in Washington. Even the NRDC's power had limits, though. Scherr could only take on a few causes at a time. Each campaign lasted two years, minimum, and some stretched over a decade. Turning away people like Candy Gonzalez was part of his job.

Still, he listened. Candy Gonzalez was a small-town lawyer from Belize's rural Cayo district. She lived in San Ignacio, a town doubly imperiled by the dam. If the structure held, it threatened to destroy the river and San Ignacio's ecotourism economy. If it broke, the flood could wipe the town off the map.

The situation was nothing new to Scherr: one more energy development destroying the heart of a pristine wilderness. But the more Gonzalez talked about the Macal and Raspaculo valleys, the more intrigued Scherr became. Jaguars, tapirs, scarlet macaws: It sounded like an incredible spot. More to the point, it sounded defensible. Among ecoactivists it's well known that a cuddly koala is easier to save than a slimy fish. The more charismatic the animal, the greater the outrage from the general public. Scherr's own whale campaign proved the point. Mitsubishi's salt factory wasn't stopped by scallops and mangroves. It was stopped by two powerful words: *baby whales.*

"Who's working on the issue in Belize?" Scherr asked Gonzalez.

"It's a group called Bacongo," she said. "We're a coalition of local environmental groups."

A good sign. Scherr knew from experience that when the NRDC operated in foreign countries, it could only join a preexisting fight, not start one themselves. If they went in without local leadership, governments cried ecocolonialism. When he consulted on foreign campaigns, Scherr often faced local reporters demanding, "What are you gringos doing here?" That's why he also kept his eyes open for American connections. If U.S. corporate money was driving a destructive project—which it often was—the NRDC felt it had legitimate standing to question the company's actions.

"Who's behind the dam?" he asked Gonzalez.

"BEL, the local power company," she said. "And there's an American company involved too. Duke Energy."

Scherr's eye flashed. "Duke Energy?" He thought for a moment. "You know, we might be able to work with you on this."

The NRDC's Washington headquarters is said to be the greenest office on the eastern seaboard. The building's air-conditioning operates without ozone-depleting CFCs. The doors are made of compressed straw, which reduces logging pressure on forests. The marblelike countertops are made of newsprint and soybean flour. Instead of wood-based particle board, the builders used a composite substrate that contains recycled junk mail. That last bit is a nice touch. The NRDC, like most big environmental groups, survives by mailing out endless batches of fund-raising letters.

It's a sophisticated workplace. The ratty couches and chipped tables typical of nonprofit offices were absent from the NRDC's Washington office. Most staffers owned more than one suit.

Ari Hershowitz was not a typical staffer. Scherr's twenty-eight-year-old protégé wore woolly Peruvian sweaters and Birkenstocks. He often went barefoot around the office. Hershowitz was a Bolivian-born neuroscientist who had abandoned his graduate studies at Caltech to join the NRDC and save the world. One of the reasons the baby whale campaign worked so well was because

Hershowitz had tramped around the fishing villages of Baja and enlisted the support of the locals.

One afternoon, Scherr appeared at Hershowitz's office door.

"Listen, what do you know about Belize?"

"I know it's south of the Yucatán."

"I met a Belizean lawyer at the Cuernavaca conference," Scherr said. "She's got an interesting project. Sounds like something we might want to get involved with."

He handed Hershowitz a file. "Here's some material I got from Jim Nations at Conservation International. He's been following the issue. He says there's a woman down there we should talk to. She runs the local zoo."

Hershowitz agreed to look into it. Using computer databases and his contacts in the power industry, Hershowitz traced the history of Macal River hydropower. Back in 1991, the head of BEL signed an agreement with the Belize government and a group of American investors to create the Mollejon Dam. The deal created a new company that would build and own the Mollejon project. That company, called the Belize Electricity Company Ltd. (BECOL), was set up as a mini-BEL, run by BEL officials but legally autonomous and financed with American money.

One of the original investors in the Mollejon Dam was Brooke Banbury, a Colorado real-estate developer. "The Mollejon Dam was a BOOT deal," Banbury explained to me. "Build, Own, Operate, Transfer. It's a standard deal in a place like Belize. We build it, run it for forty years, then transfer ownership to the government."

What wasn't standard, I would later find out, were the terms of the contract. The government granted the dam owners exclusive water rights to the Macal River and its tributaries from the Mollejon site to the headwaters high in the Maya Mountains. BECOL would never pay taxes. BEL, which distributed the power, agreed to purchase electricity from BECOL at special guaranteed-profit rates. The power from Mollejon was deemed "priority dispatch," which meant BEL had to buy all of BECOL's power before purchasing elsewhere, even if cheaper power was available. The contract also included a "take or pay" clause, which stipulated that BEL would pay BECOL $9.6 million for 120,000 megawatt-hours of electricity every year for forty years regardless of whether BECOL actually delivered the energy. If BEL couldn't come up with the $9.6 million, the government guaranteed that the taxpayers of Belize would foot the bill. The terms of the deal, known as the First Master Agreement, remained secret for more than a decade.

How did BECOL wrest such generous concessions from the Belizean government? Years later, when the contract was made public, government officials claimed that secrecy and concessions were the price of foreign investment. Without such guarantees, they said, international financiers would never invest in a country as risky as Belize. There was some truth to that. But there was also this truth: The man who negotiated on behalf of Belize's Ministry of Finance and the man who negotiated as chairman of BEL's board were one and the same—Ralph Fonseca.

"Let me tell you a story about Ralph," said Brooke Banbury. "When I went down there to work out this deal, I flew into Belize City and stayed there overnight. I figured I'd get some sleep before meeting Ralph in Belmopan the next morning." At the Chateau Caribbean, the woman behind the desk recorded Banbury's passport number and handed him his key. And then she said something funny.

"Mistah Brooke," she said. "I really like your eyes."

"Well . . . thank you," Banbury said. The desk clerk held his gaze.

"No, you don't understand," she said. "I *really* like your eyes."

Weird, Banbury thought. But whatever. This is Belize.

The next morning Banbury drove to Belmopan. Ralph Fonseca greeted the American investor with a hearty handshake and a pointed message.

"You know, Brooke," Fonseca said, "I really like your eyes."

Banbury was taken aback. Then he smiled. Fonseca was sending a message: In Belize, my eyes are everywhere. "I get the point, Ralph," Banbury said.

Ari Hershowitz turned up little of this in his initial research. All he knew was that BECOL owned the Chalillo project, which meant the money backing the proposed dam didn't come from

BEL. It came from foreign investors. Those investors had changed over the years. Brooke Banbury's investment group sold out to Dominion Resources, which sold its interest to Duke Energy. Duke's ownership made the Chalillo case appealing to Hershowitz and the NRDC. Duke's headquarters were in Charlotte, North Carolina, a day's drive from Washington. Duke took pride in its image as a good corporate citizen. When it came to pollution, the company wasn't without sin. No energy company was. But word among Ari's green-group colleagues was that the company took environmental issues seriously. You could work with Duke.

The money trail established, Hershowitz continued his research. He called Sharon and listened to her stump speech on the evils of Chalillo. He asked colleagues at Conservation International and the World Wildlife Fund what they thought. He looked into the official status of the scarlet macaw. At the end of two weeks he presented his findings to Jacob Scherr. Hershowitz leaned toward joining the fight against the dam. There was one thing he couldn't guarantee, though. It was a question the NRDC asked before committing to any campaign: Is this fight winnable? "I honestly don't know if it is," Hershowitz told Scherr.

"I don't know if we have the budget to take on another big project," Scherr said, "but I think we need to go down there and see what's going on."

At the end of a terrible year, Sharon found herself with one last onerous chore. It was late December 1999, and a rare dry season storm drummed on the *oficina* roof. She sat at her desk composing an apology to Barry Bowen. Sharon's infamous "Barry World" letter to John Briceño hadn't gone over well with Bowen. Through the grapevine Sharon heard that he'd taken to deriding her in front of guests at his Chan Chich Lodge. She knew Bowen couldn't be swayed against the dam, but Sharon needed his support—or at least his neutrality—on the dump. She swallowed her pride and scribbled out a peace offering.

"My suggestion of placing the dump in Barry World was not

meant to be offensive," she wrote. She stared at the blinking cursor. Then she opened up and confessed.

"I've had the worst year of my life," she wrote. "I'm watching one of the most incredible habitats left on earth be threatened by a project with no economic integrity. I'm dealing with over 30 people working at the zoo who feel their careers and their jobs will vanish and be replaced by a garbage dump. I've watched my mother die a horrible death from cancer this year, horrible. Please give me an ounce of credit for keeping some semblance of bloody humour through all of this."

In early January 2000, Ari Hershowitz and Jacob Scherr flew to Belize City. Sharon met them at the airport.

"I can't tell you how great it is to have you guys down here," Sharon said. She tossed their luggage into the truck bed. "So listen. I know you're meeting with the folks at Bacongo in the morning. That's right around the corner from your hotel. I'll pick you up after that and take you to the zoo, give you a quick tour, and then we can head out to Chaa Creek."

As Scherr chatted with Sharon in the front seat, Hershowitz rolled down his window and watched the country come into view. He'd traveled through Mexico, Peru, Guatemala—all over Central and South America. Belize he couldn't figure out from a glance. The children he saw walking along the highway seemed less gripped by poverty than those in Guatemala. But the roads, the houses—everything seemed less improved in Belize, more primitive.

Sharon stopped in front of the Chateau Caribbean. "Before you go, I brought you some reading material," she said. She handed Scherr an inch-thick report belted with a rubber band. "This is a feasibility study on the fifty-five-thousand-ton garbage dump the government wants to build next to the zoo as a thank-you for the work I'm doing to stop the dam."

Scherr and Hershowitz glanced at the report and then at each other. Both knew what the other was thinking: What garbage dump?

The next evening, Scherr and Hershowitz sipped coffee on the mahogany deck of the bar at Chaa Creek, Mick and Lucy Fleming's resort. There were more famous watering holes in Central America but few more enchanting. Perched on a hillside overlooking the Macal River, the open-air bar offered all the amenities of a luxury resort amid the steamy chaos of the jungle. Guests lounged on hand-embroidered pillows while watching basilisks scurry up gumbo limbo trees. Blue morpho butterflies perched on the bar rail. At night, old ship lanterns salvaged from the set of *The Mosquito Coast* bathed the bar in a romantic yellow glow. An eclectic mix of biologists, businessmen, American honeymooners, European birders, and type-A tycoons swapped anecdotes over tropical cocktails. Mick and Lucy spread hostly cheer, and occasionally Mick would tell about the time Francis Ford Coppola, who owns the nearby Blancaneaux Lodge, swung by for dinner and, during the course of conversation, mentioned the movie *Apocalypse Now.* "I wasn't even thinking about who directed it, right? And I blurted out, 'Christ! Slept straight through that one.' "

Scherr and Hershowitz nursed cups of coffee and waited for the leaders of the dam opposition to arrive: the Flemings, Candy Gonzalez, Meb Cutlack, Kimo Jolly. Sharon had driven Scherr and Hershowitz to Chaa Creek, but an emergency at the zoo called her home.

Hershowitz dropped a file of research clippings on the table. The NRDC boys had done their homework. Scherr flipped open a legal pad. "So," he said, "what's the process in Belize?"

Blinks all around. Mick Fleming spoke. "What process would you be referring to?"

"The legal process," Scherr said. "I mean what kind of approval do you have to get to build a dam?"

Nobody could say for sure. Belize had only adopted its Environmental Protection Act seven years ago. The law had never been tested.

"I know they're required to publish an environmental impact assessment," Candy Gonzalez said.

"And who approves that?" said Scherr.

"It goes through the Department of the Environment and has to be approved by NEAC," said Gonzalez.

NEAC was the National Environmental Appraisal Committee, the same group that had excoriated Tony Garel over the Mile 27 dump.

Scherr scribbled "NEAC" on his pad. Over the years he'd learned that every environmental campaign contained pressure points. Pinching them hard enough and long enough could disable a destructive project. Two questions usually revealed the pressure points: Who's funding the project? Whose approval must be won? NEAC was a possible pressure point. He and Hershowitz discussed other points with the group. Duke Energy, which owned the rights to build the dam, and Fortis, which owned the Belizean electric utility, were obviously the companies to go after.

The evening dragged on. Scherr ordered another coffee.

Long after the others had gone, Meb Cutlack stayed to talk politics with Scherr and Hershowitz. A briefing with the *Reporter* columnist was due diligence for anyone considering an investment in Belize. The country's official history could be glossed in a couple of pages of the *Rough Guide;* those seeking a deeper understanding could pick up Assad Shoman's *Thirteen Chapters of a History of Belize;* but the real history of Belize was contained in the stories passed across barstools and kitchen tables. A snippet of cocktail gossip, a clipping from *The Reporter,* an editorial in *Amandala,* a quip on the Love FM morning show, a chapter from Shoman, ruminations from Meb: That was Belizean history. You had to know which businessmen owned which politicians, which daughter of a prominent family was the mistress of which government minister, where and when ancient rivalries were born. In a nation this small, the social fabric was as complex and intertwined as the ecological web of life. "You gotta watch who you joke about," a young UDP politician once told me, "because that man may be the half-brother of the man you're talking to."

Said Musa was the prime minister, Ralph Fonseca was the

power behind the throne, but if you really wanted to know Belize you had to know the story of two men: George Price, father of the country, and Michael Ashcroft, the Baron of Belize.

For the past fifty years, George Price was Belize and Belize was George Price. Sometimes I'd ask people why Belize hadn't fallen into crushing poverty like Haiti, or dissolved into civil war like Guatemala. Almost always, "Mr. Price" was the answer. "Because of Mr. Price."

As a younger man, Mr. Price had been a dead ringer for Gregory Peck in *To Kill a Mockingbird*. In old photos he exhibited a lanky stoop, which enhanced his thin, solemn Atticus Finch dignity. His face was an ethnic riddle. A Scottish father and a Maya mother produced a son of no tribe and all tribes at once. He studied in a Catholic seminary but never heard the calling. Even after he chose politics over the priesthood, Price remained a man of the cloth in temperament and habit: frugal, abstemious, and, it was widely believed, celibate. In 1978, Graham Greene stopped in Belize on his way to Panama, where he was writing his portrait of dictator Omar Torrijos, *Getting to Know the General.* Greene and Price toured the country in Price's blue Land Rover. "As we drove across Belize," Greene wrote, "I was reminded again and again of the priest who lived in the heart of Price. His hand wave closely resembled a blessing." Belize was Price's church, Belizeans his congregation.

Now in his eighties, Price is officially retired but keeps a hand in Belizean politics, offering advice and counsel from behind the shuttered windows of his family's clapboard house on Belize City's Pickstock Street. Twice I tried to visit him, but both times I was turned away at the door by his sister. "Mr. Price regrets that he is too busy to see you," she told me.

Mr. Price has been busy for more than half a century. In 1950, he and his confederates launched Belize's independence movement by leading protests against Britain's colonial economic system. In response, England loosened its grip, allowing local elections and nominal home rule. Mahatma Gandhi liberated India with nonviolent civil disobedience. Price and his confreres adopted a less direct strategy. They decided to annoy the British out of Belize. PUP nationalists hummed "God Bless America" at official British ceremonies. They refused to hang a portrait of King George VI in the Belize City Council chambers. At a ceremony commemorating the British victory in the Battle of St. George's Caye, Price stopped in the middle of a speech praising Queen Elizabeth, said, "et cetera, et cetera, et cetera," and walked out.

Other sixties revolutionaries adopted powerful symbols: the AK-47, the clenched fist. In Belize, George Price adopted the symbol of an embroidered shirt. Colonial officials in British Honduras traditionally worked in coat and tie, the uniform of London, even on the hottest tropical afternoons. Then one day George Price showed up in a guayabera, the cool short-sleeved shirt popular in Cuba and Mexico. Suits and ties, he declared, were colonialist. Real Belizeans wore the guayabera. Overnight, PUP loyalists burned their ties and donned guayaberas.

As Belize's first independent leader, Price could have run Belize as Castro ran Cuba, as Duvalier ran Haiti, as Stroessner ran Paraguay. Instead, he did something extraordinary. He gave himself the opportunity to lose. In 1984, three months before the national election, Price's grip on power looked tenuous. Polls indicated he was headed for a Churchillian fate. Having brought Belize to nationhood, Price was about to become the victim of what he once called the "revolution of rising expectations." Progress brings dissatisfaction among the people, he said: "The more they get, the more they want." As election day neared, the opposition UDP held a strong lead. "Price's defense minister was preparing to turn his troops out against the UDP," Meb Cutlack once told me. "Price heard of this, and he fired the defense minister. If Price had left him in, it would have been awful, bloody, and there would have been no election. Price realized that. So he fired the man, went on with the election, lost fair and square, and handed over power."

Price's example set the tone for the next fifteen years. Neither party enjoyed a sustained majority. Every five years the voters tossed out one party and brought in the other, then swapped them

again five years later. Price, in fact, regained the prime minister-
ship in the early 1990s. All this happened with little corruption
and no violence. Then in 1996, a new generation of PUP leaders
took the reins. Price anointed Said Musa as party leader, along
with Ralph Fonseca and Fonseca's crony Glenn Godfrey. "Mr.
Fonseca's father, Rafael, had been a close friend of Mr. Price's,"
Amandala editor Evan X. Hyde once wrote. "But more important,
both Ralph and Glenn were like adopted children of Mr. Price's."

Price's frugality was legendary. As prime minister he always
flew coach and wrote on used envelopes to save paper. He wanted
no money for himself. But leaders of the new generation weren't
like Mr. Price. They cared about money. They liked getting it and
they liked spending it. When they came to power they found an
infrastructure designed to reward both themselves and their
cronies. The Musa-Fonseca-Godfrey PUP steered lucrative contracts to friends and big-money donors. International aid packages and Wall Street bonds turned into million-dollar personal
loans that never got repaid. The good little country turned into a
thieves' banquet.

How does something like that happen? It's impossible to know
what goes on in the minds of men. But some insight may be gained
from the tale of Michael Ashcroft, Baron of Belize, the most mysterious and powerful crony of them all.

The son of a colonial civil servant, Ashcroft spent part of his
childhood in British Honduras before returning to England for
schooling. As a young man he built up a profitable cleaning business and parlayed that success into a string of acquisitions that
paid off handsomely. Ashcroft had a genius for deal making. He
took over a failing tent manufacturer, the Hawley Group, and
used its corporate shell to create a conglomerate worth $200 mil-
lion. In 1984, he moved the company to Bermuda to escape England's burdensome tax code, thus pioneering the practice of
corporate offshoring. Three years later, Ashcroft purchased the
American burglar alarm company ADT for $1 billion. He moved
ADT to Bermuda, too. Then in the late eighties, Michael
Ashcroft returned to Belize.

He came bearing a brilliant idea. Ashcroft had seen how off-shoring worked in Bermuda. Why not set up a similar scheme in Belize? Belizeans knew little about offshoring, but that didn't matter. Ashcroft flew in his own lawyers to write the legislation. Backed by George Price and the PUP, the bill sailed through the legislature.

Ashcroft's advice came at a price. The Belize government agreed to let any and all of Ashcroft's businesses operate in the country tax-free for thirty years. Ashcroft responded by buying up half of Belize. He took over the troubled Belizean branch of the Royal Bank of Canada, renamed it Belize Bank, and quickly grew it into the nation's biggest lender. He bought Channel 5, Belize's leading television station. He bought the Fort George Hotel (later renamed the Radisson), the country's biggest hotel. When the government privatized Belize Telephone Ltd. (BTL), Ashcroft snapped up the shares and turned the utility into a hugely prof-itable monopoly. His influence could be felt in both town and country. Ashcroft's agricultural business controlled nearly half of Belize's citrus crop.

Where others saw a poor, underdeveloped country, Ashcroft saw an underperforming property with enormous potential as a base for his brand of swashbuckling capitalism. Aided by Price and the PUP, in the 1990s Ashcroft turned the sovereign nation of Belize into his own tax-free holding company. Ashcroft's invest-ments so pleased Belize's leaders that they named him "Ambas-sador Extraordinary and Plenipotentiary to the European Community." Later, the post of Belize's ambassador to the United Nations, and all the diplomatic immunity it conferred, were also transferred to his portfolio. "Ashcroft was the master," Belizean cabinet minister Mark Espat once said in a rare moment of can-dor. "The government of Belize was the puppet."

Though he maintained a seaside mansion in Florida, a town-house in London's posh Belgravia district, and his own hotel in Belize, Ashcroft often lived and conducted business aboard his 148-foot yacht, the *Atlantic Goose*. The land of his childhood, how-ever, remained his spiritual base. "If home is where the heart is,"

Ashcroft once wrote, "then Belize is my home." The tycoon's influence grew so pervasive, and his reputation so fierce, that Belizeans took to naming their toughest dogs "Ashcroft."

In 1993, Belizean voters turned George Price out of office. His successor, UDP leader Manuel Esquivel, moved to strip Ashcroft of his tax-free status. Ashcroft retaliated by threatening to crash the Belizean economy. His bank could call in its loans. He could shut down the phone lines. He could wreck the citrus industry. His financial resources dwarfed those of the Belizean government. Ashcroft had a personal fortune worth somewhere near $2 billion, more than three times Belize's gross domestic product. Prime Minister Esquivel backed down.

In the late 1990s, Ashcroft entered British politics as treasurer of the Conservative Party. After contributing more than $2 million to the Tory war chest, the party bestowed upon Ashcroft a knighthood and a life peerage. When he returned to Belize aboard the *Atlantic Goose* in 2000, he stepped ashore as Lord Ashcroft, Baron of Belize.*

Things didn't go so well for Lord Ashcroft after that. Some believe Musa and Fonseca grew tired of watching His Lordship increase his fortune on the backs of Belizeans. Others believe Musa and Fonseca wanted to increase their own fortunes on the backs of Belizeans. Not long into Said Musa's term, about the time Musa decided to move forward on the Chalillo dam, Musa and Fonseca granted a phone license to their longtime political ally Glenn Godfrey. Though it had no phones, no lines, and no service, Godfrey's start-up, called Intelco, was awarded a $20 million contract to provide phone service to the Belizean government. Michael Ashcroft, furious, hauled the government into court. When His Lordship bought BTL, he apparently understood monopoly to mean monopoly.

---

* Actually, his official title is Lord Ashcroft, Baron of Chichester. Ashcroft floated the idea of taking the name Baron of Belize during the nomination process, but the idea caused such an uproar that he soon retreated and settled for Chichester, where he kept a country estate.

~

Corruption is a virus that enters a system from the top down. Michael Ashcroft brought more than the concept of corporate offshoring to Belize. He introduced the idea that fair play is a sucker's game. In any society, lawful behavior depends on social enforcement. If everyone decided to rob and steal all at once, there wouldn't be enough police to stop us. What does? Other people. It's like jaywalking. Stand on a corner with five strangers. The light is red. Everybody waits. Then one person sprints across. He shows it can be done. Two others follow. Suddenly those of us standing on the curb don't feel so much like upstanding citizens. We feel like chumps. That's how it is with corruption. Once the top people get away with it, the floodgates open. "Government is the omnipresent teacher," U.S. Supreme Court Justice Louis Brandeis once remarked. "For good or ill it teaches the whole people by its example. Crime is contagious. If the government becomes a law breaker, it breeds contempt for the law; it invites every man to become a law unto himself." In the halls of Belmopan, ministers who didn't cut secret deals and line their pockets weren't the good guys. They were the suckers.

Jacob Scherr and Ari Hershowitz left Belize not knowing what to do. During the flight home they discussed the pros and cons of a Chalillo campaign. The dam was a fiasco: environmentally devastating, economically unsound, geologically suspect, and stinking of monopoly profiteering. Scherr had seen this sort of thing before. In 1976, Philippine dictator Ferdinand Marcos borrowed $2.3 billion to build the Bataan nuclear power plant near Mount Pinatubo. The plant never produced a single megawatt, but Marcos pocketed $80 million in kickbacks from the contractor, Westinghouse. As of 2005, the interest alone on the project's $2.3 billion debt continued to suck $155,000 out of the government treasury every day of the year.

Was Chalillo winnable? Jacob Scherr thought so. He and Hershowitz had identified a number of pressure points: Duke Energy, NEAC, Fortis, and Belize's Department of the Environment. Local activists were already fighting on the ground. And they had the passion of Sharon Matola, the beloved Zoo Lady of Belize.

Hershowitz wasn't convinced. "There are a lot of downsides to it, Jacob," he said. "This is a tiny country whose environmental activists can be counted on two hands. We'd need to have a strong, committed group in Belize, and I'm not sure how strong or committed Bacongo is." Belizeans were notoriously reluctant to oppose their own government. "Folks here don't like to stand up for things," Kimo Jolly told them. "People lose their jobs, people get killed." Hershowitz laid out his concerns. "People tell us they're opposed to the dam," he told Scherr. "But how many of them are willing to stand up and say it publicly?"

Then there was the issue of the garbage dump, which irritated Hershowitz. He'd gone down to fight a dam, not a dump. He was in no mood to open a two-front war in a country where winning one was an iffy proposition.

"Don't worry about the dump," Scherr told him. He knew a guy who could handle it. If they were going to take on the dam, they couldn't do it without Sharon—and if the dump went forward she'd be ruined.

They broke off their conversation. Hershowitz shut his eyes for an hour. Scherr made notes in his schedule book. In the end, Hershowitz conceded. Scherr had twenty years' experience on him. Besides, no environmental campaign was perfect. This one was just a little less perfect than others.

By the time the plane touched the tarmac at Dulles, Scherr and Hershowitz were agreed. The NRDC was in.

CHAPTER 11

*E*XTINCTION IS A PROFOUND IDEA. Ancient naturalists never imagined such a thing, even as the evidence lay before them in the form of fossils. "It seemed inconceivable that any forms of animate being that *could* exist, and that evidently *had* existed, should subsequently have been allowed to disappear from the face of the Earth," Martin Rudwick observed in *The Meaning of Fossils.* It wasn't until 1667 that British naturalist Robert Hooke picked up an unfamiliar seashell fossil and put two and two together. "There have been many other Species of Creatures in former Ages," Hooke concluded, "of which we can find none at present."

That wasn't easy to say. In fact, it verged on heresy. In the seventeenth century, to claim that a species had been snuffed out was to imply a flaw in the Creator's design. A slippery slope led to a denial of God's existence, perfection being among His inherent qualities. Desperate for theological consistency, scientists settled upon what might be termed the "shy descendants" theory: Extinct species found as fossils must exist, yet undiscovered, in the wilderness or in the sea. It was a reasonable idea. Every month, it seemed, naturalists were returning from expeditions with crates full of new species.

It fell to French naturalist Georges Cuvier, father of modern paleontology, to prove that there were no shy descendants. In 1796, Cuvier presented the scientific world with evidence that the Indian and African elephant were two distinct species. Then he turned to a fossilized mammoth, another species entirely. The mammoth was found in northern Europe, an area scientifically well scoured. Cuvier essentially turned to his audience and said, So where's *this* thing hiding?

Cuvier proved the fact of extinction, but its cause remained an open question. Cuvier thought a series of natural disasters had wiped out ancient forms of life, leaving behind fossils like organic tombstones. He wasn't far from the truth. It's now widely accepted that the earth has experienced five mass extinctions in the past 440 million years. Species of ancient sea urchins disappeared in the Ordovician extinction (440 million years ago), early fish in the Devonian (365 million years ago), nearly all sea creatures and three-quarters of land vertebrates in the Permian (245 million years ago), ancient squid and clams in the Triassic (208 million years ago), and dinosaurs in the Cretaceous-Tertiary extinction (65 million years ago). The first four were likely caused by climate change, usually a planetary cooling in which sea levels dropped and glaciers covered vast stretches of dry land. The leading theory on the fifth extinction holds that the dinosaurs were killed off by a meteor crashing to earth and disrupting the planet's ecosystem.

Until the mid-1800s, extinctions were assumed to be acts of God or nature—not humans. Then paleontologists dug up evidence suggesting that fantastic creatures roamed North America ten to fifteen thousand years ago. Saber-toothed cats hunted ground sloths. Cheetahs lurked amid early forms of camels, horses, and long-horned bison. Woolly mammoths browsed in herds. Beavers the size of black bears dammed countless freshwater streams. Then they disappeared. Between 13,000 and 11,000 years ago, more than two-thirds of all large North American land animals (38 of 54 species) went extinct. In 1860, British paleontologist Richard Owen, a rival of Charles Darwin's, fingered the likely culprit. The great megafaunal extinction, he wrote, was at least partly catalyzed by a new destructive force unleashed upon the land: "the spectral appearance of mankind."

Today, paleontologists pretty much agree that climate change and human overkill combined to wipe out the great North American menagerie. The global warming that marked the end of the last ice age—10,000 to 12,000 years ago—transformed eastern North America from an open grassland to the hardwood forests we know today. With their food supply dwindling, large grazers like camels, horses, and mammoths were already in trouble. Humans finished the job. American geoscientist Paul Martin has suggested that early man, armed with stone-tipped spears, swept down from Alaska to South America in a few centuries, eliminating entire species of large animals in blitzkrieg extinctions. Put crudely, our ancestors hunted and barbecued their way down the continent until all the biggest, dumbest game was gone.

After that initial extinction pulse, things mostly held steady for the next 10,000 years. Then the numbers started diving again. Of the approximately 6,000 modern species of mammals, 70 have gone extinct since the year 1600. Today, 1 in 6 mammals faces a high risk of extinction. On its 2006 Red List, the World Conservation Union put 162 species of mammals in its highest category, critically endangered, reserved for species on the edge of destruction. Of the approximately 10,000 known species of birds, 135 have already gone extinct. Twelve hundred are threatened with extinction. Parrots are particularly vulnerable. Of the 372 parrot species tracked by the IUCN, 19 have already gone extinct and 48 are considered highly endangered.

Humans are expert destroyers because we've developed so many efficient ways to kill things off. We slaughter them outright, as we did with the woolly mammoth. We destroy their habitat by turning forests into farmland and paving meadows into strip malls. We sail to isolated islands and introduce all sorts of nasty things—cats, rats, seeds, disease. Those introduced agents infect, eat, or outcompete local species clean out of existence. Lately we've come up with a method that may be our most effective yet: global warming. All over the world, habitats are changing in minute but critical ways as a result of climate change caused by the greenhouse gases produced by human industry. Polar bears, considered vibrant and abundant only a few years ago, were recently added to the IUCN's Red List because of the melting of polar ice. After eleven thousand years we've effectively re-created the conditions that brought about the last great megafaunal extinction. Back then, natural global warming reduced habitat and food supply, and humans killed off the already-weakened species. This time we're reversing the order. Having softened up thousands of species with overkill and habitat destruction, we're bringing in human-induced global warming to finish the job.

~

Perhaps the most shocking thing about extinctions is how fast they can happen. A decade after paleontologists began to consider human-forced extinction possible, the U.S. government declared war on the North American bison and showed just how quickly and easily it could be done. Prior to the coming of European settlers, sixty to seventy-five million bison roamed the Great Plains. Tribes of the interior West relied on the great herds for food. To starve those tribes into submission, in 1871 the federal government declared open season on the bison and inaugurated what historian Martin Garretson later called "the most remorseless and ceaseless slaughter of wild animals ever known." After twelve years of carnage, fewer than a thousand bison survived. Had it not been for the wise husbandry of a few cattle ranchers who took in and protected the last survivors, *Bison bison* would exist today only as stuffed museum exhibits.

Birds have been known to disappear faster than the buffalo. During World War II, emaciated Japanese soldiers occupying Wake Island, a scrub-covered Pacific isle, ate the flightless Wake Island rail right out of existence. In New Zealand, the Stephen Island wren occupied a one-square-mile outcropping of rock between the nation's North and South islands, the smallest natural range of any bird on earth. In the late nineteenth century, a new lighthouse keeper arrived on the island with his pet cat. The cat both discovered the Stephen Island wren and rendered it extinct in a matter of months.

It's no accident that those extinctions occurred on islands. Ninety percent of all bird extinctions in the past four hundred years have happened on islands. Like all animals, birds evolve to fit the conditions around them. On islands with no natural predators, protected by water, escape by flight became unnecessary. With the passage of time, wings evolved into useless appendages. That worked out fine until humans arrived. Rats, cats, pigs, and hungry soldiers found the flightless birds easy picking and tasty eating. The problem predates European exploration. More than half of Hawaii's endemic land birds went extinct before Captain

James Cook established European contact in 1778. Centuries before Cook, Polynesians migrated from island to island, bringing chickens, dogs, pigs, and rats in their twin-hulled catamarans. Some birds were eaten outright; others were done in when the Polynesians cleared forests to grow coconut palms and taro.

It's possible to kill off continental birds, too. It just takes more effort. The Carolina parakeet and the passenger pigeon were the starlings and crows of their day. The parakeet, the only parrot indigenous to the continental United States, once prospered in forests from the Great Lakes to the Gulf of Mexico. The passenger pigeon ranked among the most populous birds on earth. In the 1830s, John James Audubon described a migration of pigeons passing overhead in a flock so thick "the light of noonday was obscured as by an eclipse." The parakeet was done in by its taste for ripening fruit; orchard keepers considered them pests and shot the birds on sight. The fatal flaw of the passenger pigeon lay in its inability to evade the gunsights of sport shooters. "So vast was the population, so seemingly complete its grip upon survival that the supply of birds appeared inexhaustible," Errol Fuller wrote of the passenger pigeon in his book *Extinct Birds*. "In a hunting competition once organized, over 30,000 dead birds were needed to claim a prize." Like the American buffalo, the parakeet and pigeon were shot and shot until the last ones left were scooped up and protected in zoos. Unlike the buffalo, the birds didn't make it. The last surviving passenger pigeon died in the Cincinnati Zoo in 1914. The Carolina parakeet was last spotted in the Santee River country of South Carolina in 1938. None have been seen since.

Given the ease with which more numerous birds have been wiped off the map, what chance does the scarlet macaw stand? It's a complicated question. First, nobody knows exactly how many macaws still exist. In Central America there aren't many. Furthermore, the macaw displays several classic characteristics of doomed species. First, it's a big bird. In the animal world, size has its disadvantages. Big animals need more space, which means there are fewer individuals per acre. Big animals have longer reproductive cycles.

Scarlet macaws hatch at most two chicks per year, and only one usually survives past fledging. In a world where camouflage and the art of not being seen are crucial to survival, big bright birds colored like stoplights get seen. Scarlet macaws live within loosely bunched flocks. They don't leave home and spread themselves far and wide across the countryside. This, too, bodes ill. One of the reasons the passenger pigeon went extinct was that the species had evolved in such a way that its survival depended on a critical mass of birds working together as a flock. Once the massive flocks were broken, the remaining birds couldn't sustain themselves. Macaws feed together in predictable locales. When you see one, you're likely to see them all. One idiot with a shotgun could do a lot of long-term damage.

It's not all bad news, of course. The scarlet macaws of Belize aren't flightless, and much as Belizeans may wish it otherwise, the nation is not an island. Another thing the macaw has going for it is its brain. It's a very smart bird. Whether it will use that intelligence to create new strategies for survival has yet to be seen. A recent documentary, *The Parrots of Telegraph Hill,* illustrated the ability of once-domesticated parrots to re-wild themselves by living on their own in the suburbs of Berkeley, California. On the other hand, the macaws of Central America have shown no interest in adapting to cleared farmland, cane fields, or villages and towns. As development has encroached on their habitat, the birds haven't been able to survive amid new predators and changing food sources. In a world of adapt or die, they're dying.

Finally, scarlet macaws are profoundly charismatic. That counts for a lot. They are beautiful and curious and endlessly fascinating to watch. They're featured on stamps and postcards and promoted as national symbols. Nearly four centuries ago the English traveler and author Thomas Herbert praised their striking appearance: "I must give the parrots a particular salutation, they made me so admire their feathres [*sic*], and are so catholickly beloved and pointed at." Today they're inexorably bound up with our vision of the vast forests of Latin America. That charisma can cut both ways. It may inspire people to protect Central America's few remaining flocks. It may also increase the value of wild macaws to those who would capture and sell them.

Those are complex factors, but the issue isn't really so in-scrutable. We've seen this pattern over and over again. If you kill enough individuals, eventually the entire species will disappear. If you take away a bird's nesting and feeding ground, it will go away that much faster. To Sharon, the question of the macaw's survival was a no-brainer. "If we keep destroying habitat like this, that bird is a goner," she told me one of the first times we met. "It's not that tough to understand. Once it's got no place to eat and no place to breed, it will go extinct."

CHAPTER 12

*I*N THE SPRING OF 2000, Jacob Scherr sent NRDC garbage expert Allen Hershkowitz to Belize to investigate the landfill the government wanted to build next to Sharon's zoo. Hershkowitz spent two weeks looking into the matter, then told Sharon and Tony Garel what he found.

The existing dump, just outside Belize City, was an environmental disaster. It sat on a narrow strip of land—historically a lagoon—between the Western Highway and the Caribbean Sea. Rain fell on the open dump and fermented into a poisonous stew that drained into the Caribbean. During dry spells the garbage caught fire and burned for days.

That said, the proposed landfill at Mile 27 would be worse. The new dump would store household trash, toxic chemicals, solvents, pesticides, even medical waste, in open pits that would likely leach into the Sibun River. Developed countries require such pits to have watertight liners that prevent leakage into the water supply. Stantec, the Canadian engineering company designing the new dump, wanted to do without liners. Naturally occurring clay in the soil, they said, would seal off the garbage toxins. "Bad smells and predators will be the least of your worries," Hershkowitz told Sharon and Garel. "You're going to have a poisoned river on your hands."

Stopping the dump would be difficult. The Belizean government wanted the dump, and evidence of Mile 27's flaws probably wouldn't change the government's mind. The only good news was that funding for the dump came from the Inter-American Development Bank, and most of the bank's money hadn't yet been released to Belize. There were two options: Stop the funding or move the landfill to an alternate site.

"What about Mile 24?" said Garel.

Mile 24, a site on the northern side of the Western Highway east of the zoo, had been considered by the government but was rejected in favor of Mile 27. On Garel's advice, Hershkowitz checked it out. He liked what he saw. Mile 24 was situated on higher, drier ground. It drained away from the Sibun River; the nearest waterway ran seven miles to the north.

Garel brought Brian Holland into the game. He asked the geologist to test the soils at Mile 27 and Mile 24. Holland spent two days at the sites. "If you're just looking at the geology, Mile 24 is vastly superior to Mile 27," Holland told Garel. "And you know that 'impermeable clay' that the Stantec engineers want to line their pits with?" he said. "Take a look at this."

Holland set a lump of clay from the Mile 27 site on the table. Garbage juice, as he understood from Hershkowitz, was highly acidic.

"Now, what do you think will happen when that acid encounters this clay?" he said. Holland pulled a lime from his pocket and sliced it in half.

"This is citric acid," he said. "Pretty weak stuff."

He squeezed the lime over the clay. The clay began fizzing. After a few seconds it dissolved into goo.

Brian Holland's soil report convinced Jacob Scherr to go after the money. That meant a visit to IDB headquarters in Washington.

The Inter-American Development Bank, or IDB, was founded by the Organization of American States in 1959 as a sort of regional World Bank. Although the IDB and the World Bank have similar missions—fostering development and reducing poverty— there's a subtle difference. World Bank policies are mostly dictated by lenders, developed countries like the United States and the United Kingdom. At the IDB, borrowing countries hold a 50.02 percent majority when policies come to a vote. As a result, there's a tension at the IDB between the desire for transparency and the many shades of gray that exist on the ground in develop-

ing countries. The IDB isn't without its problems, but in the development world its reputation is much cleaner than the World
Bank's.

Sharon and Brian Holland flew to Washington to lobby against
the Mile 27 landfill. It was vital that they go. As Allen Hershkowitz reported to Jacob Scherr, "there's a capture of local IDB by
the forces that want to build this thing." In development vernacu-
lar, the term "capture" indicates that an official has, as some used
to say, gone native. Scherr believed the bank's representative in
Belize was more interested in maintaining good relations with the
Belizean government than in looking after the bank's interests
and environmental goals. If Sharon could talk one on one to IDB
officials in Washington, she might change some minds. Scherr set
up a meeting with Robert Kaplan, the IDB's chief environmental
officer. Kaplan was an experienced, technically astute executive.
He knew a whitewashed environmental assessment when he saw
one, and he also understood the realities of development work as
it's practiced in the field. Most important, he had clout. Environmental sustainability was written into the bank's mission. If Kaplan found any IDB-funded project in defiance of that mission,
that project was in trouble.

Kaplan welcomed Sharon and Holland into his office. Working
from a legal pad, he ran through the project from the bank's per-
spective. Kaplan considered Mile 27 a promising site, though he
was skeptical of Stantec's environmental report. The bank hadn't
reached a final decision on the landfill. The IDB got into the project, Kaplan said, to improve public health, reduce environmental
contamination, and enhance Belize's ecotourism profile. As far as
the bank was concerned, public health and ecotourism were the
landfill's raison d'être. If the dump poisoned the river and destroyed the zoo, its être contradicted its raison.

"Now," said Kaplan, "I'd like to hear your concerns."

Sharon nodded to Brian Holland. On the elevator ride to Kaplan's office they'd agreed that he should go first.

"Stantec points to geology as one of the primary factors in
choosing Mile 27," Holland said. "But what they aren't telling you
is that there are serious problems with the geology at Mile 27."

The clay that the Canadian engineers claimed would act as a natural liner was actually China clay, he told Kaplan. China clay is also known as kaolin, a fine white clay commonly used in ceramics. "They never bothered to spend sixty-five dollars to get it properly tested," Holland said. The biggest problem, he continued, is that kaolin reacts chemically with acids. He described the lime test he'd performed for Tony Garel.

Kaplan took notes and listened. Holland summarized his Mile 27 survey, then turned the floor over to Sharon. She began with a description of Mile 27 and the Sibun River. "Local villages draw their drinking water from that river," she told Kaplan. "If you paddle down on a Saturday, you'll pass a dozen women washing their clothes on the bank. Children play in the river all day. Old men fish for dinner." She talked about garbage juice and toxic waste. She talked about the Belize Zoo and what it meant to ecotourism and the nation's environmental awareness. Mile 27 made no sense, she said, unless you knew the politics behind it.

She laid out the saga as briefly as she could. She mentioned the macaws, the tapirs, the wild river, and the dam. Sharon could get worked up about Chalillo, but this time she held herself in.

Sharon looked Kaplan in the eye. "We can sit here and talk all day about the pros and cons of Mile 27," she said, "but in the end those reasons won't matter. This isn't about solving a garbage problem. This is about solving a dam problem. This is about the government silencing anybody who stands up. This zoo is my life's work. I've spent fifteen years building it up from nothing. When I came to Mile 28 in 1982 all that was there were orphan animals and bush. I bottle-fed some of the animals as babies. Those animals are grandparents now. Those animals, they change people's lives. Before the zoo was there, most Belizeans went their entire lives without seeing a tapir. If they saw a jaguar, they shot it. If they saw a macaw, they roasted it like chicken. They don't do that anymore, and do you know why? Because they take their kids to the zoo on Sundays and they see the birds and they read the signs and they find out there are fewer than two hundred macaws alive in the entire country. Belizeans aren't stupid. It's just that nobody gave them the information. Nobody came along and said, Say, you know what? These macaws are extremely rare and they're *yours*. They're Belize's birds. You should be proud of them."

Her voice was on the verge of cracking.

"Every day I get up and find a way to feed those animals, pay my staff, and save what's left of a few birds and wild places in Belize. And all it's gotten me is a lesson in dirty politics: If you oppose the ministers they will run you out of business." Tears welled in her eyes.

"The government doesn't want the dump at Mile 27 because it's got good clay," she said. "The government wants the dump at Mile 27 because I live at Mile 28."

Kaplan didn't speak. He let Sharon's passion dissipate in a respectful silence. Late afternoon light slanted through the window. Finally he spoke. "Are there alternative sites?"

"Sure," said Brian Holland. "There are sites with thicker clay sequences. Less permeable. Higher ground. Mile 24 is quite promising."

"Would you be willing to work with us on this?" Kaplan asked.

"Whatever I can do," Holland said.

Kaplan jotted something in his legal pad.

"Well," he said, and stood in a *time's up* gesture. "I'm glad you came to see us. We'll certainly take your concerns into consideration. I'll discuss them with our people in Belize and see if we might take a closer look at the project."

Back in the elevator, Sharon looked like a woman who'd been fired. "A closer look," she said. "That's it? A closer look?"

Holland searched in vain for optimism. You couldn't fight these guys. The IDB was one of the most powerful institutions in the Western Hemisphere. Robert Kaplan dealt with billion-dollar loans. What was one little zoo to him?

Holland put his arm around Sharon's shoulder. "We gave it our best shot," he said.

CHAPTER 13

ATER THAT SPRING, strange letters began arriving at the office of Duke Energy CEO Rick Priory. A few trickled in at first, and then more and more showed up. E-mails and postcards, too. Hundreds, then thousands, then ten thousand. All from people upset about something called Chalillo. Each bore a version of the same message: Duke was up to some bad business in Belize.

Belize? Priory barely knew that Duke operated in Belize.

He asked C. Norwood Davis, Duke's director of environmental health and safety, to look into it. Davis called the NRDC. Jacob Scherr was happy to talk. Davis proposed a meeting. The sooner the better, he said.

Duke Energy wasn't the greenest company in the world. A few months earlier the U.S. Environmental Protection Agency had charged Duke with massive violations of the Clean Air Act. But within the energy industry, Duke was known as a reasonably clean operator. One of the proudest achievements of Rick Priory's tenure was the creation of the company's code of business ethics, a twenty-six-page document that featured statements such as "We tell the truth" and "We are environmentally responsible." This was a full year before Duke's rival, Enron, collapsed as a result of massive financial fraud. In its corporate literature, Duke proudly noted that it was the first U.S. energy company to hire its own staff biologist, back in the 1930s. And now the NRDC was painting Duke as bird killers and jaguar haters over . . . what, exactly?

"Chalillo," Scherr told C. Norwood Davis. Davis and a handful of Duke officials gathered with Scherr around a conference table in the NRDC's Washington office. "It's a proposed six-megawatt dam in Belize. You own it."

Duke officials knew that much. But they didn't know a whole

lot more. A few months earlier Duke had purchased the entire Latin American portfolio of Virginia-based Dominion Resources for $405 million. The package included hydro, natural gas, and diesel power-generation companies in Argentina, Bolivia, Peru, and Belize. While $405 million is a lot of money, the Dominion buyout wasn't even the biggest deal Duke made *that week*. A few days earlier the company had spent more than $800 million to ac-quire power companies in Brazil and El Salvador. In one week, the company spent $1.2 billion to acquire more than 1,200 megawatts of total generating capacity. The fact that one of the deals in-cluded a little-known company called BECOL, which operated a tiny 25-megawatt dam in Belize, went unnoticed. Until those let-ters started to come, BECOL didn't even register on Duke's radar.

Scherr explained what was at stake in the Macal River valley. He offered the Duke officials copies of John Reid's economic study. Chalillo didn't make economic sense for Belize or for Duke, Scherr argued. "Duke is the most important part of this overall scheme," he told them. "We'd like you to play a more affirmative role in putting an end to this project and promoting environmen-tally acceptable alternatives." Cheap bagasse was there for the burning, he said. Belize could plug into the Central American grid. More sensible alternatives were available.

The meeting spurred Duke to send a fact-finding team to Be-lize. The few executives in Charlotte who'd given any thought to BECOL saw the company as a nice little earner and a possible beachhead from which to expand into the wider Central Ameri-can market. In Belize, however, they heard a different story. Said Musa, Ralph Fonseca, and BEL executives didn't want to connect to the Central American grid. They only wanted to build Chalillo. The dam had become the government's idée fixe. Duke officials demurred. They weren't sure Chalillo made sense.

Soon after the Duke team left Belize, word reached Fortis, BEL's owner, at the company's headquarters in St. John's, New-foundland: Duke was having second thoughts about Chalillo.

Fortis CEO Stan Marshall didn't hesitate. He picked up the phone and called Duke himself. "Look, are you going to do the upstream storage or not?" he demanded. "If you're not going to develop it, then let us buy out Mollejon and we'll do it ourselves!"

Marshall was a robust figure, sunny and bluff and built like a beer truck. A small-town Newfoundland boy made good, Marshall's charisma and hard-charging attitude had propelled him to the top job at Fortis at the age of forty-three. Stan Marshall was a demanding boss, but he was also the kind of guy who could swap jokes over a beer and a basket of fish in a cod shop in St. John's. Investors liked him, too. Since taking over as CEO, Marshall was steadily growing profits and expanding the company by snapping up obscure small-market power companies like BEL.

Duke officials wouldn't commit to anything. Marshall was told they'd get back to him.

Jacob Scherr also called executives at Duke. Were they willing to kill the project? "I don't have an answer for you," C. Norwood Davis told him. "But I will tell you this. We've been doing some research, and we're not convinced that the scarlet macaw is an endangered species."

Pressure continued to mount against Duke. That fall Scherr flew to Amman, Jordan, to attend a worldwide conference of the World Conservation Union (IUCN). Scherr lobbied the IUCN to adopt a resolution calling on Duke to abandon the Chalillo project.

Opposing the resolution was Belize's delegate to the conference, Jose "Pepe" Garcia. Garcia had a solid environmental record in Belize. As a civil and sanitary engineer, he'd improved the country's water systems and codrafted Belize's first environmental protection laws. He was also a staunch ally of the PUP government and a proponent of Chalillo. Like so many of his countrymen, Garcia wore a number of hats in his day-to-day work. He was an environmental and engineering consultant; he was also the president of the Belize Audubon Society. There were rumors that Garcia was being considered to oversee the development of the dump at Mile 27. Pepe Garcia was no great fan of Sharon Matola. In Amman, Garcia played the anticolonialist card against the dam opponents. He framed the issue as a fight between wealthy

American environmentalists and a poor, struggling nation. "This motion," he declared, "is a threat to the sovereignty and the environmental laws of Belize." In the end, Garcia wounded but could not entirely defeat the resolution. The IUCN adopted a statement that urged Duke to scrap Chalillo—unless the dam's environmental impact assessment showed that the project wouldn't cause "significant degradation" of the natural environment. At the time, the clause seemed a minor technicality.

The IUCN vote gave the fight against Chalillo a boost of international legitimacy. Not long after it passed, in fact, Duke Energy's hometown paper, the *Charlotte Observer,* ran a story on the controversy. The *Observer* doesn't have the national clout of *The New York Times* or *The Wall Street Journal,* but CEOs never like being portrayed as nature-haters in their local newspapers.

Duke officials all but threw up their hands in exasperation. "It's not our project," a company spokesperson told the *Observer.* "This is something that was going on long before we got there."

Meanwhile, Stan Marshall wanted to make sure Duke understood that it *was* their project, and that it was time to build or get out of the way. A few months earlier, after Fortis bought BEL, the Fortis CEO had discovered the secret "take or pay" contract drawn up by Ralph Fonseca. The deal required BEL to pay BECOL $9.6 million a year regardless of whether the Mollejon dam actually delivered any power. In fact, Mollejon had never delivered as much power as the contract stipulated. Every year BEL and its ratepayers—Belizeans who earned less than $100 a week— paid BECOL more than $1 million for electricity that didn't exist. Stan Marshall put an end to that. He ordered BEL to stop paying BECOL immediately. Suddenly Duke Energy's steady little Belizean earner became a money loser.

When that didn't get Duke's attention, Marshall tightened the squeeze. Not only would his subsidiary, BEL, not pay Duke's subsidiary, BECOL, but now Marshall wanted Duke to return the millions of dollars BEL had paid for phantom power. Caught between an obstinate government, a hostile corporate partner, and angry environmentalists, Duke executives met to consider the question that ruined fortune-seekers have been asking themselves for 350 years: What are we doing in Belize?

At the end of that meeting, a Duke official called Newfoundland.

"FORTIS BUYS BECOL," announced the front page of *The Reporter*. The terms of the deal were simple. Fortis paid Duke $62 million for the Mollejon Dam and the right to build Chalillo. At a press conference announcing the sale, Stan Marshall beamed. "This adds value to our investment in Belize," said the Fortis chief executive. "The acquisition will be accretive to earnings from the outset." Translation: The deal will be profitable from day one.

The sale also pleased BEL chief executive Lynn Young and senior engineer Joseph Sukhnandan. The only thing standing in the way of Chalillo now was an environmental okay from the government.

In Washington, Jacob Scherr dialed the Belize Zoo and got Sharon on the phone.

"Hey, Jacob," she said. "I guess you heard the news."

"You sound down, Sharon," he said. "Don't you see? This is great news! We've demonstrated to Belizeans that if you stand up to these companies, things can change. The pressure worked. We got Duke out!"

Sharon sighed. She wondered if Duke's surrender would prove to be a pyrrhic victory. She tried to put up a cheery front. Scherr and Hershowitz had worked so hard for this. But she couldn't mask her fear.

"Now Fortis has all the power," she said.

CHAPTER 14

AFTER FORTIS ACQUIRED Duke's interest in the dam, life became increasingly unpleasant for Sharon. In Belize there is an old Creole saying: *Dis fu wi.* This for we. Keep it in the family. Airing internal conflicts before foreigners brought shame upon the nation. When Sharon asked the IUCN to censure Belize, the government of Belize retaliated.

Norris Hall led the charge. In the *Belize Times,* the government spokesman derided Chalillo's opponents as wealthy white foreigners determined to keep Belizeans hungry and poor. The Zoo Lady wasn't the kindly animal lover Belizeans thought she was, he suggested. After all, what kind of person takes the nation's jaguars and tapirs, the pride of Belize, and locks them up in "her prison for animals"? In a column headlined "ENVIRONMENTAL IMPERIALISM," Hall portrayed Sharon and her allies as a third wave of foreign invaders. First came the Spanish, then the British, and now the American Greens. Hall painted the dam's Belizean opponents as ignorant Uncle Toms. "Stop being fools," he wrote. "It is about time our Belizean brothers and sisters stop doing the 'native dance' and stop cozying up to the hoaxes being played out before our very eyes."

For most of his career, Norris Hall had been known as one of Belize's leading intellectuals. He had been a longtime PUP operator, but never the party's attack dog. Some considered him a pioneering environmentalist, and indeed, Hall sat on the board of the Belize Audubon Society. But something about Chalillo—or maybe it was Sharon—turned him as crazy as a peach orchard boar. When he wasn't foaming over Chalillo, Hall wrote columns praising Zimbabwe dictator Robert Mugabe. At the time, Mugabe, whose twenty-year reign of terror has been marked by violence and corruption appalling even by African standards, was in the pilot phase of a project that would eventually wreck Zimbabwe's economy and starve its people: He encouraged black war veterans to seize white-owned farms at gunpoint. That sounded like a brilliant scheme to Norris Hall, who wondered whether the adoption of such a program in Belize might redeem the sins of the nation's colonial past.

As Hall wrote, "Our friends from abroad should understand that while they are welcomed as partners in our development, any attempt at neo-colonialism or long range attempts to meddle in what we intelligently consider sustainable development will not be tolerated."

The message to Sharon was clear: If you think the dump is bad, wait until we come for your zoo and your house.

"Are you feeling that fire in the belly?" wrote Hall. "Let it burn! burn! burn!"

"I'm ignoring it," Sharon told anyone who asked. This time there would be no "Sharon Matola responds . . ." ads in the local papers. The only way for her to win the battle was by refusing to take up arms. Her friends stood by her. Meb Cutlack defended her in *The Reporter*. Children continued to visit the tapirs and sing out the Zoo Lady's name. But in the territory beyond Mile 29, Hall's attacks began to take effect. PUP loyalists read what Norris Hall had to say and nodded their heads. Mm-hmm. We've seen this one before. The foreigner. The white one. Coming down here, telling us what to do. Making her money while we make none. Where's she getting the money for that zoo? Why is she driving that fancy truck?

The attacks escalated. "The NRDC should now be recognized as a terrorist threat to the state of Belize," wrote Hall. "Such individuals should be considered *persona non grata*." The words were Norris Hall's, but their power came from a certain minister standing behind Hall. "Norris doesn't write anything without Ralph's okay," one Belmopan insider told me. Norris Hall wasn't arguing with Sharon. He was granting dispensation to PUP loyalists to have at her.

Intimidation, arrest, and murder are common hazards in the world of environmental activism. Over the years the position that

Sharon occupied in Belize—the charismatic leader of a rising environmental movement—has proven to be a perilous role. The list
of martyrs to the cause grows every year: Chico Mendes, the
Brazilian rubber tapper and rain-forest crusader, murdered in
1988. Ken Saro-Wiwa, executed by the Nigerian government in
1995 for protesting Shell Oil's destruction of traditional farm-
lands and fishing areas. Rodolfo Flores and Teodoro Garcia, tor-
tured in 1999 by the Mexican military for fighting to save
Mexican forests. Digna Ochoa, Flores and Garcia's lawyer, murdered in her Mexico City office. When you start looking into
these cases, disturbing patterns emerge. Chico Mendes had gone
to the United States to testify against destructive development
projects financed by the Inter-American Development Bank.
Shortly after his testimony, the IDB suspended the financing.
Local ranchers and politicians accused Mendes of hindering economic progress. Not long after, Mendes was killed by a shotgun
blast to the chest.

Unsatisfied with the intensity of Norris Hall's attacks, beer
magnate Barry Bowen weighed in. "If citizens of Belize influence
powerful world organizations against a development project,"
Bowen wrote in the *Belize Times,* "I consider their actions sedi-
tious."

He didn't name Sharon, but he didn't need to. There was only
one citizen of Belize who fitted the description. Bowen depicted
Sharon and her allies as deadly tommygoffs scheming in the grass.
"Like snakes, they provide limited value to Belize but do create fear
in people who are afraid of their hissing and poison," he wrote.

Not to be outdone, Norris Hall came roaring back. "An eco-
scam which has racist connotations and which is designed to keep
this country and its people poor and undeveloped continues to be
perpetrated by Sharon Matola, her white elitist connections
abroad, and a handful of foreigners in this country who continue
to try to dampen the aspirations of an entire nation of Belizeans
as we continue the struggle to pull ourselves out of poverty," he
wrote.

"These people," Hall concluded, "must now be put into our
cross-hairs as enemies of this state."

CHAPTER 15

ATER THAT YEAR, on an evening in September, Sharon stopped her truck at the zoo's back gate. She kept the engine running and the headlights on as she fumbled with the latch and swung open the chain-link gate. Her rubber boots squished in the soggy ground. She climbed back into the truck, eased it through the gate, then repeated the procedure to close it. To Sharon, the back gate was one of the thousand reasons she loved living in Belize. She and her staff built it with their own hands. An alarmed remote-control gate might be more efficient and secure, but you didn't need one out here. That was the point. What you needed was a strong latch and a sense of personal responsibility.

She hustled past the commissary. Clutched to her chest was a thick bundle of papers. She took the steps to her *oficina* two at a time, tossed off her raincoat, and dropped the papers on her desk with a thud. The report was titled "Belize Solid Waste Management Project Environmental Impact Assessment." The dump's EIA.

She read through it with her heart in her throat. The EIA could make or break the dump. After her meeting with Robert Kaplan in Washington, the IDB had insisted that Stantec take a closer look at alternatives to Mile 27. According to the EIA, Stantec had done that. The Mile 24 site looked promising. It was on high ground and had "good potential for landfill development," Stantec reported. To reach the site, however, the engineers said they'd need to build a $400,000 access road. That wasn't good. Sharon read on. Mile 24 was a problem, the report said, because the government claimed to have received an application to build a housing development on the exact same site.

She turned page after page. There is an art to reading an EIA.

Often the most important data is tucked away in small type on late pages. In this case, though, Stantec wanted to be sure nobody missed its conclusion. In big bold letters the consultants confirmed their earlier site selection: THE PROPOSED MILE 27 WESTERN HIGHWAY SITE WAS SELECTED AS THE BEST LOCATION AMONG ALL THE ALTERNATIVES.

Sharon called down to Punta Gorda.

"Brian? Have you read this thing?" she said.

"Yeah," said the geologist. "It's not promising."

"Let me get this straight," she said. "They can't put the dump at Mile 24 because of some phantom never-gonna-happen development, but it's okay if they want to truck their garbage right next to the zoo?"

"That's what they're saying."

She bowed her head. "They're gonna kill me with this. They really are."

Holland flipped through the EIA. The report was full of holes. Stantec hadn't considered Mile 24 and Mile 27 on an equal footing, as Kaplan had requested. They hadn't done any field work on Mile 24, as far as he could tell. Stantec hadn't even gone back and done their geology homework—one of Kaplan's main requests.

"Look at page 3.6," Sharon said. "They say Mile 27 has high ground and good drainage. Now turn the page to 3.7, where they admit that the Sibun is the water source for people downstream of the dump." She read from the report. " 'Protection of this water source would be less costly than for the Mile 24 site due to onsite retention of storm water.' You can have a site that retains storm water. Or you can have one with good drainage. You can't have both!"

"Sharon, I—"

"The cost of the road," she said. "They're willing to poison the river to save—"

"Sharon, will you—" Once she got revved it was hard to slow her down.

"—a few dollars on a stupid road!"

"Sharon, this report is so bad it may play to our advantage," Holland told her. "Hear me out. Think of the things Bob Kaplan and the IDB demanded in a revised EIA. I'm not seeing any of them here. Mile 24 isn't fully investigated. The data in their geological studies contradicts the conclusions they draw. I don't see how Kaplan can let this pass."

Later that month, Hurricane Keith made its way across the Atlantic Ocean on a course for Belize. Sharon, Tony Garel, and the other keepers corralled the animals into concrete bunkers, then went home to ride out the storm. The hurricane smashed the Belizean cayes head-on. Tin roofs sailed around the resort town of San Pedro. Palm trees toppled. Phone lines went dead. Belize City lost power. Out at Mile 29, though, things remained relatively calm. The animals slept soundly. The next morning Sharon met Garel at the zoo.

"Tony," she said, "you know how Stantec keeps going on about how high and dry Mile 27 is?"

Garel nodded.

"I wonder how dry it is today," she said.

Garel smiled. "You get your camera," he said. "My truck or yours?"

Two days earlier a caravan of Belizeans fleeing the coast had created one of the first traffic jams in the history of the Western Highway. But now, with the worst of the hurricane past, the road stood empty. Water pooled everywhere. Sharon and Garel picked their way east in the truck, rumbling over palm fronds and gunning the engine to crash through small lakes. At Mile 27, they left the truck on the highway and slogged over the marshy savannah to the dump site. Knee-deep water ran into their boots.

The site was worse than Sharon expected: a wetland set for ducks. Muddy water filled Stantec's test pits and streamed south like tap water overtopping an ice tray. The emotions within her were two parts hope, one part dread. Evidence of the overflowing pits might tip the balance against Mile 27. On the other hand, if the dump went forward, this confirmed that the garbage juice would run straight to the river.

Garel stood next to the pits. Sharon backed away to capture the scene. She snapped three photos, then considered taking more from another angle. Garel turned his back to the wind and braced himself against the rain. "Take your time," he said, gritting his teeth. "I got all day out here."

The shoddy environmental assessment, the geological issues, the Hurricane Keith photos—they all added up to a body of evidence too great for the Inter-American Development Bank to ignore. Word went out from Washington to the IDB's man in Belize: Mile 27 is a problem. The bank's local representative began quietly looking into the potential of Mile 24. The bank ordered a new comparison of the two sites carried out by an independent firm in Canada. The IDB didn't trust Stantec.

Meanwhile, Tony Garel worked the riverside villages. In Belize, politics is practiced shack to shack. Show a minister that voters in river villages will turn him out if a dump poisons the water, and you'll get his attention. On afternoons and weekends, Garel walked door to door through villages upstream and downstream of Mile 27. The people knew Garel and Garel knew the people and what he told them was simple and direct. "They gonna put a garbage dump right next to the river," he said. "You drink from that? Your children swim in that? Help us out. Sign one petition. Let Belmopan know you're unhappy about the dump."

And so near the end of 2000, on the day that the National Environmental Appraisal Committee met in Belmopan to consider Stantec's Mile 27 EIA, hundreds of villagers along the Sibun River woke early and boarded buses bound for the capital. On luggage racks above the seats they stowed signs that said SAVE THE SIBUN and NO POISON OUR WATER. Three hundred people turned out, one of the biggest demonstrations in Belmopan's history. They chanted for TV news crews and said impassioned words in defense of their river.

The protest had no effect on the vote. NEAC approved the EIA.

Sharon didn't attend the protest. Her absence was a tactical necessity, as the government's campaign to vilify her was having an effect. If she showed up in Belmopan, government officials would dismiss the demonstrators as hapless dupes of American ecocolonialists. The tall white woman would be fingered as ringleader, Exhibit A. Without Sharon, reporters from Channel 5, Channel 7, Love FM, KREM, and the four newspapers would be forced to get their sound bites from Tony Garel and Bacongo director Daedre Isaacs, Belizean-born locals with homegrown credibility. When Brian Holland met with Belize's local IDB representative to discuss the dump, the bank official opened with a rant against Sharon. "This woman at the zoo is stopping all progress in Belize!" he said. "She is first against hydropower and now is holding up the waste management program. I cannot understand it."

Every politician in Belize witnessed or heard about the anti-dump demonstration. And it wasn't just another parade of UDP party hacks. The people holding signs and chanting were villagers from La Democracia, Gracy Rock, and Freetown Sibun. They were voters from Ralph Fonseca's home district.

The Mile 27 landfill went into quiescence. Rumors circulated about an IDB-sponsored survey of the Mile 24 site, but neither Sharon, Tony Garel, nor Brian Holland was told about it. The Belizean government was tight-lipped. Sharon couldn't figure out what was going on. "The matter is being taken into consideration" was the only thing the government would tell her.

Then one day, months after the NEAC vote and demonstration, a British military officer showed up at the front gate of the zoo.

"Ms. Matola?" the man said, offering his hand. "I'm Colonel Tim Earl, private secretary to Her Royal Highness Princess Anne."

Her Royal Highness, only daughter of Queen Elizabeth II, would visit Belize in the coming month, the colonel said. He was her advance man. Princess Anne fondly recalled her visit to the zoo in 1989, Earl said, and she hoped to spend more time with the Zoo Lady and her animals during the four-day royal visit.

"How wonderful," Sharon said. "Tell me what I can do."

Colonel Earl explained the intricacies of royal protocol. Sharon led him down the gravel path past the macaws and around the peccary pen.

"Tim, I wonder if I might ask a favor of Her Royal Highness," she said. "We're in a bit of a bind here at the zoo. The government wants to put a fifty-five-thousand-ton garbage dump next door, and . . ."

Colonel Earl listened. "I have to tell you," he said, "in practice Her Royal Highness only sends messages of support to those charities of which she is a patron. Otherwise she would be continually doing so and it's unfair to meet some requests while refusing others. But I will discuss it with her."

Shortly after his return to Buckingham Palace, Colonel Earl sent Princess Anne's itinerary to Belizean officials. She planned to meet with Prime Minister Musa, tour a Mennonite village, dine with Governor-General Sir Colville Young, and donate a half-million dollars' worth of British military equipment to the Belizean Defence Force. In between, Princess Anne would call at a few rural villages. Nothing unusual. One stop, though, caught the eye of ministerial aides in Belmopan: Thursday, 1000–1130 hours—Belize Zoo.

An hour and a half with Sharon Matola? That spelled trouble.

Relations between former colonies and mother countries are rarely unstrained. Those between Belize and Great Britain are notoriously fragile and bitter, and never more so than during a royal visit. Though Belize has been independent since 1981, Queen Elizabeth remains the nation's official head of state. It's a purely ceremonial title, to be sure, but that doesn't lessen its effect on Belizean national pride. After all, Belize still depends on Great Britain. British soldiers hold Guatemala at bay. Belize receives millions in British aid every year. That dependence remains psychologically dormant until one of the royals makes a visit and brings all the old resentments tumbling out. Why, exactly, were Belizeans expected to honor the British? Was it for the mahogany missing from the forests? Was it for the roads unpaved? The hospitals unbuilt? Was it for an economy warped by centuries of colonialism?

Matters weren't helped by the handover of power in 1981. Belize hadn't forced England out so much as England had finally, with palpable relief, shed the tiny colony. Neither Queen Elizabeth nor Prime Minister Margaret Thatcher could be bothered to show up for the September 21, 1981, transfer of power. Instead, England sent Prince Michael of Kent, the queen's cousin, a talisman of insignificance. Prince Michael doesn't often represent the crown at state events, but when he does, one can be assured that the event is of the utmost irrelevance to world affairs. Prince Michael has represented the queen at the funeral of the president of Cyprus, a treaty ceremony in Brunei, the coronation of King Mswati III of Swaziland, and at ceremonies in the Ukraine marking the 150th anniversary of the Crimean War. On its proudest day, Belize received its independence from a second-rate royal in a shaggy beard. The queen herself finally came to Belize in 1994. When asked about her visit, Belizeans today smile and say, "She come to see if anything was left worth taking."

Despite that hostile undercurrent, Princess Anne still held power in her person and her position. Her mother's portrait graced every Belizean dollar bill. A minority of Belizeans still held pro-British sentiments. And, of course, Belizeans expended an extraordinary amount of energy worrying what the rest of the world thought of them. A sharp comment from Her Royal Highness on an issue like the Mile 27 dump could prove embarrassing to Prime Minister Musa. It might prove financially painful as well. The U.K. government was considering granting debt relief to Belize. Musa didn't want to give England any reason to delay the deal.

Not long after Colonel Earl released Princess Anne's itinerary, Sharon called the zoo from a wildlife conference in Mexico City.

"Claudia? It's me. Any messages?"

"Yah, Sharon, lots," said Claudia. "Mister Shoman called twice. He sounded angry." Assad Shoman was a close adviser to Prime Minister Musa.

"He must have seen Princess Anne's schedule," Sharon said. "They're wondering what she's going to say when she's here at the zoo. Let them wonder."

In fact, Sharon knew exactly what Princess Anne was prepared to say. Her Royal Highness wasn't a patron of the Belize Zoo, but she was a patron of the Durrell Conservation Trust. That trust was founded by Sharon's old friends Gerald and Lee Durrell. With Lee Durrell's help, news of the zoo's plight had gotten through to the princess. Sharon had learned that the queen's daughter was ready to stand before a microphone and call upon the Belize government to move the Mile 27 dump.

She did not return Assad Shoman's call.

Some nights in Belize, when the clouds knit together and block out the moon and the stars, the land settles into a disorienting darkness. It was on such a night that Sharon closed down the zoo, hopped on her motorcycle, and rode home. Her headlamp jostled through the night like a searchlight, picking up the sparkling eyes of roadside creatures. The bike coughed to a stop in her driveway. She swung the kickstand down but didn't see that its heel lined up with a pothole. The Kawasaki crashed down on her, buckling her knee. The impact popped the fuel tank lid. In the dark she couldn't see the gasoline, but she heard it glug and felt its evaporative coolness on her skin. Soaked and reeking, she struggled to get out from under the 350-pound machine. Her dogs barked and recoiled at the smell. Eventually she freed her legs and crawled away, then felt her way back to the bike, planted her feet, and tried to tug it up. The motorcycle wouldn't budge.

"Dammit, dammit, dammit!" She kicked the fuel tank. Pain shot from her knee. She made her way to the house and called Richard Foster.

"Richard? I need your help," she said.

She sat and waited, and while she waited she cried. You can do that when you're alone in the bush. She didn't want anybody's pity. She wasn't feeling sorry for herself. She had just come to the end of a long day at the end of a long week at the end of a long year. The dump was going in. The dam was going up. Nothing was going right. Even her own motorcycle kicked her down. She loved Belize. She loved living in the jungle. But sometimes this life was hard to bear.

The next morning she rose early and rode her scraped motorcycle to the BFBS studio. Sharon was filling in for the morning host, who was on vacation. For three hours she hid behind the mask of her radio persona and lost herself in the pleasure of playlists and public service announcements. When the shift ended, her troubles returned. Princess Anne would arrive in two weeks. Sharon ticked off a mental list of all that had to be done. New signs had to go up. The reptile room wanted a scrub and fresh paint. Would they have to feed Her Royal Highness? Oh, god. Probably not, but they'd better have refreshments on hand. Maybe Tony could make a supply run to Chetumal.

She got to the zoo around noon. Claudia Duenas spun in her chair when she heard Sharon on the office steps.

"Sharon! Did you hear the news?"

"What news?"

"They're moving the dump."

Sharon tensed. Rumors like this were invariably false—the result of some chance encounter with a low-level minister who promised what he couldn't deliver. "How do you know?"

"Tony heard," said Duenas. "Government announced it this morning. He's on his way back from Belmopan right now."

Tony Garel appeared thirty minutes later. It was true, he said. "No empty promise this time. Cabinet put out a press briefing. I got it right here."

Sharon scanned the release. The government, "on the basis of a technical assessment," had agreed to relocate the dump to Mile 24, away from the zoo.

"I don't know if I believe it," she said.

"Believe it," said Garel. "You believe it." He grinned.

"Stay right here," she said. She ran out the door and into the commissary.

"One for you, one for me," she said, handing Garel a cold Heineken. They clinked bottles. "Cheers, my friend," she said. They sat and drank and savored the victory.

"Anybody told La Democracia?" Sharon said, referring to one of the Sibun River villages downstream of Mile 27. "Gracy Rock? Freetown Sibun?"

Garel nodded.

Sharon leaned back in her chair. Quiet came over the little shack. It felt good.

The phone rang. "If that's Jacob, tell him I'm not here," she said. Garel looked at her quizzically. "I just can't speak right now," she said.

He lifted the receiver.

"Tony! It's Jacob Scherr. Congratulations!"

Garel smiled and winked at Sharon. He took glad tidings from Scherr and read the press briefing into the phone. "No, she's not here," he said.

Sharon mouthed a silent thank you and slipped out of the office. At the bottom of the stairs she shucked off her boots and socks and walked barefoot through the zoo, her zoo, her still-living zoo.

Part II

PERMANENT CONNECTION

CHAPTER 16

WITH THE DUMP DEFEATED, Sharon turned her attention back to the dam. A lot had happened over the previous months.

The government put the state-run water utility, Belize Water Services, on the auction block. At Sacred Heart Junior College in San Ignacio, Kimo Jolly used the sale as a teachable moment. Would privatization be good or bad for Belizeans? His students organized a debate, and news of that debate reached the ears of certain ministers in Belmopan. Certain ministers were displeased. In fact, certain ministers were fed up with Kimo Jolly. He'd already embarrassed the government by publicizing Chalillo's numerous flaws. He wouldn't be allowed to do it again with the water sale.

The principal of Sacred Heart, a school supported by state funding, told Jolly to cool it. "The school got word from a minister that we wouldn't get any more money from government unless we cleaned up our act," Jolly later told me. "They said the school was getting a reputation as a breeding ground for ecoterrorism, that I was sabotaging the country's chances for development. In Belize, some topics are politically sensitive. If something's making a minister some money, no one is allowed to talk about it."

The school's privatization debate went on as planned. The next day Kimo Jolly was fired. *The Reporter* splashed the news on its front page, and there was talk of a lawsuit, but in the end nothing came of it. Jolly lost his job, outrage was expressed, and the world moved on. Two months after his firing, the Belizean government sold the nation's water utility for $25 million to Cascal, an international water consortium run by the British Biwater corporation. Not long after the purchase, Cascal named a new chairman of the privatized Belize Water Services: Norris Hall.

Other Belizeans stepped up to fight the dam, undeterred by
Kimo Jolly's cautionary example. Bacongo director Daedre Isaacs,
a former television reporter, openly challenged the government
and BEL. She and Sharon gained a valuable ally when BEL senior
engineer Ambrose Tillett resigned from the company and de-
nounced BEL for deceiving the public. One of his statements later
became a slogan on T-shirts worn by the dam's opponents:
"Chalillo is a lie."

Tillett knew something that Sharon, Ari Hershowitz, Jacob
Scherr, Daedre Isaacs, and Tony Garel didn't know: Fortis and
BEL were playing a fixed game. In December 1999, shortly after
Fortis acquired BEL, Fortis CEO Stan Marshall appeared at BEL's
annual meeting. Reporters asked Marshall what he planned to do
about Chalillo. Would Fortis build the dam? "Our position is that
if it is proved to be the best choice economically and environmentally," Marshall replied, "we are going to do it."

Stan Marshall was nobody's fool. "Of course the dam will be
economical," Tillett explained to Sharon. "Economical for Fortis!
For Belizeans buying their power, not so much."

Tillett believed the GE "least cost" study, which BEL cited to
justify the dam, was rigged. "It was reverse engineered," he said.
"The GE consultants knew BEL wanted the dam, so they started
from that point and worked backward. They set the estimated
cost from other power sources so high that hydro would appear as
the cheapest option. Of course they can't let anybody see the report."

In his public comments, Marshall framed Fortis and its Belizean subsidiary as impartial actors in the drama. Expert economists and biologists would advise the company on the wisdom of
proceeding with the dam, he said. Fortis, he implied, would rely on
their good judgment. The company had no interest in building a
financially foolish and ecologically destructive dam.

"What he doesn't tell you is that BEL is paying those consultants," said Tillett, "and they're paying them to say what BEL wants
to hear."

The privatization craze that swept through Europe and Latin America in the 1990s was originally hailed as free-market capitalism's great and good victory over socialism. Privatization forced bloated state utilities to operate efficiently—that was the claim. Competitive markets wouldn't tolerate lazy employees, poor service, and political featherbedding. In some cases that was true. But in many other countries, especially in South America, privatization became a convenient way for politicians to line their own pockets and pay off their contributors and cronies. Instead of opening up competitive markets for power, water, and phone service, states often ended up creating private monopolies. Michael Ashcroft's BTL, for example, charges some of the highest phone rates in the world. It's cheaper for a Belizean to catch a bus to Guatemala and talk to a friend in person than to place a twenty-minute call.

How do you sell a power utility in a tiny developing nation? One way is to take out an ad. The Belize government posted a notice in the back pages of *The Economist*. Five suitors showed interest. A Taiwanese company sent a scout over to have a look. "BEL and government were already moving forward on Chalillo," recalled Ambrose Tillett, "but the Taiwanese official didn't want to hear about it. 'We've had experience with dams,' he said. 'No matter how good they look on paper, in reality they're always more expensive.' The Taiwanese wanted gas turbines. No hydro. So as far as the government was concerned, Taiwan was out."

Chalillo had become an obsession to BEL and the Musa government. Any company unwilling to build the dam found itself shut out of the privatization sweepstakes. Chalillo's proponents based their arguments on energy and national security, but those like Tillett who had more experience in the energy industry believed there was another driving force, one that nobody dared mention: The construction of Chalillo could make some people very rich.

Dams have always been occasioned by economics—power for industry, or water for crops—but dam construction has, historically, rarely been lucrative in and of itself. That changed in the 1930s with the Hoover Dam. Stopping the Colorado River required more manpower and expertise than any one company could offer. The six engineering firms that banded together to get the job done were paid $52 million by the U.S. government. Of that, an estimated 20 to 35 percent—$10 to $18 million—was profit, making the dam one of the most lucrative construction projects in American history. Hoover Dam was the proving ground for some of today's global engineering corporations, including Bechtel and Morrison-Knudson. Chalillo was a small project, of course, but it still required an influx of tens of millions of dollars, money destined to be divided among many subcontractors. This invites the sort of graft incidental to large public works projects. As money passes from contractor to subcontractor, it tends to leak into the pockets of well-connected businessmen and government officials.

"None of the companies considering the purchase of BEL wanted to build Chalillo," Tillett said. "They couldn't see how it made sense. Then came Fortis, this Canadian company. Their expertise was in small hydro projects. They saw the world in terms of rivers and dams. So of course they thought Chalillo made perfect sense. I went out in the field with Fortis's chief engineer. We checked out Mollejon, the power lines, the site at Chalillo. I kept asking him, 'How's Chalillo going to fit? It doesn't make economic sense!' and he kept saying, 'I need to check the numbers.'"

There was only one way the numbers would work, Tillett said. "If you can get the government to give you a guaranteed market, a guaranteed price, you can make money." What Fortis needed was guaranteed profit. When the sale of BEL was announced, however, there was no mention of profit assurances. All the Belizean public knew was that their power utility had been sold to a company based on a cold northern island called Newfoundland.

Even as the government continued to paint Sharon as a white devil and a traitor, the anti-dam movement gained traction. As born-and-raised Belizeans, Ambrose Tillett and Bacongo director

Daedre Isaacs couldn't be tarred as easily as a white American. Tillett and Isaacs also knew one thing: Most Belizeans don't care about a few acres of bush, but when you talk about their money, they're all ears. Working with Ari Hershowitz and the NRDC, Bacongo took out ads claiming that Belizeans already paid the highest electricity rates in Central America, and that the cost of Chalillo would only send them higher. This campaign struck a chord.

In response, the power company took out counter-ads claiming that Belizean power rates were actually among the lowest in the region—the region being the Caribbean, not Central America— and that Chalillo would keep those rates low. The framing was brilliant. By lumping Belize in with the Caribbean rather than with Central America, BEL didn't just put its power rates in a more favorable light. The ad was nothing short of a nationalist appeal. We won't give in to Guatemala, the ad implied. We're not Central American. At BEL we stand for independence and sovereignty. We're Caribbean.

Even as she recognized the power of Bacongo's argument, Sharon couldn't hide her displeasure. "I've never understood why money is so important to people," she once told me. It wasn't that she was naïve when it came to cash. Every year she had to bring in $250,000 to keep the zoo running. But she couldn't understand why others didn't value the wild Macal and Raspaculo rivers as much as she did. It pained her that Chalillo might not be stopped on the basis of environmental conservation alone. "The manner in which you and Ambrose are approaching this is so vital, but losing sight of the environmental importance of this area is a huge loss for Belize," she wrote in an e-mail to Daedre Isaacs.

"I agree, Sharon, we need to hammer the environmental side," Isaacs replied. "It does have a value. But in our national accounting system there is no value attached to that financially—that is our whole problem."

Tillett and Isaacs brought new energy to the anti-Chalillo campaign. They connected with the Belizeans Sharon couldn't reach.

They spoke with authority and integrity. The government couldn't neutralize them with smear tactics. So another route was taken.

One day during their usual lunchtime meeting, Tony Garel greeted Sharon with a face drawn by defeat. "Did you hear about Daedre?" he said.

"What about her?"

"She left Bacongo," he said. "Going to work for Ralph."

"You're joking."

"No joke. He made her an offer too good to refuse."

Aside from Garel and Ambrose Tillett, Daedre Isaacs was the most articulate and respected Belizean fighting the dam. "He bought her off," Sharon said. "She's going to give everything we know to Ralph."

Tony cocked his head. "I don't think so," he said. "Daedre's a professional. When she took the job she told Ralph she's not going to talk about Chalillo."

Sharon threw up her hands. "So that's how he plays," she said. "If you can't beat them, hire them." She went into her office and shut the door.

In the spring of 2001, shortly after the Belizean government decided to move the proposed dump away from the zoo, Ari Hershowitz called Sharon. He and Jacob had been thinking, Hershowitz said. Fortis CEO Stan Marshall didn't seem to care what Belizeans or Americans thought of his company, but it might be a different story in his hometown of St. John's. Fortis's annual shareholders meeting was coming up in May.

"The local papers will be covering the meeting anyway," Hershowitz said. "We might as well give them something to talk about. Let's bring Belize to Newfoundland."

CHAPTER 17

*I*N MAY 2001, Sharon, Ari Hershowitz, and Ambrose Tillett traveled to St. John's, Newfoundland, to present their cause to the company's shareholders at the Fortis annual meeting. Working through a local intermediary, the Sierra Club of Canada, Hershowitz requested a meeting with Fortis CEO Stan Marshall. To Hershowitz's surprise, Marshall agreed. On the day before the shareholders meeting, the two sides gathered around a large conference table at Fortis headquarters, a glass-and-steel monolith near the harbor in downtown St. John's.

Stan Marshall sat at the head of the table flanked by Norris Hall, Fortis chief engineer John Evans, and BEL chief executive Lynn Young. Three representatives from the Sierra Club of Canada sat with the dam opponents.

"Mr. Marshall, I'm Ari Hershowitz of the Natural Resources Defense Council. And this is Sharon Matola, director of the Belize Zoo."

"The lady from the zoo." Marshall offered a big smile and a handshake. He let everyone find a seat before addressing the group.

"So tell me," he said. "What do you all have against dams?"

Ari Hershowitz answered. "We're not against all dams," he said. "There are characteristics of certain dams that make them worse than other dams—"

"Forget that!" Marshall said. "I've read your literature. I looked at one of your anti-dam sites on the Internet. They had a list of the worst dams in the world. You know what it said? Number one was the Three Gorges. Next on the list was this tiny little dam in Belize. It doesn't make sense."

He fixed Hershowitz with an angry stare. His real enemy in all this, Marshall believed, was the NRDC. "You know what I think?

I think maybe you went looking for something to do. You came upon this project in Belize and decided to attack it."

John Bennett of the Sierra Club snapped back. "Yes, that's exactly what we did," he said. "We spun a dial and it landed on Fortis, so we decided to come to Newfoundland and attack you."

Hershowitz shot a look at Bennett that said, Dial it back.

Marshall let the comment pass. "I can't see the point of talking with you if you're against all hydro projects per se. I bet you couldn't name a single dam that meets your approval."

"That's not true," said Hershowitz. "It depends on the dam. With Chalillo you've got a proposed dam that would destroy an incredible site of natural diversity and abundance. We've got letters on file from dozens of scientists around the world backing us up. In return, Belize would only gain six megawatts from Chalillo and a little more from Mollejon. That's to say nothing of the dam's questionable economics."

"Questionable economics? If this didn't make business sense we wouldn't do it. The GE report proved it was economically viable," Marshall said.

"Nobody in the public realm has been able to see that study," Hershowitz said.

"It's part of the public record."

"Then why can't the public see it? One of the reasons we're here is to ask for a copy of the GE report and the contracts between BEL, BELCO, and the Belizean government. Those should be part of the public record."

"And they are!"

"Well, if they're part of the public record, then there shouldn't be a problem with us picking up a copy of those documents today," said Hershowitz. "We can take them to a copy shop around the corner, or if you'd like to photocopy it here we'll be happy to wait."

Lynn Young spoke up. "The GE report is proprietary information," he said. "All other documents that are part of the public process have been released."

The room began to feel stuffy. Sharon tried a new gambit. "If we're talking economics, let's talk economics," she said. "Belize is a

developing country, and the tourism industry, particularly the na-
ture-based tourism industry, is our highest foreign exchange
earner. We employ thousands of resort workers, tour guides, drivers, and chefs. Belize isn't a country with a lot of big factories. Sustainable tourism is our big hope for economic stability. The
macaws that nest in that valley are one of our biggest draws."

"Ms. Matola, with all due respect, I don't know where you're
coming up with these claims about the scarlet macaw," Marshall
said. "I've checked the IUCN Red List. The bird isn't on it."

Sharon's jaw tightened. "The scarlet macaw is on the CITES
list as an endangered species," she said. "There are fewer than two
hundred of them alive in Belize and they breed in the very spot
you're going to flood."

Marshall answered. "We have an environmental assessment
going on right now. When that report is finished, we'll look at it
and determine whether the dam would cause untoward damage to
the environment. If it does, we won't go forward with the project."

He continued. "The only reason we're involved in this dam is
because your government, the democratically elected government
of Belize, asked us to be involved. Now it seems to me a lot of people have opinions about this project. Which they're entitled to. I,
on the other hand, operate on facts. When all the facts are in, we
will look at them, and if we think this is an environmentally acceptable project, we will follow the proper procedures with the
Belizean government to ask permission to develop the site. We're
involved because it's good business. But the final decision rests
with the Belizean government."

Sharon stole a glance at Norris Hall. Hall's presence at the
meeting left no doubt as to what the Belizean government's final
decision would be.

Hershowitz tried another tactic. "One of our concerns is that
we've never gotten a clear sense of which standards Fortis is ad-
hering to. You're a Canadian company building a hydro project
overseas. We feel the project should adhere to accepted international standards that—"

"We are using international standards," Marshall said.

"Those involve open public hearings and fully transparent studies. That hasn't been done. You justify the dam with documents the public can't see."

"We're a Canadian company and we live up to Canadian standards," Marshall said.

"Canada also requires full transparency," John Bennett reminded him.

"International standards require you to use best practices on this project," said Hershowitz. "Will you do that? Or will you just do whatever you can get away with?" Hershowitz knew his question crept into provocation. He wanted to let Marshall know the project would be watched every step of the way.

Marshall's face reddened. "What you people forget is that ultimately, in a democratic society like Belize, the people affected surely have to be the ones who decide. Not the NRDC. Not Stan Marshall in St. John's. I can bring my views. You can bring your views. But ultimately the local people have to be the ones who decide. That's what irritates me. You come to me as if I'm the one who decides. I've always said it's really a matter for the Belizeans."

Sharon smirked. Marshall's idea of Belizean democracy was a far cry from reality.

Norris Hall sensed his cue. "I would like to address my fellow Belizeans for a moment," he said. He turned to Sharon. "And I mean my fellow *Belizeans.*" It was clear that the Zoo Lady was not a member of the club. "I look around this table and I see a lot of faces from Canada and the United States but not many from Belize. That does not surprise me. From the start this dam has been opposed by foreigners and outsiders who show a total lack of respect for our environmental laws and our nation's sovereignty.

"When BEL was privatized, the government selected Fortis because of its excellent track record in the hydroelectric industry and its record of environmental stewardship," Hall continued. "The company has proven to be a good corporate citizen of Belize. We have more than one-third of our population plagued by poverty. There is a great need for more electrical power at reduced rates to stimulate development. Without electricity we cannot attract investment and industry. And investment and industry are the only ways to create employment and do something more than pay lip service to the alleviation of poverty."

He turned to Tillett. "Isn't that true, Ambrose?"

Ambrose Tillett thought before he spoke. He had to choose his words carefully. Using the word *corruption* could kindle a firestorm back home.

"Norris, if you really want to alleviate poverty, Chalillo should not even be on the agenda," Tillett said. "If you want to alleviate poverty the first thing that should be done, *the very first thing,* is to institute the honest, transparent administration of government. If you don't have that, it doesn't matter how much money you put to fighting poverty, because whatever you start out with is going to end up in—"

He caught himself before the words "some minister's pocket" tumbled out. "That money will be . . . misallocated. Resources wasted.

"Once you have an honest administration," Tillett said, "then you need to build capacity in people. Invest in them—education, training. Government loves big infrastructure projects because they are visible. Look at all those houses we built, look at that big dam, everybody see? But dams don't address the fundamental issue. At the end of the day you and I, *fellow Belizeans,* know that poverty won't start disappearing until we have a government that opens its books and shows the people what it is doing."

He addressed Lynn Young. "Lynn, you know those power purchase contracts must be made public. And yet they are not. Why? Why, man?"

Young held the company line. "We've made everything public," he said.

"But have you made the Mollejon power contract public?"

"It's all out there. A copy is filed with the public utilities commission."

Hershowitz jumped in. "Then you wouldn't mind giving us a copy, would you?"

Silence. Stan Marshall stood. "I think we should wrap this up," he said. "We're getting nowhere."

As the group slowly made its way to the elevator, Hershowitz buttonholed Fortis engineer John Evans. "Here's my card," he said. "Will you send me a copy of the power purchase contract?"

Evans indicated he would.

They rode the elevator in silence. Sharon pushed through the revolving door into a chill Atlantic wind. She looked downhill to the harbor and saw the road disappear into the fog. This was no place like home.

"How do you think it went with Marshall?" Hershowitz asked.

Sharon thought before she spoke. "We're in for a hell of a fight with this guy."

Fortis's involvement remained one of the great mysteries of the Chalillo affair. What were these Newfoundland pole-and-wire guys doing in the middle of the Central American jungle?

I once asked Stan Marshall about it. "We have more in common than you might think," he said, meaning Newfoundland and Belize. And it was true. The more you looked into their past, the more the two former British colonies seemed to be running along parallel tracks in history. Both shipped the bounty of their land— timber from Belize, fish from Newfoundland—to the mother country and received little in return. Newfoundlanders, like Belizeans, carried within them a deep sense of historic injustice. They were accustomed to being swindled by faraway powers, and they felt the wounds dealt to their ancestors as if they had absorbed the blows themselves.

In fact, Newfoundland even had its own Chalillo. Near the end of World War II, explorers journeying to the remote interior of Labrador came upon one of the last pristine wonders of the world: Hamilton Falls, the third largest waterfall on the planet.

Labrador is eastern Canada's wild outback, with a population of about thirty thousand spread over an area the size of England. Separated from Newfoundland by the Strait of Belle Isle, it has long been tied to its southern neighbor by culture and history. (The province's official name is "Newfoundland and Labrador.") Hamilton Falls wasn't exactly undiscovered—Labrador's bush pilots, fur trappers, and Inuit people knew of its existence—but the photographs brought back by the 1944 expedition alerted the outside world. The photos revealed a massive flood roaring off a hardrock plateau. One headline asked: "HAVE WE FOUND ANOTHER NIAGARA?"

Were it discovered today, Hamilton Falls would be preserved in a national park. But in the 1940s and 1950s, thoughts turned to hydropower. Newfoundland's premier, Joey Smallwood, recognized the waterfall's power potential. Smallwood was to Newfoundland what George Price was to Belize: a charismatic founding father, brilliant at retail politics and tireless in defense of his people and province. He didn't have much money to work with, certainly not enough to build a dam capable of blocking Hamilton Falls. So Smallwood flew to England to drum up interest. Emerging from a meeting with Smallwood, ex–prime minister Winston Churchill declared: "It is high time the Hamilton Falls had a bridle." Using Churchill's blessing as his calling card, Smallwood gained the backing of the Rothschild banking family, whose scion Edmund de Rothschild became one of the lead investors in an international consortium known as BRINCO, the British Newfoundland Corporation. In gratitude, Smallwood renamed the falls Churchill Falls. With financing complete, only one thing stood in the way: Quebec.

Newfoundland suffered Quebec as Belize suffered Guatemala. Newfoundlanders saw their neighboring province as a bully always stealing the bread off Newfoundland's plate. In the 1920s, Quebec attempted to wrest Labrador from Newfoundland, claiming that the territory lay within the natural boundaries of French Canada. You can see their point. On a map of Canada, Labrador seems strangely jigsawed out of Quebec. Newfoundland's claim rests on its traditional use of Labrador's shoreline and interior as summer fishing and hunting grounds. The two neighbors battled all the way to the Privy Council, the highest court for Commonwealth nations, where the Law Lords declared Newfoundland the rightful owner.

Though Smallwood promoted the Churchill Falls dam as a way

to bring electricity to Newfoundland's rural outposts, the BRINCO bankers knew the tiny province wasn't their primary market. The real money would be made by sending surplus power south to Montreal, Toronto, and New York City. To do that they had to string wires across Quebec. It was a classic neighborly ease-ment conflict, and Quebec played Newfoundland like a finely tuned fiddle. Relying on the advice of BRINCO's negotiators, Joey Smallwood put his signature to a contract in 1966 that gave Quebec control of the Churchill Falls power once it crossed the Labrador border, and Hydro-Quebec, the province-owned elec-tric utility, the right to buy the power at a ridiculously low fixed rate for sixty-five years. Hydro-Quebec could then sell it for profit on the open market. Between 1975 and 1995, with the 5,400-megawatt dam up and running, Hydro-Quebec's profit from Churchill Falls averaged $600 million per year. Newfound-land received a little more than one-thirtieth of that amount. To this day, Newfoundlanders consider the theft of their Churchill Falls power one of the greatest swindles in the history of North America.

Fortis grew out of that history. The company was founded in 1924 as Newfoundland Light and Power, a small private utility. About half of Newfoundland's power came from twenty-two small hydroelectric dams, most of which put out between 4 and 7 megawatts, similar to the capacity of Chalillo. In 1987, the com-pany reorganized itself into a holding company called Fortis, after the Latin word for strength. The new corporate structure allowed Fortis to pursue ventures outside its traditional business. The company expanded into banking, hotel ownership, and land de-velopment.

In 1993, Newfoundland premier Clyde Wells proposed priva-tizing Newfoundland & Labrador Hydro, the state-owned power utility. (Newfoundland & Labrador Hydro produced the power and sold it to Fortis, a private corporation, which distributed it.) Although most of the Churchill Falls profits go to Quebec, New-foundland & Labrador Hydro owns the dam itself. It also owns the potentially lucrative rights to a long-planned, never-built second dam. Behind the scenes, Premier Wells began talking with Fortis about buying the company. No introductions were necessary. Wells was familiar with Fortis. Prior to winning the premiership he had served as chairman of the board.

Outraged by the appearance of self-dealing—and mindful of the Churchill Falls debacle—the people of Newfoundland rose up and defeated the privatization scheme. Wells resigned in 1996. His successor, Brian Tobin, declared a moratorium on new hydro development to save Newfoundland's dwindling Atlantic salmon runs.

Stan Marshall took over as CEO in 1995, shortly after the privatization fiasco. Unable to expand Fortis's hydro operations at home, Marshall looked abroad for continued growth. He bought small power companies in Canada and the Caribbean. "When I heard Belize wanted to sell its power company, I flew to Belize City myself," Marshall told me. "I felt very much at home. To me, it was a tropical version of Newfoundland when I was a kid."

When Fortis took over the Chalillo project, Jacob Scherr shifted the NRDC campaign. The postcards, e-mails, letters, and phone calls that had bedeviled Duke CEO Rick Priory began arriving at Stan Marshall's office. Most were brief pleas to scrap the dam, but others attacked Marshall and his company with a combination of righteousness and rage. A number of scientists wrote letters appealing to the CEO's sense of moral and civic duty. "We bore the brunt of the NRDC's wrath," Marshall said. "Their whole strategy has been to make my life miserable, and at that they have succeeded in droves."

When talking about the Chalillo battle, Marshall often brought up the story of Brigitte Bardot and Newfoundland's swilers, as seal hunters are known. "In the winter, when the men couldn't go out for cod, they'd go on the ice for seal," he told me. "Rural Newfoundland depended on the seal fishery. Then in the seventies, Brigitte Bardot came over to denounce the swilers. She knew nothing about it. But that didn't matter. In the space of a few years the global environmental movement had wiped out the hunt."

To Stan Marshall, Chalillo wasn't about the destruction of

nesting grounds or the dam's questionable economics. It was
Brigitte Bardot redux: wealthy know-nothing foreigners mucking
about in other people's business.

Once Marshall fit the issue into that context, there was no
backing down. "I told the government of Belize, 'The easiest thing
for me would be for you guys to cancel the dam. It'd make my life
easier. But if you don't, I will pursue it to the end.'

"What the NRDC wants is to harass me to the point where I
decide to walk away," Marshall told me. "Anybody who knows me
knows that's not going to work."

The day after her meeting with Marshall, Sharon and a group of
Canadian environmentalists picketed the St. John's Holiday Inn,
site of the Fortis annual meeting. Standing in a foggy drizzle, she
passed out leaflets asking shareholders to stop the construction of
the dam. Ari Hershowitz and some activists from Newfoundland's Memorial University held up pictures of jaguars and scarlet
macaws and chanted, "Fortis forget it!" A few shareholders
stopped to chat, but most took one look at the flyer and tossed it
in a trash can near the door. The protesters weren't allowed inside.
Fortis owned the hotel, so it set the rules. Security guards moved
the activists off the property and left them chanting on the sidewalk.

Somebody had a radio, and at the top of the hour they huddled
to hear the headlines on Radio One: "CBC News. In St. John's
today, endangered species activists from Belize will speak out on
behalf of the scarlet macaw at Fortis Incorporated's annual meeting. . . ." A cheer went up. The report described the Chalillo project and ended with a pledge from Stan Marshall: "The head of
Fortis has promised the project will not go ahead if it is not environmentally sound and economically viable."

Sharon spoke up. "We'll hold you to that, Stan."

Inside the hotel ballroom, Stan Marshall announced that Fortis had posted record earnings of $30 million in the year 2000.
Gross revenues were up 15 percent. Net earnings had climbed 27
percent. The company was bringing in more money than ever be-

fore, and keeping more of that money as profit. The shareholders were pleased.

During the question and answer session, John Bennett from the Sierra Club of Canada grilled Marshall about Chalillo. Bennett had slipped into the meeting with the help of a sympathetic shareholder. Why, he asked, did Fortis insist on destroying one of the last pristine areas in Central America?

Marshall glared at Bennett. "Mr. Bennett, I met with you and explained our position," he said. "There are studies being conducted regarding the environmental impact of the project, and we will evaluate those facts when they are available to us. Fortis is a good corporate citizen."

Bennett pressed him. "Why would you go ahead with the dam when your own consultants have pointed out that it's not economic?"

"On the contrary," said Marshall. "Our consultants have concluded that hydro is the least costly option."

Bennett continued. "If you're talking about the GE consultant's report, that hasn't been made public. And we're left to wonder why. The Sierra Club and other environmental organizations from across Canada are asking you to release all the documents related to this project."

An angry flush rose in the CEO's cheeks. "As I said, Mr. Bennett, a report is being carried out. It will be submitted to the government of Belize, and it will decide on such matters. Next questioner." Bennett returned to his seat.

Marshall moved on to other business, and the shareholders dismissed the concerns of the protesters from Belize. Chalillo was just a small dam in a faraway place most of them had never heard of. As long as it boosted earnings, they were all for it.

CHAPTER 18

STAN MARSHALL'S COMMENT about the scarlet macaw nagged at Sharon. There were fewer than two hundred macaws in all of Belize. CITES listed the bird in its most-endangered category. The World Parrot Trust, the global authority on the world's 330 species of parrots, also classified the Central American scarlet macaw as endangered. How could it not be on the Red List?

Back in Belize she dug into the issue. In the United States, federal and state agencies maintain their own lists of endangered and threatened species. Developing countries like Belize don't have the resources to carry out the research needed to compile their own lists. Instead they rely on the IUCN Red List of Threatened Species, the world's most comprehensive record of the global conservation status of plants and animals. According to the IUCN's online database, Stan Marshall was right. *Ara macao* was listed as a "species of least concern." The IUCN didn't worry about the bird.

That was a problem.

Endangered species status can be a powerful tool. In fact it's a proven dam stopper. During construction of the Tellico Dam in the early 1970s, a University of Tennessee ichthyologist discovered a previously unknown species of perch known as the snail darter, which lived in the Little Tennessee River. The U.S. Fish and Wildlife Service listed the three-inch fish as endangered in 1975, just as the $100 million dam was about to close its gates and turn the Little Tennessee into a reservoir. Doing so would have wiped out the snail darter's only known habitat. The ensuing three-year battle ended up in the U.S. Supreme Court, which ruled that construction would have to stop. "It may seem curious to some that the survival of a relatively small number of three-inch fish among all the countless millions of species extant would require the permanent halting of a virtually completed dam," wrote Chief Justice Warren Burger. But the strong provisions of America's Endangered Species Act "require precisely that result."*

Without endangered status, Sharon's campaign to save the macaws would be crippled. Conservation resources were limited. A brutal triage took place every day around the world. Money and effort flowed to the most endangered species; those of least concern could fend for themselves. In a world of diminishing biodiversity, you had to save the most threatened species first. The same dynamic played out in the media. Reporters wanted to know if the macaw was endangered. If not, why should their readers care?

Sharon started asking how a species got on the Red List. It turned out that the IUCN didn't compile the bird list itself. It subcontracted that work to BirdLife International, a London-based conservation group. BirdLife officials told her a change in status required rigorous documentation proving that the macaw met a strict set of declining-population standards. The process could take years.

She didn't have years. The dam would go up in months. Sharon worried that the macaws would suffer the fate of the Tasmanian tiger. The tiger, a striped wolflike marsupial, roamed the Tasmanian outback for thousands of years. Humans hunted it to near extinction by the beginning of the twentieth century, and in the 1930s a movement arose to protect the animal. In 1936, the Tasmanian tiger finally received officially protected status. A few months later it went extinct.

Sharon set the process in motion by collecting letters from bird

---

* The snail darter proved to be a dam stopper but not a dam killer. Soon after the Supreme Court decision, the United States Congress passed special legislation exempting the Tellico Dam from the Endangered Species Act. The dam was completed in 1979. The reservoir wiped out the fish's Little Tennessee River habitat, but other populations were later found in creeks and rivers in the Tennessee River drainage. Efforts to bolster those populations resulted in the snail darter's status being upgraded from endangered to threatened in 1984.

experts. All agreed that Belize's subspecies of macaw, *Ara macao cyanoptera,* should be considered for endangered status. Richard Bateman, London's Natural History Museum official who oversaw the NHM's Belize research station, strongly recommended that the IUCN upgrade the bird's status. Ernesto Enkerlin, president of Mexico's National Commission on Protected Areas, wrote that without upgraded status, "the Central American populations known to be a distinct subspecies would be decimated in a short time." One of the strongest letters of support came from Valdemar Andrade, director of the Belize Audubon Society. "The Society would like to pledge support for upgrading the status," he wrote. Based on recent research, the society considered the macaw population vulnerable within Belize. "This species warrants that status upgrading," he concluded.

Not long after Andrade wrote that letter, Belizean government officials caught wind of Sharon's strategy. Realizing that endangered status for the macaw could halt the development of Chalillo, they moved to block any change in the bird's protection level. The Belize Audubon Society's position inexplicably changed. In the group's next newsletter Valdemar Andrade announced that the society's board, led by BAS president Pepe Garcia, had voted to support the construction of Chalillo. Audubon Society officials believed the habitat of the Macal Valley was replicated elsewhere in Belize. The macaws were birds. They would fly away and find other nesting sites. Reversing its earlier position, the society announced that "the scarlet macaw population in Belize is stable." The species didn't warrant a status upgrade after all.

The reversal stunned Sharon. She knew enough about bird politics to realize the difficulty of what lay ahead. The Audubon Society is recognized as a world authority on bird conservation. In most countries the group acts as a rigorous independent critic of government environmental policies. Not so in Belize. Years earlier the government had turned over management of Belize's national parks to the Belize Audubon Society. In environmental circles this unique setup was often heralded as a model public-private partnership. And in some ways it was—Belize didn't have enough money to protect its national parks, and the Audubon Society did an admirable job. The downside was a certain level of capture of the Audubon Society by government officials. The society carried all the power and prestige of the Audubon name, but in truth it had become an arm of the Belizean government. "People in Canada, in the U.S., and the U.K. are going to hear that the local Audubon Society says the macaws are doing fine, and what are they supposed to think?" Sharon told me. "They don't know the situation here."

Sharon continued to petition BirdLife International, but without the Audubon Society's support she got nowhere. Alison Stattersfield, a species coordinator for BirdLife, told Sharon that the situation was complicated. Belize's scarlet macaws were, it seemed, simultaneously endangered and not endangered. "In a global context, scarlet macaw (*Ara macao*) does not meet the IUCN Red List criteria for threatened status on the basis of its overall population numbers," Stattersfield wrote in an e-mail message. "In the regional context the subspecies *A. m. cyanoptera* has been assessed as meeting the IUCN Red List criteria for 'Endangered' status by several independent experts." Stattersfield agreed that the subspecies had been nearly extirpated from Central America. "In the next ten years, remaining populations will probably disappear except for those in highly protected areas," she wrote. In short, Stattersfield wrote, Belize's scarlet macaws were a subspecies of "global concern," but there was nothing BirdLife or the IUCN could do about it.

In questioning the macaw's Red List status, Sharon had entered one of the most contentious debates in science. At its core, the status of Belize's scarlet macaws hinged on a fundamental question: What is a species?

The problem went back at least as far as Carolus Linnaeus, the father of scientific taxonomy. Up until the 1730s, there was no common system for naming plants and animals. Biologists used chaotic jumbles of Latin to identify individual species, with little rhyme or reason to the name. Linnaeus, a Swedish botanist, established a common standard with the publication of his *Systema*

Naturae in 1735. Under the Linnaean system, each species carried two Latin names. The first identified its genus, the second its species. The scarlet macaw, *Ara macao,* was included in the first edition of *Systema Naturae.* Linnaeus organized the world logically, beginning with the most general classifications (the kingdoms: animal, vegetable, mineral) and narrowing to the most specific, the species. The system wasn't perfect. Linnaeus himself recognized that within some species there existed different varieties of individuals—what we today would call subspecies.

The species concept changed over time. Linnaeus classified plants based on their reproductive organs, which proved to be unworkable for a universal system of organization. Science ultimately paired Linnaeus's naming scheme with the more useful method practiced by his predecessor, the seventeenth-century British naturalist John Ray. Ray categorized species based on morphology, the form and structure of an organism.

Morphology worked well for a while, but it had an inherent flaw: Species evolve. One of Linnaeus's most famous dicta, "The invariability of species is the condition for order," is also famously wrong. Linnaeus himself realized his error late in life, when his research into plant hybridization opened his mind to the possibility of new species coming into existence. For Charles Darwin, working a century after Linnaeus, fixing permanent names to species was beside the point. He considered species to be an arbitrary stage in the ongoing evolutionary process. For Darwin, the notion of defining a species as permanent and unchangeable made as much sense as defining a person as always and exactly the way they are at the age of twenty. Species were status reports.

A more viable species concept emerged in the twentieth century. In 1908, British zoologist Edward Poulton proposed interbreeding as a species criterion, but it wasn't until Ernst Mayr, a German-American evolutionary biologist and ornithologist, refined the idea in his 1942 book *Systematics and the Origin of Species* that it firmly took hold. Mayr's definition in *Systematics* remains the clearest and most widely embraced species concept today: "Species are groups of actually or potentially interbreeding natural populations which are reproductively isolated from other such groups." In other words, if they can't interbreed, they're different species.

Mayr's definition ushered in a rare period of consensus. Through the 1970s the scientific community seemed content to stick with Mayr's biological concept. Coincidentally, it was during this time that the U.S. Congress passed the Endangered Species Act (1973), the landmark law that spurred the passage of wildlife protection laws around the world. In the past thirty years, though, the species debate has been reinvigorated by scientists proposing new variations. At last count there were at least twenty-two different species concepts competing to overtake Ernst Mayr's standard.

When it comes to subspecies, things get even murkier. Ask ten scientists to define subspecies and you'll get ten different answers. It's a hazy concept that has never been satisfactorily pinned down. The best way to think of it may be this: A subspecies is evolution in action. It describes a distinct population that differs from the rest of the species in a clearly observable but minor way. Subspecies differ in a physical characteristic but may not be reproductively isolated. They're halfway to becoming a new species. "What counts," writes E. O. Wilson, "is that somehow a group of individuals occupying some part of the total range evolves a different sex attractant, nuptial dance, mating season, or any other hereditary trait that prevents them from freely interbreeding with other populations. When that happens, a new species is born."

The northern Central American scarlet macaw had grown larger than its southern relatives. It diverged slightly in wing color. Whether those traits prevented the two types of macaw from interbreeding, nobody knew. There were no researchers camped in the Nicaraguan jungle trying to find out.

When it comes to subspecies, biologists divide into lumpers and splitters. Lumpers allow for minor variation within a species; they don't believe in subspecies. This tends to keep population figures high and widespread. Splitters believe in subspecies, which tends to break up species into smaller, isolated populations—and makes them appear more vulnerable to extinction.

BirdLife International and the IUCN were lumpers. "We

cover more than ten thousand species of birds," Stuart Butchart explained to me. Butchart was the global species coordinator for BirdLife. "We have a staff of fifty, and we rely extensively on partners and experts in the field. We don't have the resources to effectively go to the subspecies level."

BirdLife was so busy with higher-priority parrots that it had all but forgotten about the scarlet macaw, and the group's assurances about the bird's health were deeply flawed. The source for BirdLife's Least Concern designation was Josep del Hoyo's massive ten-volume series *Handbook of the Birds of the World*. In del Hoyo's volume on parrots, published in 1997, he included an extensive discussion of the scarlet macaw's conservation status. After asserting that the bird was "common over much of its range," meaning that it was doing fine in South America, del Hoyo went into great detail about the bird's tenuous and threatened survival in Central America. "It is now mainly confined to one area in Belize," he wrote; "it is extinct in most of Guatemala save the Peten; it is extinct in El Salvador; it is extinct or virtually so on the Pacific slope of Honduras and Nicaragua. . . ." On and on he went. And yet what BirdLife lifted from the book was this: "The species is described as 'common' in at least parts of its range (del Hoyo et al. 1997)."

The scarlet macaw data in del Hoyo's book dated from the early 1990s. In the years since, at least half a dozen researchers had published warnings about the species's dwindling populations in Central America. But officials at BirdLife assumed macaw populations were so healthy that they neglected to assign a specialist to check in on the bird now and then. Nobody was watching.

To be sure, there were plenty of parrots in more desperate shape. The echo parakeet, a native of the southern African island of Mauritius, had dwindled to a population of fifteen. A single Spix's macaw existed in the forests of Brazil.* But while the con-

---

* It's now been several years since the last noncaptive Spix's macaw was seen. The species is now categorized as extinct in the wild. Conservation efforts have raised the echo parakeet's population to more than a hundred birds.

servation community's attention was diverted, the common scarlet macaw was disappearing from Central America with uncommon speed. When all the populations of *Ara macao cyanoptera,* the subspecies of scarlet macaw that occurred north of southern Nicaragua, were added up in the late 1990s, the total came to fewer than two thousand birds.

Sharon continued to press BirdLife to reconsider the macaw's status. She sent feather samples from Blue, the little rescued macaw, to a researcher at Columbia University in New York City. DNA tests revealed substantial differences between Blue's genetic makeup and that of the larger *Ara macao* species. "The thing is, you can't just say: 'There we are!' " Sharon told me. "All it told us was that we needed more testing. It's a skewed sample—it's just one bird. As a scientist you can't base anything on that." BirdLife's ban on subspecies designations meant the scarlet macaw could go extinct in Central America without anyone knowing. As long as the bird's South American populations stayed healthy, it would remain listed as a species of least concern. The Belize Audubon Society continued to assure BirdLife that the macaw population in Belize was "stable." Unless Sharon could present conclusive proof that the threatened subspecies had transformed into its own species, BirdLife and the IUCN could do nothing to help her.

By the summer of 2001 it had become clear to Fortis and the Belizean government that local opposition to Chalillo would rise or fall on two questions. The first was whether the dam would raise electricity rates. BEL chief executive Lynn Young saw the issue as one of the biggest threats to Chalillo. "Most people don't care how green their energy is," Young once told me. "What they care about is how it's going to affect their wallet."

On that score, hydropower's recent history didn't inspire a lot of confidence. In a study of seventy-one hydroelectric dams built in developing countries in the 1990s, economists Robert Bacon and John Besant-Jones found an average cost overrun of 27 percent. Power companies typically underestimated the price of the

dam to justify its construction, then raised electricity rates once it
was built to cover the budget shortfalls.

To defuse the issue, Young stood before his fellow Belizeans and
promised, again and again, that Chalillo would keep power rates
low. The dam's opponents argued the opposite. Both sides made a
case for an unprovable claim. Ultimately it came down to a question of whom Belizeans trusted, and the dam's opponents didn't
have a leader with the stature of Lynn Young. The BEL chief executive pulled off a brilliant one-man marketing campaign that
paired an enticing message—"Chalillo will lower your electric
bill"—with one of the strongest brands in Belize. That brand
wasn't BEL; it was his own family name. His father, Sir Colville
Young, the governor-general of Belize, was known as a man of
integrity who had devoted his life to teaching and public service.
Lynn Young had built on that foundation while rising to the top of
BEL. In Belize, the Young surname connoted intelligence, dignity,
and honesty. To be sure, Sharon had a strong reputation in Belize.
But in the eyes of most locals, Lynn Young was Belizean. Sharon
wasn't.

The second issue was whether the dam's benefits outweighed
its environmental cost. Here the smooth reassurances of Lynn
Young couldn't make the problem disappear. For that, Fortis relied upon one of the most abused and misunderstood documents
of modern times: the environmental impact assessment (EIA).

The modern EIA grew out of the United States' National Environmental Policy Act of 1969, the landmark law produced by the
environmental foment of the sixties. NEPA was a revolutionary
document. For the first time ever, a national government declared
that it would act in such a way as to "encourage productive and en-
joyable harmony between man and his environment." To that end,
the act forced federal agencies to stop and consider, in a written
impact assessment, the environmental effects of any major project
prior to proceeding. NEPA's success in the United States inspired
the adoption of similar laws in countries around the world.* Belize

* In the United States they're called Environmental Impact Statements, or
EISs.

included an EIA requirement in its 1992 Environmental Protection Act.

In theory, EIAs sound great. In practice, they can be deeply flawed. EIAs aren't intended to be stand-alone gatekeepers. They're reports that make policy makers stop and consider the environmental consequences before approving major projects. As they've evolved—especially in developing countries—EIAs often provide little more than the illusion of environmental checks and balances. Many of the world's largest construction firms now operate lucrative environmental consulting arms that produce slick project-justifying EIAs for the worst sorts of developments.

Belize's Environmental Protection Act requires developers to submit EIAs to NEAC, the National Environmental Appraisal Committee. To prepare Chalillo's EIA, Fortis hired Amec, a global engineering firm based in London. Chalillo was a small job for Amec, which was at the time the world's third largest engineering and construction company. Amec's environmental division alone boasted two thousand employees in ninety offices worldwide. The company's fee would run anywhere from $200,000 to $400,000, about one percent of the cost of the dam. Despite the fact that Fortis had just posted an annual profit of $30 million, the company considered Amec's fee a bothersome expense. To defray that cost, Amec hatched a scheme to make the taxpayers of Canada foot the bill. The company assigned the project to its Montreal office, then applied for foreign aid from the Canadian International Development Agency (CIDA). CIDA normally funds projects like health clinics in Tanzania. In June 2000, CIDA awarded Amec's Canadian division a $167,500 grant to prepare the Chalillo EIA. The grant was later increased to $312,000.

Fortis CEO Stan Marshall had pledged to abandon Chalillo if the EIA consultants found the dam to be environmentally unsound. But those consultants were hired for one reason: to declare the project environmentally sound. That understanding was spelled out in the contract between Amec and the Canadian International Development Agency:

The Firm [Amec] shall seek to achieve the following objectives in carrying out the activity: The Firm shall seek to interest the Client [Fortis] in assigning implementation of the Project [Chalillo] to the Firm, or to interest the partner in continuing its cooperation in implementing the Project.

Amec wasn't hired to produce a balanced assessment of the pros and cons of Chalillo. It was hired to persuade the Belizean government to greenlight the project.

The trick was to find biologists willing to sign off on an EIA that gave the all-clear. In the United States that's not a problem. As the tobacco companies can tell you, plenty of scientists are happy to sell their scruples to the highest bidder. Environmentalists often deride these pliable researchers as "biostitutes." If biostitutes can't be found, an EIA consultant can subcontract the scientific studies to reputable researchers and then hide or misrepresent the findings. Often this is done through summary fraud, in which dire findings in the scientific data are ignored or contradicted in the report's executive summary. The deception usually works because most researchers sign nondisclosure agreements that prevent them from talking to the press.

Biostitutes weren't easy to come by in the jungles of Central America. In all of Belize there were only a handful of biologists qualified to undertake the wildlife study called for in the EIA. Most of them were already skeptical of Chalillo. Amec and Fortis offered the job to Chris Minty, a biologist with London's Natural History Museum.

Minty, a tropical soil and river expert, ran the museum's Maya Mountain research station located a few miles from Chalillo. He was no biostitute. Minty had worked with the Belizean government on plenty of environmental projects, and he knew how to keep his science rigorous and clean without making enemies in the development world. He was a friend of Sharon's but he'd stayed away from her anti-dam crusade. He avoided the subject whenever he saw her. Minty took the job on one condition: There would be no nondisclosure agreement. Amec flew Minty to Montreal to meet with Raymond Goulet, the Amec official heading up the Chalillo EIA project. Goulet was adamant that Minty sign an all-encompassing confidentiality agreement. Minty balked. "It would've put my team in an impossible position," Minty later recalled. "Imagine if we'd found a new species. We'd have to clear it with Amec before publishing anything." With few other options and the clock ticking, Amec agreed to Chris Minty's terms.

Minty and his team spent four months in the Macal River valley. They noted the animals that came and went, what they ate, and where they slept. Amec asked the biologists to focus on the tapirs, crocodiles, and scarlet macaws living in and around the river, so they spent days charting nesting areas and following tapir trails. They worked their fingers through tapir scat and probed the dark recesses of crocodile dens. At the end of four months, Minty typed up a 105-page report that confirmed Fortis's worst fears. Nearly everything Sharon Matola claimed about the Macal River valley was true.

Minty's team reported that the area to be flooded by the dam's reservoir "contains a rare and discrete floral floodplain habitat which acts as both a conduit and critical habitat for resident and non-resident fauna and avifauna." The valley teemed with rare wildlife, most of which would be wiped out by the reservoir. Few of the researchers had ever encountered such a robust and intact ecosystem. The experts concluded that the scarlet macaws nesting in the area did indeed constitute a distinct and endangered subspecies. Minty's researchers disagreed with Sharon on only one point. She estimated the macaw population at two hundred. They cut that number in half. Minty's team believed Belize was down to its last one hundred scarlet macaws.

There was more. Tapirs used the river as a critical food cache, Minty wrote. When the dry season sun withered their accustomed plants, the mountain cows retreated to the damp riverbanks where cane grass grew. The researchers found the river crawling with young Morelet's crocodiles, indicating that the reptiles used the area as a breeding ground. Bird surveys indicated that the flood zone functioned as a critical way station for neotropical migrants making their annual journey between North America and

South America. Tennessee warblers, western tanagers, Baltimore orioles, and more than eighty other long-distance travelers stopped in the Macal Valley because the naturally flooding river provided richer food than the surrounding jungle.

Blocking the river, Minty warned, would destroy the local food chain. Riparian grasses and shrubs would disappear, along with the tapirs and peccaries that ate them. With the tapirs and peccaries gone, jaguars and pumas would have no reason to visit the river. The river's fish and shellfish would likely disappear, leaving the area's otters without food. The effect on migrating birds would be substantial but nearly impossible to document. They'd have to go farther afield for less nutritious food. Fewer would survive their hemispheric journey, but it was difficult to quantify. The damage, Minty wrote, "will be major, long-term and regional in extent."

When it came to the scarlet macaw, Minty was blunt. If the dam went in, he wrote, Belize's macaw population was doomed. Without their accustomed nesting sites, few if any of the birds would breed. After one or two years, the population would fall into irrevocable decline. "It is likely," he wrote, "that they will eventually become extirpated from Belize."

Minty's report presented a major problem for Amec and Fortis. Here were researchers from London's renowned Natural History Museum laying out clear evidence of the dam's devastating environmental impact—in Fortis's own EIA! Raymond Goulet, the Amec official overseeing the EIA, was not happy. He met with Chris Minty in Belmopan and tried to persuade the biologist to reconsider his conclusions. Minty wouldn't budge.

Goulet had one thing going for him: He didn't have to prove Chris Minty wrong. The company's EIA only had to provide cover to Fortis and the National Environmental Appraisal Committee. Amec could do that by labeling Minty's report a "supporting document," downplaying its importance and hoping that few NEAC members or reporters would bother to read it. Chris Minty and the Natural History Museum had no control over the main body of the EIA. Nor did they have any say over how their material was handled in the EIA's three-page executive summary. That was where the fate of Chalillo would be sealed.

Working out of Amec's Montreal office, Goulet and other officials put together a 1,500-page masterpiece of spin and obfuscation. Again and again Chris Minty's findings were ignored, warped, or outright contradicted. About the tapir, Belize's beloved mountain cow, the Amec team wrote that "measures are required to mitigate potentially significant adverse impacts" to the animal. This despite Minty's statement that "any costly efforts to rescue and relocate tapirs would have little effect."* Where Minty predicted that the dam would wipe out native fish and shellfish along a twelve-mile stretch of river, the EIA's main report predicted that "downstream fish communities would benefit from a more stable flow regime." On the scarlet macaw, Minty's team was unequivocal: *Ara macao cyanoptera* was an endangered subspecies that would be wiped out by the dam. That information was translated in the main report as: "If the Belize population represents a distinct subspecies, significant adverse residual effects are likely to result from Project development. If the Belize population is not a distinct subspecies, significant adverse residual effects to the macaw are unlikely."

As deceptive as the main report was, it positively brimmed with integrity when compared to the executive summary. A reader brings certain assumptions to a 1,500-page environmental impact assessment. One assumes that the main report accurately reflects the data in the supporting documents. One expects the executive summary to offer a truthful précis of the main report. The Chalillo EIA did neither. In its three-page summary, Amec presented the dam as a slam dunk. "The impact analysis," the consultants wrote, "shows that the Project will provide positive

* *Mitigation* is a magical word to companies like Amec and Fortis. The term holds out the promise of well-funded programs to save or transplant wildlife impacted by the dam. In the real world, those programs usually disappear once the dam goes up. In many cases, power companies pledge to monitor the wildlife situation, as if documenting the destruction of biodiversity compensates for its loss.

impacts related to labour force, economy, flood control, reliability of power supply, increase in power self-sufficiency, and a decreased cost of electricity." The dam's only adverse impacts, they wrote, "include effects to plant and animal species at risk." In the hands of Amec's prose stylists, Chris Minty's conclusion that Chalillo would "most probably force the local extinction of some species of internationally important conservation concern" became a single digestible word: "effects."

To convey the pros and cons of Chalillo, Amec included a chart in the executive summary. It looked like this:

TABLE 1
SUMMARY OF PROJECT ADVANTAGES AND DISADVANTAGES

Adverse Predicted Impact	No Predicted Impact	Positive Predicted Impact
Plant species at risk	Population	Labour Force
Animal species at risk	Tourism and Recreation	Economy
	Transportation and Public Safety	Flood Control
	Heritage and Archaeological Resources	Reliability of power supply
	Water quality	Increased power self-sufficiency
	Disease vectors	Decreased cost of electricity
	Mercury levels in fish	
	Ground water quality	
	Surface water quality	
	Air quality	
	Parks and forest reserves	
	Sediment quality	
	Saline intrusion	
	Aquatic resources	

The chart was a brilliant piece of work. Anybody who's served on a board of directors will recognize it. It's meant to be the last piece of data a board member sees before voting. Information design guru Edward Tufte would call it "visual information for executive decisions." A more blunt description might be "visual fraud." On a design level it falsely flattened each issue, giving equal weight to the extirpation of the scarlet macaw and saline intrusion in the Macal River system. On a factual level the chart failed the most rudimentary truth test. Its assertions contradicted data in the EIA itself. The impact of the dam on the local labor force was listed as positive. On page 231, Amec predicted that long-term employment at the dam was "unlikely to exceed twelve people."

For those twelve jobs the dam put at risk hundreds of Belizeans employed in the Cayo district's ecotourism industry. "Heritage and Archaeological Resources" were listed as being unaffected by the dam. At the time, archaeologists from North and South America were pleading with Fortis and BEL not to flood the potentially significant Mayan ruins in the reservoir zone. Water quality and mercury levels in fish were listed as having no significant impact. In the EIA, Amec wrote that "increased mercury levels in fish are predicted to occur for several years after impoundment" and that anyone eating those fish more than three times a week would fall ill.

None of that mattered. What counted was the chart's visual effect. At a glance, the boxed summary conveyed this message: The dam's positive and neutral impacts vastly outnumber its negative effects. Who could vote against such a thing?

In the early autumn of 2001, NEAC welcomed a new face to its twelve-member committee. The two NEAC seats reserved for nongovernmental organizations rotated annually among a number of local groups. As it happened, the seat that year fell to the Belize Institute of Environmental Law and Policy, a small group of environmental lawyers whose meetings usually took place around kitchen tables. They sent their vice president, Candy Gonzalez, the San Ignacio lawyer who had first drawn Jacob Scherr and the NRDC into the fight.

The Chalillo EIA was Gonzalez's first assignment. She brought home the report, divided into five thick three-ring binders, and set it on the kitchen table. Her husband, George, asked her, "You really going to get through all that?"

"I'm going to try," she said.

And then a strangely fortuitous thing happened. Candy Gonzalez contracted dengue fever. The mosquito-borne virus is extremely painful. Eighteenth-century American settlers called dengue "break-bone fever" because the pain felt like God cracking the victim with a rolling pin. Dengue can be fatal, but in most cases the fever passes and the victim survives. The only treatment is lots of water and bed rest. So Candy Gonzalez climbed into bed with the Chalillo EIA. With a fan at her feet and Post-it Notes beside her, she propped herself up on pillows and spent ten days reading every last word, number, chart, and footnote of the "Macal River Upstream Storage Facility Environmental Impact Assessment."

NEAC's members were charged with approving or denying the dam's environmental permit. In theory, they could vote according to duty and conscience. In reality, they had jobs, families, and futures to consider.

"There will be unbelievable pressure on these individuals to approve Chalillo," Meb Cutlack wrote in *The Reporter.*

The NRDC sent each member a thirty-page report highlighting the dam's problems and the EIA's errors. Prime Minister Said Musa let it be known how he expected the panel to vote. "At the end of the day, we are left with the compelling evidence that the building of the Dam offers the best alternative for Belize's energy security," he said in his September 18, 2001, State of the Union address.

Those who crossed the Prime, as Musa was referred to in the halls of Belmopan, did so at their peril. Shortly after that State of the Union speech, a cabinet minister named Jorge Espat spoke out against the corruption, cronyism, and privatization deals that he believed were crippling the country. "Too few control too much, and too many have too little—a condition made worse by the conversion of public assets into unregulated private monopolies," he said. The next day Jorge Espat found himself out of a job.

More environmental pressure came from outside Belize. Sharon ran into Harrison Ford at a Conservation International board meeting in Guatemala. The actor knew the Zoo Lady from the *Mosquito Coast* set, where Sharon had worked as the film's animal wrangler. Ford, a Conservation International board member, asked what she was up to. Sharon told him about Chalillo, and he offered to help. A few weeks later Ford wrote an op-ed piece that ran in the *Globe and Mail,* Canada's national newspaper. "Fortis, based in St. John's, is turning a blind eye to the ecological devastation the dam would wreak on the area's lush flood plains, undisturbed since the time of the ancient Maya," he wrote.

Fortis CEO Stan Marshall fired back. "This is misleading information," he told Canada's *National Post*. "Look, I can't take on Harrison Ford. What am I going to do, hire Darth Vader?"

Jacob Scherr and the NRDC drafted their own in-house celebrity. Robert Kennedy, Jr., son of the former U.S. attorney general and nephew of the late president, took Scherr up on an offer to come down and see the Macal River for himself. Through his work as a senior attorney for the NRDC and as president of the Waterkeeper Alliance, Kennedy was America's most famous environmental advocate. His name drew instant recognition around the world. The Belizean press flocked to him, and after seeing the Macal and talking to the locals, Kennedy gave them plenty to quote. "This dam is the absolute worst face of globalization," he said. Chalillo combined three of his great passions: rivers, good government, and corporate malfeasance. At a "Save the Macal River" rally in San Ignacio, Kennedy urged Belizeans to stand and fight for their river. "Fortis is stealing from you," he told them. "They're doing it by destroying this wonderful river and by taking an obscene profit out of this country. You already pay the highest energy bills in all of Central America, and this dam is going to make those bills go even higher." Kennedy possessed an extraordinary presence. His voice was oddly strained, like that of a man perpetually fighting off a cold. Somehow this made him sound all the more impassioned. His words were simple but eloquent, and his tone carried a righteous outrage. "Before you put a dam over one of the people's waterways, you first have to do a series of reports," he said. "The people who created those reports on behalf of Fortis lied to the public, they lied to the government agencies. That's an act of fraud. It's an attack on democracy, on the economy, and on the soul of this country.

"What Fortis is doing is wrong," Kennedy concluded. "In twenty years of environmental advocacy, this dam is one of the most harebrained, reckless schemes I've ever seen."

In late October 2001, the National Environmental Appraisal Committee met in a conference room at the Department of the Environment's central office in Belmopan. Candy Gonzalez brought a box containing all five volumes of the EIA, bristling with Post-its. As the committee began discussing the EIA and the dam, Gonzalez realized she couldn't protest every last error and untruth in the report. She spoke from a position of weakness. Though a naturalized Belizean, in the eyes of many around the table she was just another white American expat. "I had to pick my battles," she later recalled. "You can only be a pain in the ass for so long before people tune you out. You gotta let some things go."

Gonzalez remained silent as the committee discussed Amec's stream-flow estimates. Then came the subject of power rates.

"The company keeps justifying the dam with the General Electric 'least cost' study," Gonzalez said. "The study supposedly says the dam is the cheapest way to produce power. And yet BEL won't let us see the study. Why not?"

Committee chairman Ismael Fabro, head of the Department of the Environment, said he'd ask the power company to provide a copy.

The committee moved on to geology. Gonzalez raised a question. "Does it bother anyone else that this dam would be going up in an active earthquake zone and yet there's no emergency response plan? What happens if the dam fails?"

That concerned other committee members, too. The previous year a magnitude 6.4 earthquake centered near Guatemala sent shock waves into Belize and damaged buildings in San Ignacio. In the EIA, Amec reported the seismicity of the Macal Valley as "moderate to high." But the consultant's geologists found no faults of any significance near the dam site. The map provided in the report showed faults in other parts of the Maya Mountains, but none near Chalillo.

A voice came from the far end of the table. "While we're talking about geological concerns, there's something I think we should address." It was Andre Cho, a young geologist representing

Belize's Geology and Petroleum Department. The Belizean-born Cho had only recently graduated from the University of the West Indies. He was still learning his way around Belizean politics. "Looking over section 2.5," he said, "there appear to be inconsistencies in the data. There's no justification for slope, and there's no discussion of the possible effect of slope failure on the integrity of the dam."

Pages flipped. "I'm also concerned about the identification of the rock types at the dam site," he said. "From what I've read about the geology of Belize, the rocks the consultant identifies aren't likely to exist in that area."

"What page are we on?" someone asked.

"Site Geology, 2.5.2.2," Cho said. "Where it says, 'Bedrock Foundations.' "

The first sentence in that section declared, "Bedrock at and below the valley floor is primarily granite." That didn't make sense to Andre Cho. Only two geologic maps had ever been made of that valley. Both recorded limestones, sandstones, and shale, but no granite. Yet Amec's geologists claimed to have found granite everywhere. In one 45-meter borehole, "all but a total of 1 meter of rock was granite," they wrote. They found granite 18 meters deep at the proposed powerhouse site. And elsewhere—12 meters thick here, 11 there, 15 at a spot across the valley.

"I haven't inspected the site myself," Cho said, "but nothing I've read about the area mentions granite."

There was a pause in the discussion. Nobody knew what to do with Cho's comments. The other committee members were foresters, archeologists, meteorologists, and public health officials. Geology was outside their expertise.

"Perhaps we should have a site visit," said Chairman Fabro. Candy Gonzalez circled the Site Geology page and scrawled a question mark in the margin.

As the afternoon wore on, Gonzalez felt the EIA grind inexorably toward acceptance. Issues came and went. The committee's archaeologist expressed little concern over the Mayan ruins to be submerged in the reservoir. Again and again, problems were shunted into the black box of the Environmental Compliance

Plan, a list of mitigation measures Fortis promised to implement prior to the dam's completion.

"We keep talking about mitigation and the compliance plan," Candy Gonzalez said, "but the compliance plan doesn't exist!" A number of faces, weary and irritated, turned to her. "We talked about mercury accumulating in the fish," she said. "The best case scenario for mitigation laid out in the EIA is a plan to warn people not to eat too much fish. That's not mitigation. Mitigation means keeping mercury out of the fish in the first place. We're just telling people not to eat the poison. And that's *if* Fortis follows through on the compliance plan. Which I doubt. At the very least I'm going to have to see a written, detailed mitigation plan. If I don't, I can't vote in favor of this."

Valdemar Andrade, director of the Belize Audubon Society, agreed with Gonzalez. The room was quiet.

The committee met again the next month in Belize City. The passage of time hadn't settled Andre Cho's issues. "I had a chance to go out and look at the rock myself," Cho told the committee, "and I came away more convinced than ever that the EIA is wrong."

The committee chairman waved off Cho's concerns. "The engineers from BEL and Fortis will be here this afternoon," Fabro said. "They'll be able to clear it up."

That afternoon, Lynn Young and Joseph Sukhnandan appeared before the committee, accompanied by Fortis chief engineer John Evans and Amec consultant Jeremy Gilbert-Green. Fabro told them that Andre Cho had concerns about the EIA's geology section.

"What sort of concerns?" said Sukhnandan.

"I don't think it's accurate," said Cho.

Sukhnandan defended the report. "Highly qualified geotechnical personnel carried out those drilling and core studies," he said. "We have no question as to their competence."

Another committee member asked if the rock's identity really mattered. Could Fortis build a dam on sandstone?

"We can build a dam on anything," John Evans answered. "We can build a dam on sand if we need to."

Andre Cho backed down. He agreed that a dam could be built on the rock at Chalillo. "I just want to make sure it's accurately named and described."

Candy Gonzalez spoke up. "We want to know more than that," she said. "The geology in the EIA seems pretty important if you're building a dam. If it isn't accurate, that raises concerns about the credibility of the rest of the EIA and the people who prepared it."

"Examine the core samples for yourself," Sukhnandan told Cho. "We can show them to you tomorrow morning."

That satisfied Cho. He agreed to meet Sukhnandan at BEL headquarters the next morning.

"I might be there too," said Gonzalez.

"Wonderful," said Sukhnandan.

"And while I'm there I wonder if I can pick up a copy of the GE least-cost study," she said. "Are the members of this committee ever going to see that document?"

"You can see it any time," said Lynn Young.

"Where?"

"It's my understanding that a copy of the GE report is in the Department of the Environment library."

"It is not there."

"You are welcome to view the report at BEL headquarters tomorrow."

"I'll be there at nine."

The meeting broke up. Ismael Fabro announced that the committee would reconvene the next day at three o'clock. "I'm confident that we will have enough information at that time to make a decision on this project," he said.

Gonzalez hustled across town to the Bacongo office and called Ari Hershowitz in Washington, D.C. "Ari, we're running out of time," she said. "Fabro's going to push a vote tomorrow afternoon."

"Stop the vote," he said. "Do whatever you can. Stand up on the conference table and yell."

"Ari, I can't do that," she said. "We don't have the votes to stop it. The only thing holding it up is a question over the geology. BEL is supposed to give me a look at the GE report tomorrow morning, but I'm not holding my breath."

"Take good notes," he said.

The next morning, a security guard escorted Candy Gonzalez into BEL headquarters and upstairs to a room where Andre Cho, Lynn Young, and Joseph Sukhnandan huddled around several cylindrical core samples. Young excused himself and returned a few minutes later carrying a thick bound document. "The GE report," he said, and offered it to her.

The report was as fat as a college chemistry text. She browsed the first few pages. It was hopeless. The report was indecipherable to anyone not versed in the technology and jargon of the power industry.

Lynn Young hovered over Gonzalez as she took notes. He left the room but soon came back and announced that her time was up. Andre Cho had finished viewing the core samples and it was time for her to leave too.

She pushed through the door into the midmorning sun and realized she'd been conned. Lynn Young could now claim, truthfully, that she'd seen the GE report.

At the meeting that afternoon, Andre Cho reported that the geology still wasn't right. "The rock referred to as granite isn't granite," he said. The cores confirmed it. Whatever it was, the rock at Chalillo could hold a dam, he added. But to claim it was granite simply wasn't right.

Chairman Fabro broke in. "The issue appears to be a judgment call," he said. "Geology, not being an exact science, allows for a difference of opinion." Fabro said he'd brokered a deal with Fortis officials earlier that afternoon. The company agreed to hire a team of independent geologists to examine the rock. If it wasn't granite, the necessary engineering adjustments would be made in the environmental compliance plan. "Since the question of geology does not really affect the fact that the dam can be constructed, the committee should continue ahead and make a decision," Fabro said.

He pressed for a vote. Candy Gonzalez balked. "With all respect, there are a lot of problems with this EIA that can't be brushed aside by saying they'll be covered in the environmental compliance plan," she said. "The mitigation measures you talk about haven't been detailed. Proper public hearings haven't been held. We need to know more about—"

"Public participation?" Fabro said. Impatience rose in his voice. "This project has gotten the greatest amount of publicity of any that's ever come before this committee! There were hearings held in different parts of the country. The EIA itself includes those reports."

Gonzalez stood her ground. "There are no public hearings documented in the EIA," she said. The meetings referred to were information sessions hosted by BEL. They were packed with BEL employees. "According to Belizean law, formal public hearings must be held," she said.

Discussion ensued. Were formal public hearings required? Nobody could say for certain. The clock swept toward five. The streets outside began to bustle with Friday afternoon excitement. The weekend was getting under way. Fabro ended the debate. "After a decision is made," he said, "perhaps we may take suggestions from the public for additional mitigation measures for the environmental compliance plan."

It was time to vote. "The question is whether to give environmental clearance for the Macal River Upstream Storage Facility," Fabro said.

The final tally was eleven in favor, one—Candy Gonzalez—opposed.

An ebullient Lynn Young appeared on Channel 5 News that night. Construction of Chalillo would start in a matter of weeks, he said. "There's a lot of work to be done—the survey, the road building, setting up the camp, and all that," he said. "We expect to be able to complete the dam in eighteen months."

Sharon took the vote in stride. When it came to Belizean politics, she lacked savvy—but she wasn't stupid. Asking government officials to vote against Chalillo was asking them to commit career suicide. Besides, the same committee had voted to approve the Mile 27 dump. Look what happened there. When the Channel 5 crew came to the zoo looking for a quote, she gave them a short one.

"This isn't over," she said.

CHAPTER 19

A FEW DAYS AFTER THE COMMITTEE VOTE, the phone rang in Brian Holland's office.

"Belize Minerals," he said. "This is Brian."

He recognized the voice on the other end of the line. It was Joseph Sukhnandan. BEL's chief engineer was following up on the deal struck with NEAC chairman Ismael Fabro. "There is some dispute as to whether the rock is granite or not," Sukhnandan said. He wondered if Holland could come up to Belize City and examine the cores.

Holland considered the offer. As a rule, the geologist stayed out of Belizean politics. It was bad for business. Holland owned a small dolomite mine a few miles west of Punta Gorda. While the operation strained to turn a profit, it was nevertheless coveted by a local PUP apparatchik who was forever scheming to cancel Holland's mining license and confiscate his land. A few years earlier, before anyone had heard of Chalillo, Sharon had asked Holland to join the Belize Zoo's board of directors. He'd agreed. No worries there. The zoo was the most neutral ground in Belize. But Sharon's battles over the dam and the dump had forced him to take uncomfortable positions against the Musa regime.

"You know that I prepared a critique of the geology in the EIA for Bacongo," he told Sukhnandan. Holland wanted all cards on the table.

The news seemed to take Sukhnandan by surprise. Still, there weren't many geologists in Belize. "Why don't you send me the report and then we can decide," said Sukhnandan.

Holland's eight-page study described Amec's geological assessment as "fundamentally incorrect." Sukhnandan read it and called Holland back. He still wanted the geologist to come. Holland hadn't seen the cores, Sukhnandan noted. Perhaps that would change his mind.

"When can you come?" he asked.

Holland said he'd be there the next morning.

Holland left Punta Gorda before dawn and pulled into BEL's parking lot in Belize City just as the Caribbean heat came into the day. Joseph Sukhnandan introduced him to a young geologist named Craig Moore. BEL wanted two expert opinions, Sukhnandan explained. "Look at the cores with Craig and see if you can agree on what type of rocks they are," he said. Around them sat two dozen wooden boxes the size of vegetable crates. In each box were plugs of rock the diameter of soda cans.

Holland and Moore went to work. They held the cores and examined them with hand lenses. Almost immediately, they agreed: This was sandstone interbedded with soft black shales. Some of the moist shales were so soft that Holland could squeeze them like pottery clay. For three hours the geologists pored over the core samples, murmuring to each other and jotting notes.

Around lunchtime, Holland saw CEO Lynn Young emerge from the building. "Good day, Mr. Young!" he called out. "You have some very interesting cores here, sir."

Holland and Moore reported their findings. There was no granite in the cores.

Joseph Sukhnandan seemed distressed. "But we've had the best people in the business tell us these are granites."

"They're not the best in the business, because these are not granites," Holland said. Moore nodded in agreement.

That wasn't all, Holland said. He and Moore had discovered sequences of rock that raised serious questions about the suitability of the site. A number of cores contained soft shale, a rock with little load-bearing capacity that could compress under the dam's weight. He noticed that divots had been taken out of the cores to measure the compressive strength of the bedrock. That was fine, except that the samples seemed to be taken only from the hardest rocks in each sequence. That was like testing the strong links in a chain and ignoring the weak ones. Statisticians call this "sampling to please"—choosing data points that are more likely to satisfy the client's desires. There were signs of iron staining in some of the cores, which indicated that water had moved within the rock layers. "If water encounters the shale," he told Sukhnandan and Young, "it can create a slip surface that allows the bedrock to move. And if the bedrock under a dam moves, it will crack the concrete."

Young thanked Holland for his advice. Sukhnandan asked the two geologists to return the next day.

Holland slept in a spare bed at a friend's house that night in Belize City. Before turning in, he called Evadne Wade, head of Belize's Geology and Petroleum Department, who was Andre Cho's boss. "I'm finding the same thing as Andre," he said. "There's no granite."

Wade said that Cho would be relieved to hear it. Then Wade passed on some gossip. "I overheard a conversation in our office today," she told Holland. "Fabro found out that BEL hired you to look at the cores and he went ballistic. He told BEL to get rid of you because you're on the zoo board."

The next morning when Brian Holland showed up at BEL headquarters the core samples were gone. So was Craig Moore. "We have decided to send the core material to an independent laboratory for examination," Joseph Sukhnandan explained. "Your report and your services will no longer be required."

"Why is that?" Holland demanded.

"Are you on the board of the zoo?"

"Does that matter?"

Sukhnandan paused. "No," he said carefully.

As if on cue, Norris Hall stepped out of the building. He jokingly waved a finger at Holland. "Traitor!" he said. "Traitor!" Holland laughed and the two men shook hands. Hall turned serious. "Why is there a misunderstanding about the rock?" he said. "We have the best people in the business looking at this."

"Norris, that doesn't matter," Holland said. "There's a serious problem with the geology."

Sukhnandan assured both men that the lab would sort it out.

After BEL dismissed him, Holland worked political back channels to alert others to the geology problem. He called John Woods, an influential Belize City businessman. A former chairman of BEL, Woods guarded his reputation as one of Belize's least corruptible citizens. In the late 1990s he took over the privatized Hattieville Prison, Belize's notorious penitentiary, and turned it into a model of penal reform. Woods heard the geologist's concerns and made a few inquiries. A few days later he called Holland back. He'd spoken with BEL and Amec, Woods said. "The Canadians say you're wrong," he told Holland.

"John, I'm not imagining this," the geologist said. "Either it's sandstone or it's granite. It's not a matter of interpretation."

That evening Holland sat on his porch and mulled over his predicament. For two years he'd steered clear of Chalillo. That was Sharon's battle. Lobbying the IDB to move the Mile 27 dump had made him no friends in Belmopan. Holland worried about the consequences of taking on Musa and Fonseca. Look what the PUP machine was doing to Sharon's reputation. She told friends she was holding up fine, but Holland heard different. Keepers at the zoo grumbled that Chalillo was taking up all of her time. The Zoo Lady was dam-obsessed and sullen. Bills weren't getting paid.

Against that risk stood the obligations of professional duty. Brian Holland was a geologist, and that title has a certain ethical charge. He'd seen the core samples with his own eyes. Saying nothing while Fortis built a 150-foot-high dam on unstable bedrock—or at least on misidentified samples—would be more than a calculated career move. The dam sat directly upriver from San Ignacio. Silence would be unconscionable.

His wife, Anne, joined Brian on the porch. He laid out the situation. "I'm going to have to go public," he told her.

"Didn't you send BEL your report?" she said.

"They're ignoring it. The Canadians have them convinced that I'm wrong."

Anne nodded.

"I'm not going to be popular," he said. "You know what they've done to Sharon. It could affect your work."

Anne worked on development projects in southern Belize. She was a steely Danish woman with an even temperament and a no-nonsense, pragmatic outlook on life. She got along well in Belize.

Anne waved away his worry. "Do what you have to do," she said.

Early the next morning, Brian Holland called Sharon.

"I had a look at BEL's core samples," he said. "The geology is worse than I thought."

"How much worse?"

He told her about the fractures and slippage potentials he saw. He told her about the granite question. "They don't even know what kind of rock they're dealing with," he said.

She didn't follow much of what he said. Sometimes Holland talked as though he were in a roomful of geology students. Quaternary this, quartz vein that. "So you're telling me this isn't a good place to build a dam," she said.

"I'm telling you this is a terrible place to build a dam."

Sharon spread the word. In an e-mail to Ari Hershowitz, she urged him to take another look at Holland's critique of the EIA. Hershowitz had scanned it without paying much attention. He'd gotten one whiff of Brian Holland and dismissed him as just another American industrialist ripping up the jungle in search of gold. Holland ran a strip mine. Hershowitz had spent years fighting guys like him. But now he reconsidered. If the geology was as flawed as Holland thought, Chalillo wasn't merely an environmental issue. It was a matter of public safety. Human lives were at stake.

Sharon called Mick Fleming at Chaa Creek. Fleming called Meb Cutlack at *The Reporter*. Cutlack rang Holland. "I hear there are problems with the rock at Chalillo," the reporter said. "Can you tell me what you know?"

"I can do better than that," Holland said. "I can show you."

Holland and Cutlack spent the next day bushwhacking to the dam site. At the river Holland pointed out the offset in the northern bank, which indicated seismic activity. He showed Cutlack the various sandstones and shales that Amec had misidentified as granite.

Cutlack took it all down in his notepad. "Are you absolutely sure about this?" he asked.

"See for yourself," said Holland. "You can carve this stuff with your hands." He scooped a divot with his fingers.

That Friday, *The Reporter* hit the streets of Belize City with Cutlack's story bannered on page one. "CHALILLO A NO-GO" said the headline. "STUNNING NEW REVELATIONS WILL SOUND DAM'S DEATH KNELL!"

CHAPTER 20

ABOUT THE SECOND WEEK OF JANUARY 2002, a rumor swept through Belize: Bulldozers were rumbling up the Chiquibul road on their way to Chalillo. Sharon called Meb Cutlack to see what he knew.

"Nothing more than you do," he told her. He held the cell phone in his right hand and steered the car with his left. "I'm headed up there now. It sounds like the bastards have jumped the gun."

Thirty miles up the road, Cutlack came upon a crew of bearded Mennonites operating heavy equipment. It was an odd sight but not unusual in Belize. The country had many Mennonite communities, each practicing its own degree of asceticism. On one extreme you had the Barton Creek Mennonites, once described to me as "No trucks, no tractors, no teeth." Barton Creek Mennonites traveled by horse and buggy and abstained from all luxuries of modernity, including dentistry. Other Mennonites embraced the more practical tools of technology. Some had gone into the road-building business. The "mechanized Mennonites" were respected for their hard work, construction skills, and willingness to do a job without asking questions. Their relative prosperity was also a source of resentment among some Belizeans, who referred to them as "the Moneynites."

Cutlack flagged down a bulldozer operator and asked what he was doing.

"Building a road," the man said in a faintly Dutch accent.

"Where to?"

"The dam."

"Who hired you?"

"Mr. Bowles."

Bob Bowles was an American expat contractor who operated out of an office in San Ignacio.

"And who hired Bowles to build the road?"

The man shrugged. "You'd have to ask him." He fired up the bulldozer. In the distance Cutlack watched the crown of a palm tree jerk and fall like a rabbit pulling a carrot from below.

Back at his office, Cutlack called around to see who'd given Bob Bowles the job. Legally, construction on the dam couldn't begin until the National Environmental Appraisal Committee signed off on Fortis's environmental compliance plan—the plan that was supposed to address the problems brought up in the EIA. Bob Bowles couldn't be found. A spokesperson for Fortis said the company hadn't started work on the dam. BEL executive Lynn Young told Cutlack he knew nothing about road building. "Maybe the Ministry of Works is preparing the road to Caracol," he said, referring to the Mayan archaeological site ten miles southwest of Chalillo. But officials at the Ministry of Works said they had nothing scheduled for the Caracol road.

Cutlack called Sharon that night. "What we have is a road crew, a new road, a contractor, bulldozers, Mennonites, but nobody in charge," he said. "Nobody knows, or nobody will tell me, who ordered the road."

Sharon sent an e-mail message to Ari Hershowitz and Jacob Scherr in Washington. "BEL bulldozers are moving on Chalillo," she wrote. "We're desperate down here."

Scherr called Sharon the next morning. Hershowitz would be on a plane to Belize City the next day. "Help is on the way," Scherr said.

To Hershowitz and Scherr, the road construction wasn't entirely bad news. For more than two years they'd failed to find a legal hook for Chalillo. The NRDC wasn't known for Earth First–style direct action. NRDC staffers didn't chain themselves to the axles of logging trucks. Their expertise was in the courtroom. As long as Fortis and BEL took no physical action to build the dam, there was no legal case to build.

Now that had changed. With bulldozers moving on Chalillo, the NRDC could go to court and demand an injunction halting the dam's construction. At least that was Scherr's plan. "But who's going to bring the case?" Hershowitz asked him. "Who are we going to sue? Fortis? The government of Belize? We don't even know who's building the road."

Scherr smiled. "So find out," he said. "Call me when you get to Belize City."

When he arrived, Hershowitz found nothing but problems in Belize City. Bacongo had hired a replacement for Daedre Isaacs. Jamillah Vasquez seemed like an eager, promising young director. But she was oddly difficult to reach. She rarely returned phone calls and was often out of the office. The group's legal counsel did not inspire confidence. Weeks earlier, Jacob Scherr had struggled to find a lawyer to help Bacongo take on the dam. He looked for an attorney unaffiliated with either political party. In Belize, that club could meet in a closet. Scherr couldn't find a single high-profile lawyer willing to touch Chalillo, let alone one unattached to the PUP or UDP. In the end, a well-liked but inexperienced Belize City attorney named Marilyn Williams accepted the case.

"How do we stop the bulldozers?" Hershowitz asked Williams.

She didn't have an answer. "I will have to do some research on that," she said. "I will get back to you."

Hershowitz made his way through Belize City, past the Albert Street electronics shops and across the swing bridge, to Bacongo's office on the second floor of an old colonial administration building near the Chateau Caribbean. There was a note on the door. "Back in 20 mins." The same note had been there that morning. Hershowitz banged his head against the door. "Jamillah!" he said. There was no answer.

He called Sharon from a pay phone at the Radisson. He wasn't sure why he was calling. Desperation, maybe. A yearning for a sympathetic ear. He laid out his frustration. Sharon listened and offered a suggestion. "It might be worth talking to Lois Young," she said. "She won't take the case, but I think she's on our side. Couldn't hurt."

Lois Young (no relation to BEL chief Lynn Young) was known

throughout Belize as the best lawyer money could buy. She had once been married to Dean Barrow, leader of the opposition UDP party and Said Musa's archrival. It was said that Dean was the only attorney in Belize who could match Lois in the courtroom.

Hershowitz found her office on the second floor of a building on Belize City's bustling New Road. He had to be buzzed through a fortified metal door. Lois Young's clients did not take tea at the Radisson.

Young waved Hershowitz into her office. "What can I do for you?"

He briefed her on Chalillo and the road construction. She cut him off. Yes, yes. She knew all that. She'd considered taking the case but was too busy representing Lord Ashcroft and BTL in their bid to keep Glenn Godfrey out of the phone business. She did offer Hershowitz some pro bono advice, though. "You might try using judicial review," she said.

"What's that?" Hershowitz said.

"It's used when a government breaks its own laws," she explained. American and British courts had been ruling on the constitutionality of government actions since the early nineteenth century, but in Belize the concept was just being tested. If Bacongo could prove that the Department of the Environment unlawfully approved the Chalillo EIA, she told Hershowitz, then Fortis wouldn't have government clearance to build the dam. That would be enough to stop the bulldozers.

The next day Hershowitz went to see Marilyn Williams. "What about the idea of using judicial review?" he said.

Williams gave him a hard look. "I will have to do some research on that," she said.

It was becoming apparent that Hershowitz would have to pull together most of the case himself. There was only one problem. He was a scientist, not a lawyer.

"It's easy," Scherr told him on the phone from Washington. "Just get a copy of what a pleading looks like in the Belize courts and follow the form."

Hershowitz hung up, thinking, Easy for you to say, Jacob.

Over the next week Hershowitz roamed the Cayo countryside with a clipboard, a legal pad, and a pen. By day he gathered affidavits from villagers whose lives would be affected by the dam. By night he cobbled his notes together in a crude legal brief. At the end of the week he left a packet of legal papers with Marilyn Williams and caught a flight home.

The following Monday, Williams filed papers in a Belizean court requesting judicial review of the Department of the Environment's approval of the Chalillo EIA. Meanwhile, Hershowitz briefed his boss. "We have to get another lawyer," he told Scherr. "We've got a good case, but it's going to be screwed up."

"What can we do?" said Scherr. "Nobody else will take it."

Belize's Supreme Court resides in a handsome two-story colonial structure set back about thirty feet from the Caribbean Sea. It was built in 1926 by a New Orleans firm, and its whitewashed walls, green wrought-iron trim, and clock tower exhibit a distinctive French Quarter influence. Its polished wood floors and simple pine chairs have witnessed the dispensation of justice in cases great and small, from George Price's toilet-paper trial to common machete-chop murders.

On an overcast morning in February 2002, Marilyn Williams settled into her chair for the first day of proceedings in Bacongo's lawsuit against the government. Denys Barrow and Elson Kaseke sat across the aisle for BEL and the Government of Belize. Barrow was a trimmer, more stylish version of his brother Dean. Kaseke was Belize's solicitor general, the man who'd been arrested on the approach to Reagan National Airport.

Sharon wasn't there. She had come to accept the fact that her presence sometimes did her cause more harm than good. The less Chalillo appeared to be the Zoo Lady's issue, the better. Also, Hershowitz had prepared her for the worst. She didn't feel she could sit quietly and watch the government tear Marilyn Williams to shreds.

Meb Cutlack was there. So was Norris Hall.

"All rise," the bailiff called out. "The Supreme Court of Belize

shall now be in session, the Honorable Chief Justice Abdulai
Conteh presiding."

A commanding figure in a flowing black robe appeared through a
side door and took his seat behind the bench. Abdulai Conteh,
former vice president of the small West African nation of Sierra
Leone, had a face carved from weathered mahogany: dark, thick,
and runneled with creases. It was the wise, sorrowful face of an
African chieftain topped with a flowing white barrister's wig.

The application that appeared before the chief justice was clut-
tered and confused. When Marilyn Williams presented her oral
arguments, the situation only worsened. Her line of reasoning was
difficult to follow. Some points were dropped midthought. Judge
Conteh urged the attorney to come to the meaning of her submis-
sions. "And so . . . ?" he said, looking expectantly at Williams.

Meb Cutlack sat in the gallery taking notes. He grew more de-
spondent by the minute. The case was hopeless. Bacongo would
be lucky if the judge didn't hold them in contempt for wasting his
time. After a while Cutlack slipped out of the courtroom for a
smoke.

On the second-floor veranda, the *Reporter* columnist fished a
pack of Independents from his pocket. Across the street a familiar
profile caught his eye, a tall, lanky woman hailing a taxi. "Oh, dear
god," Cutlack said to himself. He dropped the cigarette and ran
downstairs in a rumpled shamble. "Lois!" he yelled, waving his
arm. "Lois!"

Cutlack caught up with Lois Young at the taxi door. "Conteh's
hearing the Chalillo case in there and Marilyn's getting murdered," he said. "You and I know there are only two lawyers who
are capable of taking this case. And Dean says he can't do it."

"It's impossible, Meb," said Lois Young. "I'm too busy with
BTL."

"At least come have a listen," Cutlack said. "I tell you, they're
going under."

Young got out of the cab.

In the courtroom, Judge Conteh was still pulling the argument out of Marilyn Williams.

At the rear of the courtroom, Lois Young watched Williams flail. Young knew Denys Barrow and Elson Kaseke would crush Bacongo's overmatched attorney. Young left after half an hour. Outside the courtroom she opened her cell phone and called Ari Hershowitz in Washington. Hershowitz put her through to Jacob Scherr.

Young scolded the NRDC senior attorney. "I'm here watching the Chalillo case, and believe me when I say you must hire another attorney," she said. "You can't let Marilyn go and be slaughtered like this."

She proposed a solution. If the NRDC would pick up Dean Barrow's fee, Lois would call the UDP leader and insist that he take the case. Scherr agreed.

Back in court, Bacongo's case hung in tatters. Denys Barrow tore through Williams's arguments. Elson Kaseke destroyed what little was left. A less merciful judge would have dismissed the case. Chief Justice Abdulai Conteh did not. And though the judge never publicly revealed the reason for his decision, his personal history included an episode that may have played a role. Years earlier, Conteh had been party to a case that hinged on the question of judicial review. The stakes were extraordinarily high. His own life had hung in the balance.

As a young man, Abdulai Conteh possessed one of the brightest legal minds in West Africa. Sierra Leone, like Belize, was a former British colony where the most ambitious students aspired to the great universities of England. After graduating from London University, Conteh earned his Ph.D. in law from Cambridge. Upon returning to Sierra Leone he became a respected law professor, led a student protest against government corruption, and then entered politics himself. He rose quickly and was eventually named attorney general by President Joseph Momoh. Conteh's financial fortunes kept pace with his political power. Momoh was one of the more corrupt of Africa's "presidents for life," and his top ministers lived well, if not honestly. Cabinet members drove flashy new cars and indulged in foreign shopping sprees while the majority of Sierra Leoneans survived on less than one dollar a day. Abdulai Conteh kept a house in the London suburb of Finchley and sent his children to English boarding schools.

In 1991, President Momoh promoted Conteh to first vice president. The early nineties weren't an auspicious time to be first vice president of Sierra Leone. Liberian rebel leader Charles Taylor was fomenting violence throughout the region, and Sierra Leone was about to plunge into a decade of what we now know as the conflict diamond wars. In 1992, when a group of rebels staged attacks on remote Sierra Leonean villages, President Momoh sent soldiers to put down the uprising. In an oddly poetic twist, the corruption endemic to his regime proved to be Momoh's undoing. The government spent nearly $1 million per month on the anti-rebel campaign, but senior army officers embezzled so much of it that frontline troops went nearly three months without pay. Finally a group of fed-up government soldiers descended on the capital of Freetown. Their paycheck march quickly evolved into a coup d'etat.

The takeover happened so fast that Vice President Conteh had no time to dash home and grab his passport. With orders out for their arrest, Conteh and President Momoh ran to the shore, hopped in a dugout canoe, and pushed out to sea. They paddled north by night along the West African coast, stopping only when they reached the shores of Guinea, Sierra Leone's northern neighbor. Displeased to find a pair of international fugitives on their doorstep, Guinean officials issued Conteh and Momoh diplomatic passports and ordered them out of the country. Momoh fled overland to Gambia. Conteh boarded a flight to Brussels, connected to Heathrow, and eventually arrived at the front door of his Finchley estate.

Exhausted but alive, Conteh changed his clothes, collected his wits, and contacted the British government. He expected sympathy and asylum. What he got was imprisonment. Immigration officers appeared at his door and took him away.

Conteh found himself charged with entering the country on

false documents. His passport marked him as a resident of Guinea, British officials said, when clearly he was not. This was a mere technicality. Behind the scenes, British prime minister John Major had chosen to make an example of the deposed vice president. For too long African dictators and their cronies had looted their own countries, then fled to the West to enjoy the spoils. Major wanted no more asylum for scoundrels. Home Secretary Kenneth Clarke personally denied Conteh's application.

Abdulai Conteh's legal advisers appealed Clarke's decision through a process well established in the English court system: judicial review. His barrister argued that although Conteh served a corrupt government, Conteh himself had led the fight to establish multiparty democracy, which was the most important step in fighting corruption.

The judge wouldn't hear it. Abdulai Conteh may well have been reforming a rotten system from within—and about that, accounts vary—but his personal and political behavior wouldn't be considered in the case. This was a judicial review of the government's procedures, not a judgment on Conteh's actions in Sierra Leone. The government's case hinged on a technicality, but the technicality was good enough for a win.

Abdulai Conteh was expelled from England. Still a wanted man in Sierra Leone, the former vice president retreated to Gambia. Gambia threw him out too. In desperation he turned to the nation of last resort, Belize. And Belize, country of castaways, land of second chances, embraced him.

So it was that Marilyn Williams presented her case to the one judge in all of Central America who had personally suffered the sting of injustice in a case of judicial review. Williams's case could have been dismissed on her shoddy paperwork alone. But Judge Conteh was not a man inclined to reject a claim on procedural flaws. He recognized that beneath the rubble of Williams's presentation there existed a case with solid merit. The government may well have broken its own rules in the rush to get Chalillo's construction under way.

At the end of the day, the judge removed his glasses and peered down at Marilyn Williams with stern disapproval. On a more trivial issue, Conteh said, the matter before him would go no further. Bacongo's case was a mess. "But Ms. Williams," he said, "I am thinking about letting you amend this complaint." Elson Kaseke and Denys Barrow protested. Judge Conteh cut them off. "This is not a matter of formality," he said. "This is a matter of justice."

The judge advised Williams to leave his courtroom and proceed immediately to the library. Go back to your books, the judge said, and see how a proper application for judicial review is presented. "You will return to stand before me in two days," he told her. "And, Ms. Williams," he added, "you *will* be prepared."

Two days later, Marilyn Williams reappeared in Judge Conteh's courtroom. On her left sat Dean Barrow. On her right, Lois Young. Marilyn Williams had come prepared.

Young and Barrow had spent the preceding forty-eight hours stripping Bacongo's case to the bone. There were too many complainants and too much evidence. They had to have a simple claim and a clear story. Their goal wasn't to win the case immediately. All they had to do was persuade Judge Conteh to let the case proceed.

Dean Barrow presented the arguments for Bacongo, the claimant. He zeroed in on what he saw as the most flagrant violation of the law. Belize's Environmental Protection Act required public hearings on large projects like Chalillo. No such hearings had been held.

Denys Barrow, representing BEL, rose to challenge his brother. A complex weave of kinship ties made up the cloth of Belize, but the scene playing out before the spectators in the courtroom was rich even by local standards. Lois Young and Dean Barrow, former husband and wife, teamed up to battle Dean's brother over an issue that was splitting the nation. Denys Barrow argued that his brother's point was moot. The government, he said, never gave Fortis permission to start construction on Chalillo.

Eyebrows lifted throughout Conteh's courtroom. Surely the

chief justice had seen the Mennonite bulldozers splashed across the front page of *The Reporter*.

Dean Barrow pulled an ace from his sleeve. Through political back channels he'd learned that the Mennonite road builders had been hired by Ralph Fonseca's Ministry of Finance. "The government of Belize did grant approval in effect," he argued, "as it has spent hefty sums of money in some areas of the project. The Ministry of Finance issued contracts for road work to the Chalillo site even while the Environmental Compliance Plan was being developed." According to the vote of the National Environmental Appraisal Committee, construction on the dam couldn't start until that plan was finalized and approved.

The chief justice turned to Elson Kaseke, who represented the government. "Is this true?" Judge Conteh asked.

Yes, Kaseke admitted. The government had spent nearly half a million dollars to cut an access road through the jungle to Chalillo.

Meb Cutlack frowned and scribbled in his notepad.

As the afternoon drew to a close, Judge Conteh squared the papers on his desk and addressed the court. "Very important and serious issues have been raised, both in support of and against this matter," he said. It remained unclear whether the government had acted illegally in giving the go-ahead to the dam's construction. Nevertheless, the judge said, he found enough merit in Bacongo's case to allow it to proceed.

Word of Judge Conteh's decision spread quickly. By evening it was known from Cayo to the Cayes: Chalillo was going on trial. The last person in Belize to hear the news was the Zoo Lady herself. Unable to bear the suspense, Sharon had driven into the Maya Mountains and paddled upriver to spend a few days with the macaws.

CHAPTER 21

*T*HE GEOLOGY OF THE DAM SITE bedeviled the engineers at Fortis and BEL. Samples of the rock sent to three independent labs came back with inconclusive results. Two labs found no granite; one reported the presence of a granitelike rock. Evadne Wade, head of Belize's Geology and Petroleum Department, brokered a compromise. She would hire an objective third-party geologist to remap the entire site. Fortis would pay for the survey but have no control over its findings. The company agreed, on one condition: The original Amec geologist who had found the granite, Rodolfo Alvarado, had to be included on the survey team. Evadne Wade agreed.

Wade hired Jean Cornec, an American geologist with decades of experience in the mineral business. Cornec maintained an office in Denver, Colorado, but spent most of his time roaming the jungles of Central America as an oil and mining consultant. Craig Moore, the young geologist who had examined the core samples with Brian Holland, hired on as Cornec's junior partner on the job. Rodolfo Alvarado joined them.

In April 2002, the three geologists met at the head of the new Chalillo access road and walked to the dam site. When they reached the river, Jean Cornec turned to Alvarado. "Could you point out the granite, Rodolfo?"

He couldn't.

For five days Cornec and Craig Moore scoured the banks of the Macal River. (Rodolfo Alvarado did not return after the first day.) They compared their field mapping to previous geological maps of the area. They examined the drill cores inch by inch. They located the site in satellite photos and compared positions of known faults to the position of the dam site. In their written report to

Fortis and the government, Cornec and Moore confirmed nearly every one of Brian Holland's claims.

"There is no evidence of any granitic intrusion or contact metamorphism at Chalillo," they wrote. "The closest granite outcrops in the area are located approximately 1 kilometer to the northwest."

Cornec warned Fortis that the reservoir basin was well known for its karst, porous limestone that weathers into caves and caverns. If any of those caves exist below waterline, he wrote, they "will most likely make the reservoir leak like a sieve."

Seven pages into his report Cornec noted something even more alarming. "A major fault exists some 550 meters west of the left abutment of the proposed Chalillo dam," he wrote. Clear evidence existed in the bedrock. "It's like a knife going through the land," Cornec later commented. The fault was an offshoot of the well-known Cooma Cairn fault, a fifteen-mile-long fracture that was, he wrote, "the most striking geological feature visible from a space satellite in the entire country of Belize."

In the Chalillo EIA, Cornec noted, Amec reproduced the standard geological map produced by a British Geological Survey team in 1977. He compared Amec's reproduction with the original map and found a striking omission. The fault was clearly defined on the original map, but appeared nowhere on Amec's version. "The rationale for the removal is unknown," Cornec wrote, "as this fault outcrops spectacularly in the Macal river bed and left bank."

By this time it was clear that Amec's EIA was shot through with errors, misinformation, and incorrect summations. Those inaccuracies might, in theory, be blamed on sloppy work and professional laziness. But not Cornec's discovery. What the geologist uncovered was out-and-out fraud. Amec had erased the fault line.

Cornec presented his report to the Geology and Petroleum Department, which forwarded a copy to BEL and Fortis. "I wanted to use the word 'criminal' in my assessment of the map," Cornec told me years later, "but I knew that would never fly." Even his guarded language was too much for Joseph Sukhnandan and other BEL officials, who pressured Cornec to change the report. Cornec refused. "You can do whatever you want," he told me, "but if you change one word, my name comes off the report."

Cornec moved on to other projects. His report mysteriously disappeared. The remapping study was never publicly released or acknowledged. Cornec's findings weren't mentioned in any of the legal proceedings that grew out of the Chalillo battle. Sharon knew the report existed—word got around—but BEL and the government refused to acknowledge it.

Finally, fed up with the stonewalling, Sharon called Jean Cornec herself.

"Jean, we've got to get this report released," she said.

"I'm sorry," he told her. "I can't tell you anything."

Cornec had signed a nondisclosure agreement. He couldn't reveal his findings for two years. It was as if the report never existed.

At the end of their meeting in Newfoundland, Fortis chief engineer John Evans had assured Ari Hershowitz that he'd send the NRDC a copy of BEL's power purchase agreement. The agreement set the terms for the power company's purchase of electricity from the Mollejon Dam. Hershowitz waited months for the promised copy. It never arrived.

Meanwhile, Fortis and the Belizean government were secretly hammering out a new power purchase agreement. In late 2001, Ralph Fonseca and Fortis CEO Stan Marshall negotiated a forty-four-page contract for the delivery of power from Chalillo. The contract was called the Third Master Agreement, as it superseded two previous contracts for power delivery from Mollejon. The Third Master Agreement didn't become known to the public until the spring of 2002, when BEL announced that the Public Utilities Commission, the government's utility regulating body, had approved the contract. In its press release BEL claimed that the new agreement would result in lower electricity rates. The end of the announcement carried a legal notice. "Interested parties wishing to view the Third Master Agreement may make arrangements to do so with the Public Utilities Commissioner," it said.

Ari Hershowitz and Ambrose Tillett read that line, and both had the same response: Let's go view it.

Hershowitz and Tillett showed up at the commissioner's office with a copy of the press release in hand. "It says here that 'interested parties' may view the agreement," Tillett told the receptionist. "We're interested."

The receptionist handed them the agreement. "You can't copy it," she said. "Just read it."

Tillett interpreted the technical language while Hershowitz took notes. The contract laid out the protocols for power delivery from Chalillo to BEL at a wholesale price of nine cents per kilowatt-hour. "What's funny about this," Tillett told Hershowitz, "is that the GE study, the one that said Chalillo would be BEL's lowest-cost source of power, assumed that the dam would sell power at six and a half cents."

The contract gave Chalillo priority dispatch status. That meant BEL would have to buy all of Chalillo's nine-cent power before it could buy any of Mexico's off-peak six-cent power. BEL also agreed to kick back 5 percent of the gross revenue collected on Chalillo's power to the dam's owner, Fortis. All of these costs would be borne by Belizean ratepayers.

"Here's why the road got built," Tillett said. Hershowitz followed Tillett's finger on the page to where it said that "the Government shall, at the cost of the Government, design and construct the New Project Access Road, with the completion of such construction to occur no later than March 31, 2002."

Hershowitz was gobsmacked. "They hired the Mennonites because they had a contractual deadline to meet," he said.

That wasn't all. The Belizean government promised to provide security for the dam, the power lines, and the access roads at no cost to Fortis. Ralph Fonseca had turned the Belizean Defence Force into Fortis's private security guards. Those guards would come gratis, as the government agreed to exempt Fortis from all taxes and import duties.

Tillett read further. "Look at this," he said.

Hershowitz read. "The government hereby agrees to waive any

and all licenses, permits, consents, and regulatory approvals necessary or required in connection with the construction or operation of both Mollejon and Chalillo, pursuant to any law, rule or regulation of Belize."

"Does that say what I think it says?" Hershowitz said.

Tillett nodded. "They're saying Fortis is above the law. According to this contract, the company doesn't need approval for anything to do with Chalillo. None of the rules apply."

If anything went wrong with the dam, the contract stipulated that Fortis and its subsidiaries would face no liability under Belizean law. If Fortis were sued, the government agreed to defend the company in court. If the government chose not to defend Fortis, the company could hire its own lawyers and send their bills to the taxpayers of Belize. Furthermore, if the dam ever collapsed, the Third Master Agreement allowed Fortis to sell whatever was left of it, along with all legal liabilities, to the Belizean government for one U.S. dollar.

"No wonder they don't care about the geology," Hershowitz said. "If the thing collapses, they walk away free and clear."

"Not quite," said Tillett. "They walk away with an extra dollar in their pocket."

CHAPTER 22

As Lois Young prepared the court case, Sharon organized a rally in Belize City to galvanize opposition to the dam. In Belize, political rallies are daylong street parties. Live bands fill the air with Belizean brukdown, a sort of jug band zydeco. Plates of chicken and beans and rice appear out of no-where. Children squeal and chase, and stray dogs slink through the crowd seeking table scraps. Onstage, politicians peddle sun-nier days, brighter futures, and better bus service. At PUP rallies the leaders sport crisp guayaberas and the foot soldiers wear blue T-shirts. At UDP rallies everyone comes dressed in red. A big rally will attract both allies and enemies, as most Belizeans turn out for the sheer entertainment of it all.

Sharon's rally would feature music, free food and drink, and a lineup of speakers to stir the crowd against Chalillo. Bacongo took out ads in *Amandala* and *The Reporter*: "RALLY FOR THE MACAL RIVER! SATURDAY NOON," they said, and "DIS DA FU WE RIVA!"— a play on the Creole phrase meaning "This is our river."

Early on the appointed Saturday, Sharon and Tony Garel and a handful of Bacongo volunteers set up shade tents, a public address system, a stage, food tables, and soda in tubs of ice. They waited. As the morning matured, Belize City came to life. Traffic thick-ened on the BelCan Bridge. Pedestrians glanced at the tents and kept on walking. A few children enjoyed the free soda, but their mothers, fathers, aunts, and uncles stayed away. As noon ap-proached, Sharon suspected something was up. Then she saw something that left no doubt. A shiny black sport utility vehicle pulled off the street and circled slowly around the parking lot. The driver's window was down, giving Sharon a clear view of a familiar profile. It was the Big Wheel himself. Ralph Fonseca looked im-passively at the Bacongo activists. He stayed long enough for his presence to be registered. Then he rolled up his window and moved on.

Sharon grimly gathered her supporters. "We might as well pack this stuff up," she told them. "Nobody's coming. They've been told to stay away."

The rally became a propaganda victory for the government. The front page of the PUP's *Belize Times* crowed "ANTI-CHALILLO FAIR A BUST." Under a photo of an empty shade tent, the paper reported that the fair's turnout was "nothing short of pathetic."

Discouragement hit her like a hangover. Sharon didn't talk much the next week. She spent a lot of time feeding the animals, and zoo staffers knew enough to stay out of her way. All the scientific data in the world, she realized, didn't mean a damn thing if the government had the people cowed. "Doesn't anyone here have a backbone?" she asked Angel. The three-legged jaguar pawed the floor. In the musty refuge of her *oficina* Sharon wondered if she was leading a fool's crusade.

In July 2002, Lois Young presented the full case against Chalillo to Abdulai Conteh, chief justice of the Belize Supreme Court. She did it without her ex-husband, who recused himself soon after winning the initial go-ahead from Judge Conteh. God blessed Dean Barrow with a sensitive political nose, and in Chalillo he smelled a loser. If he were to have any chance against Said Musa in the upcoming national election, the UDP leader couldn't afford to be associated with the Zoo Lady's campaign.

Lois Young wasn't worried. She could do just as well without Barrow, and her robust claim before the chief justice showed it. To win the case she had to prove that the government broke its own rules in giving environmental approval to Fortis. Young asserted that the government broke the law not once but twice. First, Belizean law required a public hearing to be held prior to approval being granted. Second, that approval was based on an inadequate EIA.

Nonsense, argued the attorneys for the government and Fortis. It was the government's prerogative to decide whether a public hearing was necessary. And the EIA was far from incomplete. Ismael Fabro, head of the Department of the Environment, testified that the Chalillo EIA was the most comprehensive environmental assessment ever submitted to his office. Fifteen hundred pages, Your Honor!

After a week of testimony Judge Conteh retired to his chambers. For five months he mulled over the case. Then in early December he issued his ruling.

Conteh began his twenty-three-page decision by bringing clarity to the confusing issue of an EIA's ultimate purpose. An EIA, Conteh declared, was not intended to make a project like Chalillo environmentally foolproof. The judge quoted the British environmental-law scholar John Alder. An EIA, Alder wrote, "is intended to enable decision-makers to make an informed choice between environmental and other objectives and for the public to be consulted."

Conteh proceeded to topple one of the two pillars of Lois Young's case. The EIA in question was, he wrote, "a massive, detailed and voluminous" document. Whether the EIA was too error-riddled to be considered adequate wasn't for him to say. "The EIA may or may not be the perfect EIA," he wrote; "this is not a matter for this Court to decide." Judicial review, he said, was only meant to determine if the government's rules of procedure had been broken.

The other pillar survived. Conteh ruled that the EIA's public consultation requirement had not been fulfilled. Rather than annul the government's environmental approval of the dam, though, Conteh ordered the Department of the Environment to hold an ex post facto hearing. "I realize, of course, that this order would sound like putting the cart before the horse," the judge wrote. "But so be it. Stopping the cart would not necessarily overturn or upset it. But stop it must, until a public hearing is held."

Lois Young considered it a half victory. The bulldozers would sit idle, at least until the public hearing. If nothing else, Judge Conteh's ruling bought her time to prepare an appeal.

To Sharon it felt like a full defeat. Conteh hadn't even considered the massive errors and misrepresentations in the EIA. The public hearing would be a pro forma exercise. All Fortis had to do was hold it. Nothing in Conteh's ruling held out the promise of stopping the dam. All he'd done was slow it down.

The public hearing took place a few weeks after Judge Conteh's ruling. On a sultry night in January 2003, dam supporters and opponents packed Novelo's Convention Center, a drafty barn of a building just outside of San Ignacio. Fortis bused in BEL employees and supporters and gave them green CHALILLO T-shirts. Joseph Sukhnandan opened the evening with a PowerPoint presentation on hydroelectric power. Tony Garel and Mick Fleming spoke out against the dam.

Sharon didn't attend. Norris Hall had revived his attacks in the *Belize Times,* charging her with leading a "white conspiracy" aimed at restoring colonial control over Belize. Sharon felt that others would carry the banner more effectively.

Near the end of the evening, as spectators began drifting away in twos and threes, an old Belizean with graying hair made his way with great deliberation to the microphone. Godsman Ellis was an elder of Cayo. A native-born Belizean, he had been one of the rural district's first teachers and agricultural agents. The old man waited before he spoke, standing with the microphone in his hand and casting a quiet tension about the hall. He introduced himself. He wasn't there to revisit old debates about endangered species and water levels, he said. He had no expertise in geology or the nesting habits of birds. He rose to speak, he said, because the government's behavior in the Chalillo affair offended him. The government had colluded with Fortis in a series of sweetheart deals, he said. "Due process was not followed," he said. This was a moment for good citizens to rise in protest, to speak out and hold their government accountable. But fear silenced those voices. "The done-deal syndrome has taken over the psyche of most Belizeans, who now refrain from speaking out," Ellis said.

Whether the dam would be good or bad for the environment was not for him to say, Ellis told the crowd. Whether it would be good or bad for the economy, only time would tell. One thing was certain, however. Chalillo had exposed the rotten doings of a government determined to flout the law for private gain. "There is," he said as his allotted time elapsed, "a loud cry for practical democracy in Belize."

With the public hearing out of the way, construction began in earnest. Stan Marshall flew in from Newfoundland to turn the first shovelful of dirt at the groundbreaking ceremony. Eighteen-wheel trucks hauled bulldozers, rock crushers, and steamrollers up the Chiquibul road to the dam site.

As it happened, Amec didn't win the contract to build the dam. After years of negative publicity, the engineering giant declined to bid on the project. Amec officials looked at the company's own EIA and decided the environmental costs were simply too high. According to the company's 2003 environmental sustainability report, Amec's "detailed, professional and robust study clearly emphasizes that serious environmental damage would be unavoidable if the project went ahead and that this damage could not, in our view, be satisfactorily mitigated." Although Amec paraded its ecoconscience before its shareholders, the company neglected to inform anybody in Belize about its radical change of heart.

The contract went instead to Sino-Hydro, a Chinese engineering firm with experience on the Three Gorges Dam. Sino-Hydro was the low bidder, thanks in part to its ability to import low-paid Chinese workers. Customs agents at Goldson International Airport began noticing an influx of Chinese men arriving with hard-hats.

Meanwhile, depression closed over Sharon. She could no longer turn to the jungle for relief. She'd stopped going up the Macal and Raspaculo. "I hear rumors that the Chinese workers are poaching tapirs and having barbecues," she told me. "That just disgusts me. I can't go up there. I don't know if I can ever go back." There was no way to know if the rumors were true, but Sharon often believed the worst and most outlandish rumors about Chalillo.

She sought solace in music. She volunteered for extra shifts at BFBS. Deejaying forced her to perk up and took her mind off the dam. A lifelong fan of the Rolling Stones, one day she learned that Mick Jagger and Keith Richards's hometown of Dartford, a working-class town southeast of London, had never recognized their two most famous sons. No keys to the city, no monument, not even a plaque. "Can you believe that?" she said to me. "It's outrageous! Liverpool's tourist economy runs on shrines to the Beatles. But for the Stones, nothing." Sharon Matola would do something about that. She decided to start a new campaign—a crusade to get the city fathers of Dartford to recognize her beloved Mick and Keith. She figured she might win this one.

It was nuts. She knew people thought it was nuts. She didn't care. She needed some positive project to counter the negative energy of the dam.

Lois Young, on the other hand, poured her energies into Chalillo. She continued to work the case. She told Sharon not to give up. Young convinced Jacob Scherr that a legal appeal might work. The bad news was that they had just one final shot. The good news was that Belizean politics held no sway over the appellate judges.

For more than three hundred years, prisoners convicted by courts within the British Empire have looked to a small, obscure chamber in the heart of London for their salvation. When all other avenues of appeal have been exhausted, a condemned man may plead his case before the absolute court of last resort: Her Majesty's Privy Council.

The Privy Council has always carried an aura of mystery and power. Viscount Haldane of Cloan, an early twentieth century British statesman, once recounted a popular legend that captured its inscrutability and global reach. A traveler to a remote plateau of northern India came upon a local tribe offering a sacrifice to a faraway god. The traveler asked who the god was. "We don't know," the tribesmen answered, "except that he is a very powerful god, because he interfered on our behalf against the Indian government, and gave us back our land which the government had taken. The only other thing we know is that the name of the god is the Judicial Committee of the Privy Council."

In the year 895, King Alfred gathered a small council of advisers who became known as the King's Privy Council. The Privy Council that survives today is largely ceremonial, except in the area of law. In England the king and queen have always functioned as the court of final appeal. A busy monarch can't hear every peasant's plea, of course, so the judicial wing of the Privy Council evolved to handle the caseload. The Privy Council no longer hears appeals from within England, but in all other corners of the Commonwealth the Law Lords, as the judges are known, act as a court of last resort. At the height of Great Britain's imperial reign, the council functioned as a United Nations of judicial appeal. Viscount Haldane recalled strolling through the council's hallways in the company of "yellow men, some of whom come from Hong Kong; Burmese, who come from Burma; Hindus and Mohammedans from India; Dutch from South Africa; a mixed race from Ceylon—all sorts of people may be straying in there." Even today the Judicial Committee of the Privy Council retains one of the widest jurisdictions in the world. Only the International Court at The Hague is more cosmopolitan.

Breaking away from the Privy Council has long been seen as a milestone in a colony's road to full independence. Canada ended its appeals to the Privy Council in 1933. Australia sent its last case in 1968. Malaysia cut its ties in 1985, Singapore in 1994. Belize and a number of Caribbean countries have struggled for years to create a regional Caribbean Court of Justice. Squabbling among the island nations has delayed the court's establishment, however. In 2003 the final court of appeal for all Belizeans remained, as it had for nearly three centuries, an oak-paneled chamber in London presided over by five elderly white lords who, as far as anybody knew, had never set foot in Central America.

Lois Young drafted a petition and sent it off to the clerk of the Privy Council. Within weeks she received a response. The Law Lords would hear the case.

"Sharon," she told the Zoo Lady, "we are going to London."

CHAPTER 23

*T*HE DRY SEASON THAT YEAR seemed like it would never end. The lush savannah around the zoo turned a sickly yellow. Chickens died from the heat. So many brush fires broke out all over Belize that the smoke could be seen from space. The Macal River shriveled to a trickle. Without water, the Mollejon power-house ground to a halt. Power outages struck Belize City.

With Mollejon dry and Chalillo in legal limbo, BEL chief executive Lynn Young scrambled to find power. With Fortis's blessing he paid $9 million for a new 23-megawatt diesel-fired turbine. This further shackled Belize to the world oil market, but with lightbulbs blinking out in Belize City the company said it had little choice.

In the national elections Said Musa defeated UDP leader Dean Barrow and retained his position as prime minister. Meanwhile, the nation sank deeper into a mire of debt and corruption. Editors at *Amandala* and *The Reporter* stopped referring to the problem as "a certain minister" and began calling out Ralph Fonseca by name. It became clear that Fonseca, not Musa, was the force driving Belize to the brink of default. A political cartoonist captured the situation with a drawing of Fonseca popping out of Musa's empty head, observing, "Whoo! Lotta room in here!"

Months passed. The dam's opponents carried on with their lives. Sharon focused her energy on getting Mick Jagger and Keith Richards their due in Dartford. Chaa Creek owner Mick Fleming won the masters title in the Ruta Maya canoe race from San Ignacio to Belize City. Ambrose Tillett stepped away from the Chalillo fight and entered politics by winning the UDP's open seat in the Belize Senate. Brian Holland delivered more dolomite to banana growers and shrimp farmers. Meb Cutlack excoriated the Musa government in the pages of *The Reporter*. Bacongo director Jamillah

Vasquez quit the group and fled the country under murky circumstances. She left a note on her office door that read "Back in 20 mins."

Fortis and the government moved quickly to build the dam before the Privy Council heard the case. The more complete the project, the more difficult it would be for the lords to stop it. Lois Young appealed to the council to issue a temporary injunction halting work until the trial. The Law Lords denied her request.

In the legal case against Chalillo there existed an imaginary bar that marked the level of unlawful behavior required to halt the project. That bar rose with each passing week. By December, the dam would be so far along that Lois Young would have to present evidence of extraordinary malfeasance to win the case.

She was prepared to do that. Her evidence included a dozen affidavits testifying to Fortis's geological errors and EIA deceptions.

Prime Minister Musa grew uneasy with Lois Young's confidence. Belizean courts could be expected to defer to the almighty PUP, but there was no telling what would happen when Young brought the case before five old Englishmen in Whitehall. So Musa and Fonseca hatched a backup plan. Using their majority in the Belizean House and Senate, the PUP leaders pushed a measure called the Macal River Hydroelectric Development Act through the legislature in a single day. The act authorized Fortis to proceed with the construction of the Chalillo Dam "notwithstanding any other laws to the contrary, or the judgment, order or declaration of any court or tribunal."

UDP senator Ambrose Tillett condemned the act on the floor of the Belize Senate. "A lawless bill indeed!" he howled. "The Prime Minister is asking us to do nothing less than elevate a foreign company above the supreme laws of our country." Despite Tillett's protests, the bill passed. The lords of the Privy Council could say whatever they wanted. The law of the land in Belize declared their opinion moot.

Each side in the Chalillo dispute retained a London barrister of the highest rank. These elite attorneys are called QCs, or Queen's Counsel. Known for their experience, intellect, and high ethical standards, QC's are sometimes referred to as "silks" for the special silk robes that only they are allowed to wear in court. And so when the silk representing the Government of Belize got word of the Macal River Hydroelectric Development Act, he considered it his duty to advise his client to repeal the act immediately. The Law Lords would read it for what it was—an insult to the Privy Council and an underhanded ploy to complete the dam. The government might win over the Law Lords at trial, but not as long as the act was on the books.

Musa and Fonseca mulled over their strategy. Keeping the act could sabotage their case and would unequivocally sever Belize's centuries-old ties to the Privy Council. If they repealed the act and won the case, the dam would go up and the government could claim vindication by the highest court in the Commonwealth. Musa and Fonseca took a gamble. A few weeks after its passage, the Belizean legislature quietly repealed the Macal River Hydroelectric Development Act.

CHAPTER 24

*S*HARON ARRIVED IN LONDON bearing bad news.

"Lois Young can't make it," she told me. "She made it as far as Miami. Then she got a phone call. Her father is deathly ill and he took a turn for the worse. The rest of us caught the flight to London. Lois went home."

We met on the opening morning of the trial in the Privy Council Chamber at 9 Downing Street, next to the British prime minister's official residence. Despite its prestigious address, 9 Downing is a humble building, an anonymous Georgian row house cut up into a warren of courtrooms and offices. The Privy Council shares Number 9 with the prime minister's chief whip.

London that December was damp, gray, and miserable. The cold weather and Lois Young's absence combined to put Sharon in a dour mood.

"Excited?" I asked.

"We'll see what happens," she said, unbuttoning her coat. "I don't expect miracles."

One by one, other players in the drama arrived. Bacongo's British attorneys swept into the courtroom like crows in white wigs. The younger man, Richard Buxton, was a dashing solicitor with a passion for environmental law. His senior, Richard Clayton, was a high-profile barrister known for writing the leading textbook on human rights law. Several secondary solicitors and legal assistants trailed in. I glanced at the stairs and saw Jacob Scherr and Ari Hershowitz—K Street and Haight Street. Scherr wore a tailored suit. Hershowitz sported an old gray sweater. Meb Cutlack made the trip to give *Reporter* readers a firsthand account of the trial. Representing Bacongo was Godsman Ellis, the Cayo elder who spoke so eloquently at the public hearing. Ellis had been elected chairman of Bacongo shortly before the trial.

The forces of Fortis and the Belizean government gathered across the room. The government's case would be presented by Edward Fitzgerald, QC. A brilliant courtroom tactician, Fitzgerald specialized in two types of clients: the downtrodden and the despised. He often appeared on behalf of abused prisoners, mental patients, battered wives, and condemned murderers. He spoke for Mary Bell, the infamous British murderess. He spoke for al-Quaeda terrorists held in British custody. Two years prior to the Chalillo hearing, Fitzgerald had argued before the Privy Council on behalf of a Belizean death-row inmate. By all accounts it was a magnificent defense. Fitzgerald destroyed the government's case so completely that the Law Lords all but abolished Belize's death penalty. When Chalillo went before the Privy Council, the government of Belize went out and hired the man who had so soundly beaten them.

At eight o'clock, a door at the back of the courtroom opened and the Law Lords appeared. By custom the lords wore no wigs or robes. Their informal suits and ties made them appear all the more powerful. We're lords, their dress implied. We've got no one to impress.

They were impressive nonetheless. Lord Walker of Gestingthorpe, a tall man with a long face, modeled a snappy pinstriped suit. Lord Steyn, a South African jurist, accented his bright pink face with owlish glasses. Baron Leonard Hubert Hoffman of Chedworth, a.k.a. Lord Hoffman, was an intimidating figure with fierce eyes and a scowling mien. Lord Rodger of Earlsferry was the quiet man of the group; he had the look of a retired constable who filled his days with volunteer service on parish committees. Rounding out the group was Sir Andrew Leggatt, a distinguished barrister who, as England's chief surveillance commissioner, had the final say on whose phones got tapped by the authorities.

The key player was Lord Hoffman. A legal magazine once described him as "the most dominant personality in the Lords." His powers of persuasion were legendary. Whichever side won Hoffman over would likely carry the day.

~

"My Lords, may I begin?"

Richard Clayton bowed slightly in a gesture of respect. Five pale men looked up from their papers.

"My Lords, the respondents in this case propose to build a hydroelectric dam in the Macal River valley of Belize, which is one of the most remote, undisturbed wilderness areas in Central America." Clayton walked the lords through an outline of his case. First he established the unique character of the Macal, with its endangered subspecies of scarlet macaw and its thriving population of rare tapirs, which, he explained, "is a cross between a horse and a hippopotamus." He challenged the claim that the dam would serve the public interest ("its electrical capacity is not substantial"). Furthermore, he argued, the site posed fundamental geological concerns, "about which," he said, "some significant information has only recently come to light."

The room's wooden benches cracked with the weight of two dozen spectators straining to hear. The council chamber is a small oak-paneled box with a ceiling high enough to allow a game of volleyball. Cases are presented today exactly as they were a century ago. Barristers stand at a lectern and speak to five jurists seated at a curved bench a handshake's distance away. The intimate setup allows barristers to address the lords in conversational tones, which would be fine except that there are no microphones. For spectators, it's incredibly frustrating.

After Clayton's windup came the pitch. "My Lords, environmental approval in Belize requires a lawful environmental impact assessment, or EIA," he said. "Our primary complaint is that the EIA did not consider a number of significant impacts of the dam, and that the members of the National Environmental Appraisal Committee left those matters to be dealt with in an environmental compliance plan that did not, at the time, exist."

"Now," he added, "I wish to turn Your Lordships' attention to the Cornec report, a document which was disclosed to us for the first time last Friday."

The Cornec report? I nearly slipped off my bench.

~

At a break in the proceedings, Sharon and Jacob Scherr filled me in on the events of the previous forty-eight hours.

"We've been asking for a copy of Jean Cornec's geological survey for months," Scherr said. "We knew from Brian Holland that it was out there somewhere, but Fortis and the Department of the Environment never acknowledged that it even existed. Finally one of our requests for disclosure made it to their British lawyer, who happens to have a sense of legal ethics."

When the Belizean government hired Edward Fitzgerald, it didn't consider the fact that Fitzgerald would bring his sense of fair play along on the job. Fitzgerald asked the government if Jean Cornec had, in fact, prepared such a report. The government admitted that he had. "Fitzgerald's been around long enough to know that this kind of thing doesn't play with the Law Lords," Scherr said. "He told the government they had to disclose the report immediately."

The government stalled. They sent a few pages over, then a few more, dribbling it out as slowly as possible. The final pages arrived in Richard Clayton's office two days before opening arguments.

"It's no wonder they didn't want it to get out," Sharon told me. "Basically it proves they've been lying for the past year."

The Bacongo allies were both elated and shocked. They couldn't believe their eyes. There was no granite at the dam site—never had been, never would be. But that paled beside Cornec's biggest revelation: Amec had erased the existing fault line on the map. "This is it," Ari Hershowitz told Sharon. "We've got the smoking gun."

In the council chamber, Richard Clayton held up the Cornec report as prime evidence of the government's deception. "On page 66 of Exhibit 17 Your Lordships may see a highlighted line, which is the Cooma Cairn fault. On the next page you may see a similar map. This map was included in the EIA, but here the fault does not exist."

Clayton paused to let the point hang in the courtroom. The lords studied the two maps.

Edward Fitzgerald rose to object. "There is a fault line which has been removed, but Richard," he said, addressing Clayton, "if you're going to say the fault line is important, you must say what the significance of the fault line *is*."

Clayton was flustered. He sensed a trap. "Well . . . it is . . ."

Fitzgerald sprang it. "In fact it is not the main Cooma Cairn fault, is it?" he said.

Clayton conferred with his chief solicitor, Buxton. With every second, more air leaked out of the balloon. "Er, yes, Mr. Fitzgerald's point is well taken," Clayton allowed. The erased fault line was not the main Cooma Cairn fault. It was an offshoot.

Clayton had overplayed his hand. Fitzgerald called him on it and diverted attention from his own client's malfeasance. Jacob Scherr gave Bacongo solicitor Richard Buxton a knowing look. Edward Fitzgerald's reputation was well earned.

"My Lords."

It was Fitzgerald's turn. The government's barrister was a tall man with thick lips, an arched forehead, and glasses so large they looked like windshields. As he stood before the Law Lords, Fitzgerald was in plain discomfort. The behavior of his clients regarding the Cornec report seemed to leave him embarrassed and disturbed. At the same time, few lawyers in England were more experienced at representing unsympathetic clients.

He went to work. "Let us bear in mind that the focus of the complaint rests on the decisions themselves," he told the lords. "That is, the November 9, 2001, National Environmental Appraisal Committee vote and the later clearance given by the Department of the Environment."

The decision of that committee, Fitzgerald argued, was taken lawfully on the basis of the materials before it. "The Cornec report does not change that."

Fitzgerald's strategy was simple. The Cornec report, he contended, didn't matter. It wasn't even applicable. "The report was produced *after* the decision taken by the committee," he said. "If the report had been published prior to those decisions, the committee would have proceeded on the basis that the bedrock at the dam site was sandstone, not granite. Well, *they did.*"

Fitzgerald subtly reframed the Cornec report. Its revelations were about sandstone and granite, he implied, not about an erased fault line and a fraudulent map. The QC raised himself up to full height and grinned. He was alerting the lords. Here comes the overhead smash.

"In the minutes of their meetings, we see that the geologist, Mr. Cho, said the bedrock was sandstone, not granite. Twice in two separate meetings he raised the point. The idea that before Jean Cornec came along, nobody had any idea this might be sandstone? Not a bit!"

I glanced at Sharon. Her lips were flatlined. Jacob Scherr and Ari Hershowitz scribbled furiously and passed their notes to Bacongo solicitor Richard Buxton.

The barristers were a study in contrasting styles. Clayton, for Bacongo, played the kindly law professor. He presented facts as if delivering a lecture. Fitzgerald, for the Government of Belize, argued like a passionate member of parliament. His deep baritone fell clearly on the ears of us backbenchers.

As the afternoon light filtered through Downing Street, the full scope of Fitzgerald's attack unfolded before us. He didn't defend the EIA's deficiencies. He held them up for all to see. Will the dam reduce habitat for tapirs, jaguars, and scarlet macaws? Yes. Admitted in the EIA. Known to the committee. Will Mayan ruins be flooded? Yes. Admitted. Known. Is there a dispute over the geology? Absolutely. Known to all.

It was damage control, but it was a splendid job of damage control. Fitzgerald succeeded in blunting Clayton's sharpest points. The Law Lords weren't about to let him get off without a taste of the lash, however.

"When did the Government of Belize know about the Cornec report?" demanded Lord Walker.

"Not until about a week ago," said Fitzgerald.

His Lordship reacted as if to a nasty stench. "A week ago?" he said.

"When were you first asked for it?" said Lord Rodger.

"There was a request for various matters addressed to Lynn Young in June 2003—"

"It was 2002," said Clayton.

"The confusion seems to have stemmed from the fact that the request was sent to the wrong government department," Fitzgerald stammered. "The Department of the Environment didn't know about the existence of the report until late last month."

Lord Walker was incensed. The Law Lords did not enjoy being deceived. They knew deception wasn't part of Fitzgerald's playbook. The barrister could only deal with the facts as his client revealed them. "I must say this is typical of the way information has been *squeezed* out of the government in this matter!" said Lord Walker. He shot a withering look at Fitzgerald.

Dusk fell on Whitehall. The chamber's overhead lights flickered on. At the stroke of 4:01 the lords retired and the rest of us spilled out into the damp streets of London. The Bacongo lawyers passed through the Downing Street gates humming with optimism. "I think it's going incredibly well," said Richard Clayton.

Edward Fitzgerald offered collegial farewells as he passed by the group. "Feeling a bit bruised?" one of the Bacongo solicitors asked.

Fitzgerald offered a sheepish smile. "I knew that was coming," he said.

Sharon didn't want to talk much about the case that night. She preferred to discuss the Rolling Stones. "I'm going out to Dartford after the trial's over," she told me. "It's really close—just on the outskirts of London. The mayor wants to hear my proposal. I had a fifteen-minute conversation with Princess Anne's personal assistant about it. I don't know how much she'll be able to help."

An objective observer might conclude that the Privy Council trial represented one woman's triumph over corruption and greed. An obscure zookeeper from the Central American jungle had dragged an entire nation before the highest court in the British Commonwealth. At 9 Downing Street a dishonest government was on trial for conspiring to destroy a river through deception and fraud. That was the logical way of looking at it; but to Sharon the trial was the final death penalty appeal of the scarlet macaws. It was too painful to think about. So she turned her attention to the positive: a plaque for Mick and Keith. That's the thing.

I tried to steer her back to the trial. "Any chance Lois Young might make a late flight?"

Sharon shook her head.

"I spoke with the mayor of Dartford last week," she said. "Did you know mayors in England aren't elected?"

On the second day of the trial, Edward Fitzgerald concluded his opening arguments and called upon the attorney general of Belize. Godfrey Smith rose.

A handsome, athletic man with an easy smile, Smith wore a trim mustache that gave him the air of a Belizean Billy Dee Williams. He stood at the lectern in his black law robe and gathered a few seconds of silence.

"My Lords, the question arose yesterday as to whether this dam will serve the public interest in Belize." Smith's warm, rich voice filled the chamber. "It is true that we are not discussing the Three Gorges Dam today. But this project is significant for Belize. It will generate its own power and provide storage for water for power generation at the Mollejon Dam. We are not saying that once Chalillo is completed the cost of energy will fall." Sharon gasped. Ari Hershowitz picked up on it too. He scribbled a note and passed it to Buxton. *Not what they've told Bz public,* it said. "What it will do," continued Smith, "is stabilize the cost to Belizean consumers in the long run. That is the specific, practical public interest in this project.

"My friends at Bacongo have also raised the issue of the Third Master Agreement, the contract between the government and Fortis to build and operate the dam. With the greatest respect, to question that contract is to ignore the economic and demographic realities in Belize. If the Government of Belize had the money and wherewithal to build the dam ourselves, we would have done so. The simple fact is we do not. When a private investor comes to our country, he says, What is your population? And we tell him two hundred and fifty thousand. He wonders, How can I recoup profits in a country that small?

"Yes, BEL is under contract to purchase power from Chalillo and Mollejon first, before any others. Belize can't have it both ways. We can't ask Fortis to invest thirty million dollars in our country and at the same time tell the company, 'Well, we'll shop around for other suppliers once it's built.' That's not the way foreign investment works. To believe so is to put our heads in the sand like ostriches."

The Law Lords fixed Smith with rapt attention.

"As to the question of public consultation," he continued. "A public hearing was held. You have seen the transcript. Also, the Department of the Environment received thousands of letters of concern via e-mail."

Sharon jotted a note and handed it to Ari Hershowitz. *E-mails deleted before anyone read them,* it said. Hershowitz passed it to solicitor Richard Buxton.

"Your Lordships are aware of the consequences of granting relief in this case," Smith said. "Relief would result in considerable delay and, ultimately, abandonment of the project. The costs incurred would simply be too high. That outcome would inject a completely unacceptable level of indecisiveness in the foreign investment community. Belize cannot have it known in the international financial world that there is this lack of security."

Worry came over the Bacongo legal team. Jacob Scherr shifted uneasily in his seat. Godfrey Smith was good—very good. What began as a point of clarification had become a passionate oration. And the Law Lords were listening.

"My Lords," he continued, "Belize is a poor country. Belize is small. Belize is underdeveloped. We in the government have identified the Chalillo dam as a fundamental building block for the development of our nation. We won the national election on that basis earlier this year. As the attorney general, I can say that the Government of Belize considers it not in our national security interest to depend on a foreign power for half of our electricity needs."

There was something in Godfrey Smith's manner that imparted an almost unbearable tension to his words. You could see it in his eyes. A black man, Godfrey Smith was the highest legal officer in the sovereign government of Belize. Yet here he was, bowing before the Law Lords, five old white Englishmen who probably couldn't place Belize on a map. It angered him. The set of his jaw and the diction of his words conveyed an unmistakable message: I will do everything in my power to ensure that no Belizean will bow before this court again. You may have your say in this case. But we are not coming back.

"Finally," Smith said, "I wish to make a point about sustainable development. Your Lordships should bear in mind that over forty percent of Belize is designated as protected areas. Forty percent of our land has severe restrictions on habitation, logging, and other extractive activities. The Government of Belize fully appreciates the importance of conservation measures. At the same time, we are concerned about the level of detail called for by our colleagues at Bacongo. The acceptability of the EIA in question is extremely important. It will determine the standards for lawful EIAs in the future. This was, as you have heard, a fifteen-hundred-page document, the most extensive EIA undertaken in the history of our country. If that is deemed insufficient, the ripple effect could be devastating. We have many other projects awaiting environmental approval. Housing developments. A waste disposal site. If the standards demanded of an EIA are such that large multinational corporations cannot hope to meet them, the consequences for development in Belize would be devastating.

"We urge Your Lordships to consider this. Thank you."

With that, the lords broke for lunch.

"Quickly! Quickly!"

Richard Clayton waved his Bacongo team into a huddle. "We will have limited time for our rebuttal," he said. "I want each of you to write down thoughts, ideas, corrections, objections—anything at all. Make your points brief, and do it quickly! We will meet in the back chamber in twenty minutes."

Panic swept through the Bacongo partisans. Godfrey Smith had devastated their case. The lords were clearly moved by his appeal. The attorney general set the full weight of 350 years of colonial oppression upon the shoulders of the five learned Englishmen sitting before him. You have been telling us what to do for nearly four hundred years, he effectively told them. It is time to stop.

I caught up with Ari Hershowitz on the way out the door. He was worried. "An hour ago they were five Law Lords weighing evidence and precedent," he said. "Now they're the white guys in England telling the black guys in Belize whether they can turn the lights on or not. That's a hell of a thing to overcome."

Richard Clayton disagreed. Smith's speech had nothing to do with the law, he said. It was political bluster, nothing more. The lords would disregard it.

"If only Lois were here," said Sharon. "They're lying! And we know they're lying. But of course you can't stand up and say they're lying." She paused. "Lois could, though."

As a native Belizean attorney, Lois Young could tell the lords that foreign investors weren't driven away by environmental regulations; they were driven away by corrupt governments. Only she could tell the lords that in Godfrey Smith's "poor country," government ministers drove through Belize City's blighted Southside in shiny new sport utility vehicles and kept yachts and mistresses in Miami. Only Lois Young could explain how lucrative government contracts went only to the friends of certain ministers. Only she could speak for the Belizean people who believed that development could be both environmentally sustainable and corruption-free.

Godsman Ellis nodded. "We need Lois now," he said.

Sharon found a sheet of paper. POINTS FOR RICHARD, she wrote.

TOURISM—Cayo gateway to fastest growing tourist region.
Nature as economic engine
FLOW OF BIODIVERSITY hurt by dam; affects not just BZE but entire region
AG says 40% protected but habitat threatened by dam NOT replicated in other parts of BZE

Twenty minutes later Sharon joined Richard Clayton and his legal team in a cramped conference room. Chaos reigned as five people shouted at once. Clayton struggled to pick out a usable suggestion from the dozen thrown at him. Sharon begged him to focus on the environmental destruction. Hit the wildlife note. The tapirs! The jaguars! The scarlet macaws!

Clayton waved her off. Warm fuzzy animals couldn't save them now.

Hershowitz wanted to focus on the geology. "Let's let the lords know why it matters," he said. "What happens if the dam collapses?"

"No, no," said Scherr. He argued for attacking on international law. Godfrey Smith mentioned international conventions recognizing each country's right to set its own environmental laws. "Go after that," Scherr said. "Those international conventions include the public's right to know what's going on!"

Clayton was skeptical. "That's international law," he said, "not English law." Besides, using all of his precious rebuttal time responding to the attorney general was a losing tactic. Clayton checked the time. "Five minutes," he said. He conferred with his solicitors and returned to the council chamber moments before the lords took their seats.

"My Lords, may I express regret that Lois Young is unable to address this court."

Richard Clayton let his comment hang for a moment. He wanted the lords to know there were two sides to Godfrey Smith's story.

Clayton returned to his most damning evidence, the Cornec report. "Mr. Fitzgerald claims that everyone knew what was in the report," he said. "With respect, that is simply not the case. Geology was a fiercely contested issue. Mr. Holland's views throughout were treated as being personal to him and unsupported by the evidence. In fact, the Cornec report shows that his views were supported by *the government's own report!*"

He linked that deception to the larger issue at hand. "The whole point of this procedure," he said, referring to the environmental impact assessment and the National Environmental Appraisal Committee vote, "was to secure an informed decision, not to secure a particular predetermined decision."

For the next hour Clayton jumped hither and yon through the evidence, guiding the lords into the far reaches of his document packets ("I would ask Your Lordships to turn to Bundle 5, page 139 . . .") for bits and pieces that added up to . . . that added up to . . .

That added up to what, exactly?

Richard Clayton, normally an organizational dervish in the courtroom, was falling to pieces. He hurled fact after disconnected fact at the Law Lords as if victory might be secured by the massing of tiny truths. There were errors here, misstatements there, outright deceptions on this other page. He jumped from power rates to archaeology, from bedrock to stream flow. Clayton's attack turned scattershot and desperate. The afternoon drained away and with it exited Bacongo's optimism and hope. Edward Fitzgerald offered the lords a clear, coherent argument: The environmental assessment committee had voted with its eyes wide open. Clayton offered the lords a thousand errors in the EIA, but no overriding reason to halt the dam. By the end of the afternoon, in fact, it was hard to recall what Bacongo wanted in the first place.

Time grew short. "Mr. Clayton," a voice called out. Lord Steyn peered over his tortoiseshell glasses. "You have five minutes to put your"—Steyn paused and gazed suggestively at the barrister—"your *big* points to us." His Lordship practically stood up and waved semaphores. You've got my vote, Steyn implied. But if I'm expected to sway Hoffman, you've got to give me something to work with.

Clayton pulled himself together. "There are two sides to this debate," he acknowledged. "Many people have reservations about the dam. Many people have issues with the effect stopping it might have upon foreign investment. But I will leave with this.

The mere fact that a scheme such as this may be found to be unlawful, but nevertheless allowed to proceed, would be a radical ex-
tension of legal principles."

The Law Lords stood and filed out of the room. The legal
teams and spectators chatted quietly and made their way downstairs and out onto Downing Street. A light rain fell upon the cob-
blestones. Sharon and I pushed through the iron turnstile onto
Whitehall Street and buttoned our coats against the wind. Nobody was hungry. Everybody wanted a drink.

At a pub around the corner from Richard Clayton's law office,
the exhausted Bacongo supporters splayed themselves on chairs
and couches. Clayton was upbeat. "I think it went rather well," he
said. Others weren't so sure. "It all depends on how they received
the attorney general's speech," said Ari Hershowitz. Jacob Scherr
held a cell phone to one ear and stuck a finger in the other. "I'll be
back in *Washington* on *Monday*," he shouted. Throbbing music
bounced off the walls.

Sharon relaxed on a couch and drained a glass of wine. Richard
Buxton, the solicitor who'd fought dozens of environmental cases
over the years, sat next to her and offered some encouraging
words. "I think we have at least two of them," he said, referring to
the five lords. "Let's hope we can turn a third." Sharon asked Buxton where this case fell in the context of his career. He thought for
a moment. "Well, it's the first environmental case the Privy Council has ever heard," he said. "And," he added, "we actually might
win."

Sharon toasted that thought, then shook her head. "The odds
are against us," she said.

Buxton smiled. "The odds are always against us," he said.

CHAPTER 25

A DECISION FROM THE PRIVY COUNCIL was expected in January, so about the middle of the month I flew down to Belize and waited in one of the zoo's guesthouses. The one-room shack teetered on stilts over a crocodile pond, and when the water rose you could look between the floorboards and spy turtles paddling lazily through the yellow murk. I loved the place. At dawn I would wake to clay-colored robins trilling outside my window. In the evening I would sit on the porch watching chachalacas, vultures, kingfishers, and gray foxes wander by.

On some days I'd walk over to the zoo and hang out with Sharon. That winter she was training two hawks to perform in a birds of prey show. "Billy is a Harris's hawk," she told me one morning as we climbed into an aviary. Sharon wore thick leather gloves and carried a fistful of chopped rat. "I have to keep him away from Alvin, the roadside hawk. Alvin gets jealous if he sees me talking to Billy."

"Jealous like how?" I asked.

"Well, he'll attack me if he catches me working with Billy."

She spent half an hour training Billy to fly to her glove, eat the rat, then return to his perch. Afterward we wandered over to where Tony Garel and another keeper were designing a home for a new toucanet, a diminutive relative of the toucan. "One of the women with British Forces found the bird injured, and she nurtured it back to health," Sharon told me.

Tony Garel explained the aviary's design to Sharon. She nodded. "Can we create a small pool?" she said. "The bird likes to bathe."

Garel considered this. "Yes," he said, calculating the cost of concrete and manpower. "Over there, I think."

"Are we using nets or wire?"

"Wire," Garel said. "Nets we don't have right now."

She thought for a moment. "Can we find some?"

Garel turned away. "I'll see what I can do."

"Jacob says Fortis and the government are nervous," Sharon told me. "They really don't know which way the Privy Council will go."

"What do you think?"

She shrugged.

While we waited for the decision, I spent a lot of time in Sharon's *oficina* going through stacks and stacks of Chalillo documents. Angel the jaguar kept an eye on me. Once a notebook slipped off Sharon's messy desk and fell open to the back page. On it Sharon had scrawled a sort of Increase Your Word Power list. The notebook was new, and it gave me an idea of where Sharon's head was at.

> *inauspicious = bad*
> *confabulate = engage in spoken exchange*
> *spurious = containing fundamental errors in reasoning*
> *hebetudinous = lacking in intelligence*
> *calamitous = causing ruin*
> *kismet = fate*

On some days I caught a bus east from the zoo to Belize City or west to Belmopan. This took some doing. First I had to walk about a mile across the savannah to the Western Highway, then stand by the side of the road as all manner of rickety trucks whizzed by at sixty miles an hour. When a bus approached, an aspiring passenger was expected to flag it down like a runway worker directing a 747 to the gate. I wasn't very good at this. At first I chalked it up to overcrowding—Must be full up—but one day after two half-empty buses passed me by, a Belizean woman waiting to catch a bus going the other way took pity on me. "Tch," she said. "You got to let 'im *know*." She raised her arm and brought it down hard like an executioner's axe. A few minutes later when her bus came she stepped out into the highway and dared the driver to run her down. He stopped, and she gave me a pointed look: You see?

The coaches were old Blue Bird models exported to Belize after a lifetime of loyal service to American schoolchildren. Rides were cheap. You could cross the breadth of the country for five bucks. The bus business didn't look like a real moneymaker in Belize, but looks were deceiving. It was in fact one of the many fronts used by friends of the government to loot the public treasury. It happened like this. Belize used to have a number of different bus companies, each serving different routes. Then one day the Novelos Bus Line, the country's largest, received a $15 million loan from the government to buy out all the smaller players and upgrade its fleet. This was done by the Novelo brothers, who were tight with the Musa-Fonseca crowd. A few months later, however, something had mysteriously gone wrong. The Novelo brothers bought out their competitors and kept running the same old brukdown buses. But for some reason the company was no longer able to turn a profit. The brothers declared bankruptcy and walked away from the business. What happened to the $15 million? Nobody could say.

Often I caught the bus early enough to hear "Good Morning Belize" on Love FM. The bus drivers often played it over the PA systems. One day the host mentioned a ceremony going on in Belize City, so I went to see it.

Every year on the third Monday in January the judges and lawyers of Belize gather in St. Mary's Anglican Church for an ecumenical service marking the opening of the Supreme Court year. It's a sight. In white wigs and black robes, the counselors and jurists pack themselves into rosewood pews. The most senior judges sit up front, the youngest attorneys in the back.

I claimed an empty seat in the back just as the Reverend LeRoy Flowers warmed up his sermon. Reverend Flowers was powerful with righteousness and the Lord, but not in a dramatic Southern Baptist way. He was a man who knew how things operated in Belize, and the way things operated did not please him. For this day he drew inspiration from the fifth chapter of Amos. "Woe to those who change justice into wormwood, throwing integrity to the ground," he read, "who hate the man dispensing justice at the city gate and detest those who speak with honesty."

Flowers had us consider that. "Amos," he said, "was harsh in his criticism of the powers that be at the time." The preacher's voice was deep and steady. "In Amos's eyes the court of justice was a place where righteousness should bear fruit, where justice should be established. But Amos was upset with what he found. The justice offered to the poor was a bitter fraud." He gazed out at the congregation. "The source of righteousness," he said, "had been turned into a spring of injustice."

I knew nothing of the Reverend LeRoy Flowers, but I knew enough about Belize to understand that I was witnessing an act of courage. The pastor could have sent the judges out the door with some sweet bromides about justice and integrity. These words weren't sweet. They were sharp, pointed, and direct. He was telling the judges and government officials to clean up their act.

Having dispensed with Amos, the good reverend turned to Solomon. "Solomon was wise and just," he said, "but due to his arrogance he forsook the Lord and enslaved his people for his own gain." This was as far as Flowers felt he could push it. The minister said a few more words about Solomon and then wrapped things up with the hymn, "Now Thank We All Our God."

After the service I followed the judges as they paraded behind a boom-chime band through the streets of Belize City to the Supreme Court building. Chief Justice Abdulai Conteh led the way, his face framed by a resplendent vanilla wig that hung past his shoulders. Attorney General Godfrey Smith walked a few paces behind. At the steps of the Supreme Court building they all piled into the main courtroom to hear Smith, fresh from his Privy Council triumph, address the nation. I tried to hear too, but when I made for the stairs a burly man in sunglasses scowled and stepped in my way. "And *who* are *you*?" he demanded. I told him I was a writer working on a book about Belize. He crossed his arms.

"Why are you here?" I said I was interested in what the attorney general had to say. The man shook his head. "Very crowded up there," he said, in a way that indicated *dis fu wi, not you.* I chose not to press the point. As I walked away, he called out: "Write only good things about Belize!"

Fortunately, I had a radio with me and Love FM broadcast Smith's speech live from the Supreme Court chamber. At one point the attorney general recounted the Privy Council trial. "I cannot tell you the bad taste left in my mouth when we were told that the lords would retire to consider the advice they shall give Her Majesty," Smith said. The time had come, he said, to cut the nation's ties to the Privy Council. Belize no longer needed Her Majesty's justice.

As it happened, Godfrey Smith didn't stick around long enough to cut those ties himself. Less than a week later, Smith was fired by Prime Minister Musa for a minor scandal. The attorney general had improperly steered a lucrative contract for the renovation of the nation's law library to his own brother's construction company. It was hard to say whether Smith had been kicked upstairs or downstairs, because the very next day Musa appointed him Minister of Defence.

One day I stopped in at the Texaco station in Belmopan for a bottle of water. I paid my money and headed out the door when I saw Meb Cutlack's Chevy Geo pull in to the gas pump. He waved me over in a state of agitation.

"The dam is dead!" he said.

"The ruling came out?"

"No, no," he said. "We're still waiting. But whatever the lords say may be moot. I just spoke with Evadne Wade at the Geology and Petroleum Department. There was a tremor at the dam site a couple nights ago and a big crack opened up in the earth. Evadne's sending an inspector out there to take a look. She says if the ground's not sound, there's no way she can sign off on it."

"Have you been to the site?"

"I'm on my way now." He handed three bills to the attendant and spun gravel out of the station.

The next morning I rode a bus to San Ignacio. I wanted to hear what Mick Fleming knew about the tremor at the dam site.

Fleming caught up with me near lunchtime. "Christ, man, sorry to keep you," he said. "One of my guides got impaled on a tractor this morning."

"Holy crap!" I said.

Fleming nodded as if to say it was as bad as I imagined. "Got him right in the backside," he said. "He was left hanging there for about ten minutes before anybody found him." The man was on his way to the hospital in Belize City. It looked like he might pull through.

I said something about the hazards of bodily trauma so far from medical care. Fleming waved me off. "It's not so bad now, not bad at all," he said. "Twenty years ago there wasn't even a road to Chaa Creek. When Lucy went into labor with our daughter, the river was in high flood. We had to wait until the rain let up. Then we got into a canoe, dead of night, and paddled to the clinic in San Ignacio. Made it just in time."

Fleming told me what he'd been hearing about Chalillo. "One of the drillers came through and had a drink the other night," he said. "He's an experienced bloke, fourteen years on the job. Been up at the dam site searching for granite for months. Months! He's found nothing. The Chinese workers up there—lot of them are Nepalese, I hear—they get ten dollars a day, they don't know much."

"What about the tremor?"

"Right. A few nights ago a tremor ran through the site and opened up a crevasse on the right bank. Big enough to lose a man. The men in charge ordered the bulldozers to fill it in. Nobody was supposed to talk about it, but apparently word got out to government. Is it true? I don't know. As we say in Belize, 'If no so, nearly so.' "

"You think this'll kill the dam?"

Fleming laughed. "Nothing seems able to kill this dam. Meb thinks it will. I wouldn't bet on it."

~

I wanted to be in Belize when the decision came down, but the Law Lords wouldn't be rushed. Days passed. The turtles grazed on pond grass under my floor. Eventually I ran out of money and had to go home. The ruling came three days later.

Their Lordships sided with Fortis and the government, 3–2. The dam would not be stopped.

As expected, Lord Hoffman proved to be the deciding force. Though he was troubled by the improprieties practiced by the government and Fortis, in the end Godfrey Smith's passionate address and Edward Fitzgerald's brilliant framing won him over. Hoffman wrote the majority opinion. Belize is a sovereign nation, he wrote. Despite the inconsistencies and mistakes contained in the EIA, Hoffman believed the government had more or less followed its own rules for environmental approval.

The most astonishing aspect of Hoffman's ruling was his interpretation of the Cornec report. In Hoffman's seventeen-page opinion, the mapping fraud was magically transformed into an innocent omission helpfully corrected by Jean Cornec: "The Cornec report said that the design should also take into account the close proximity of a major fault." Then he added: "For some reason this report was not disclosed to the appellants until very shortly before the hearing" in London. When I read this, my jaw hit the floor. *Naïfs* rarely come this *faux*.

If there was any consolation for Sharon and the dam opponents, it came in an extraordinary thirteen-page dissent written by Lord Walker. He and Lord Steyn were in agreement: This case stank. "I differ, respectfully but profoundly, from the view of the majority," Walker wrote.

"In this most unsatisfactory state of affairs a few essential points are clear," he continued. First, governments owe a duty to the court—any court—to "make candid disclosure of the relevant facts" in a case such as this. The people of Belize were entitled to be properly informed about the fate of their rivers and land. "It is now apparent," he wrote, "that the respondents"—Fortis and the Government of Belize—"failed in that duty of disclosure." The government and Fortis proclaimed their studies and assessments to be transparent and public, Walker noted, while making it impossible for the public to see them. "Not even the most protracted and determined paper chase could have got at the true facts," he wrote. Second, "it is now accepted" that the early geological claims for the dam site were wrong. Those claims were not minor secondary impacts of the dam's construction. With a touch of wit, Walker pointed out, "A dam which is liable to leak, and still more a dam which is liable to prove unstable, may have a more serious environmental impact (and fewer if any countervailing advantages) than a secure dam." His third point came in answer to Attorney General Godfrey Smith: "The rule of law," he wrote, "must not be sacrificed to foreign investment."

The deception practiced by Fortis and the Government of Belize seemed to set Lord Walker's kettle boiling. To Lynn Young and Joseph Sukhnandan, His Lordship offered undisguised contempt. Both "must have known" about the Cornec report, he noted, while pretending otherwise. Walker saved his harshest words for Department of the Environment chief Ismael Fabro, who also claimed to know nothing about Cornec's findings. Lord Walker found Fabro's testimony "simply incredible" in the old sense of the word: not credible. This is as close as a Law Lord will ever come to using the word *liar* in a legal document.

Were it within his power, Walker wrote, "I would have quashed the Department of the Environment's decision to grant environmental clearance for the project." The EIA was so flawed, he wrote, "as to be incapable of satisfying the requirements" of Belizean law. With one more vote, Lord Walker would have stopped the dam.

I got through to Sharon later that morning. "It's exactly what I expected," she said. She always thought the lords would lay a spanking on the government but ultimately let the dam proceed. "That's just what they did."

"It was too daring for the Privy Council to override a developing country, I suppose," she said. She added some other things about using Lord Walker's dissent to continue the fight, but her words sounded scripted. I realized Sharon had done so many interviews that morning that she was operating on verbal autopilot. I didn't think she had any more fight left in her. Legally, the Privy Council was the end of the road.

"This is not the end," she insisted. "This is the beginning of the next chapter. Now we'll see what happens with the geology and the stream flow. You can't lie your way around the rocks and the river. In the end Mother Nature gets the final call."

CHAPTER 26

ONSTRUCTION OF THE DAM kicked into high gear. Prime Minister Musa held a press conference at the Chalillo site to mark the first concrete pour for the dam's retaining wall. "I would like to congratulate BEL and Fortis for their tenacity," the prime minister said. Ralph Fonseca, Stan Marshall, and Lynn Young stood next to him.

Six months after the Privy Council decision, Fortis announced plans for a third hydroelectric dam on the Macal River. The 18-megawatt dam at the majestic Vaca Falls, six miles downstream of Chalillo, would wipe out one of Cayo's most popular ecotourist attractions.

Things fell apart at the zoo. Money grew tight. The board of directors pressed Sharon to get the zoo's budget back on track. Staff grumbling about the Zoo Lady's dam obsession grew louder. A spate of robberies hit the zoo, and it appeared the culprits were the kids of one of the zookeepers. Her Dartford project stalled. It turned out that tourists associated the Beatles with happy love songs. With the Rolling Stones they thought of heroin busts and skull rings and Altamont. Then one night the walls of her house came crashing down. Termites had chewed their way through the pine boards and a gust of wind blew the weakened timber down.

Sharon retreated within herself. A grim fatalism smothered her can-do attitude. "What's the point?" she'd say when asked about Chalillo. "There is no point. They're going to do what they want to do. I was foolish to think I could stop them. Or even slow them down." I pointed out that she did, in fact, slow them down. "You came within a single vote of stopping them," I said.

"Yeah, but they're still doing it," she said. Sharon looked at me like I was one of the people who led her on, who allowed her to stroll merrily along on her fool's errand.

"I'm so tired of reading about the destruction of this forest, the loss of that species, trawlers ripping up a coral reef," she told me. "Every month there's more and more. It never stops. Everything is gloom and doom. I'm tired of it. I need to find something that works."

She found no relief in her private life. In one three-week span, her brother's wife was killed in a car accident, then an old personal friend died, then her father followed her mother into the grave. Emotionally, she was spent. "I felt like I was dying inside," she later told me. Sadness turned into depression. She considered leaving the zoo. The "exit Sharon" strategy, she called it.

It was hard to be around her during this time. Little things set her off. One afternoon she and I were in her *oficina* talking about what she was working on to keep her mind off Chalillo. She'd signed on to research jabiru storks living near the Sibun River, which runs a couple of miles east of the zoo, and she was building a new children's playground at the zoo. Then she saw something that broke her grip.

"Look at this!" She held up a copy of *Audubon* magazine with Pale Male on the cover. Pale Male was a celebrated red-tailed hawk that nested on the ledge of a Fifth Avenue apartment building in New York City. "Have you heard about these birds?" I nodded.

"Red-tailed hawks nesting in New York," she said. "They were going to kick them out of their nest but people rose up and protested. They held up signs. They picketed. They stopped traffic! Why? For a *red-tailed hawk*? Please. I could close my eyes and throw a rock and hit a red-tailed hawk." She slammed the magazine on her desk. "This makes me so mad I could cry. CNN's giving them worldwide coverage. Meanwhile down here these scarlet macaws are being wiped out. Wiped out! And nobody cares."

Her eyes welled and her voice cracked. She walked to the door and regained her composure.

"Red-tailed hawk. Which I think is important, and I admire everybody's effort and I'm pleased it got the cover of *Audubon*. But you know what? It pisses me off. I'm sorry about that. But it just— Jesus!"

I told her what I could. I said that what she was doing had mattered. It did make a difference even though she lost. "You started in a hole. You're so far away from the United States and our media."

"What do you mean by that?"

"The reason hawks in New York get media is because they're in New York. People can see them. Belize is not a place a lot of people can see.

"People need a compelling story to latch on to," I said. "Otherwise issues like saving the macaws don't stick in their minds."

"What about *March of the Penguins*?" she said. "People went nuts for those birds. There was so much empathy. And they live in the Antarctic."

We sat there and let a few seconds pass without talking. "Do you think it was all just about politics?" she asked.

I thought for a moment. "It was about a lot of things. Politics. Corruption. Fraud. Geography. Power. One of the things you were up against was a company that didn't have to care about its image," I told her. "It was a big company, but it's small enough, and based in a faraway enough place, that it just didn't have to care. If it was GE, Microsoft, Mitsubishi, it might have turned out differently. Those companies have to care about their public image. Duke had a public image to uphold. Fortis didn't have to care. I was at the company's annual meeting. Their shareholders are hedge fund managers and Canadian retirees. They've never heard of Belize. They don't give a damn about what goes on down here. They care about their dividend, and as long as Fortis looks after that, they're happy.

"We think that sometimes the bigger the company, the harder they are to deal with. But sometimes the bigger companies can have their chi used against them. Look at Duke. Duke got your letters and their executives asked, What the hell are we doing in Belize? So they sent people down here. And in the end Duke decided Belize wasn't worth it. Duke was a company that, from its founding, believed that being a good corporate citizen was part of their culture. And that includes the environment. They were one of the first energy companies to hire a full-time biologist. When you're dealing with that kind of corporate culture, you have a chance to change things. Fortis didn't have that. Fortis's whole corporate culture *was* hydropower. That's what they've done, that's what they do. And once they got their teeth into this there was no stopping them."

Belizeans began learning the hard way that Ralph Fonseca's privatization program would not, in fact, keep utility rates low. Shortly after the Privy Council decision, Fortis raised electricity rates 12 percent. Water rates shot up 17 percent. Phone tolls remained among the highest in the world.

Over the following months, Fonseca's secret contracts and financing schemes began to unravel. A ploy to sell Lord Ashcroft's phone company at a premium to a Florida tycoon* fell apart when the tycoon defaulted on his loan. The whole thing ended up in court, and for most of the next two years nobody really knew who owned the phone company. Meanwhile, another of the Big Wheel's secret contracts leaked its way into the press. In early 2004 Fonseca signed a hush-hush deal with Carnival Cruise Lines giving the company the right to build an enormous new terminal in Belize City. The only problem was that he had already sold exclusive docking rights to Carnival's rival, Royal Caribbean.

Other ministers got fed up. It was one thing to be corrupt; it was another thing to be corrupt and inept. In the summer of 2004, a group led by Godfrey Smith, Mark Espat, and John Briceño banded together—calling themselves the Group of Seven—and went to Prime Minister Musa with an ultimatum. Either Ralph goes or we go, they said.

---

* Although the reasons for the deal were never clear, many Belizeans believed it was a make-up gift to Lord Ashcroft. Ashcroft had bankrolled Said Musa's 2003 reelection despite Musa's move to introduce competition into Ashcroft's monopolized phone market.

Musa said he'd have to think about it.

Eventually, the prime minister negotiated a deal with the Group of Seven. He stripped Fonseca of his finance minister title but didn't kick him out of the cabinet. Things returned to normal for a while.

But then the mother of all scandals hit Belize. After the Novelos bus fiasco, people started asking how the Novelo brothers got that $15 million loan in the first place. The money, it turned out, came from the Development Finance Corporation, a government lending program set up to provide Belizeans with low-interest loans to start a business or buy a home. At least that was how the DFC was supposed to work. Following Said Musa's election in 1999, the Musa-Fonseca Group turned the DFC into their own private piggy bank. The typical scam worked like this. A government crony—call him Mr. Harmon—applies for a $3 million loan to build a resort on Ambergris Caye. The DFC gives Mr. Harmon a ten-year loan at 13 percent. It's a good deal, the banks are charging 19 percent, but that doesn't matter because Harmon isn't going to make any payments. What he does is take the cash and wait a few months. He puts a few thousand dollars into construction to make it look good, then he defaults on the loan. The government repossesses his resort, which is nothing but a cement foundation. The money goes on the government's books as a bad loan, but nobody really cares because it's government money. Meanwhile, Mr. Harmon pockets $3 million cash. There's no jail time because Belize's prosecutors have their hands full dealing with all the pedal-by shootings and machete murders. If he needs to, Mr. Harmon can hire the best lawyers in the country, because now he's got $3 million.

The scheme worked so well that by the end of 2004 the DFC had racked up $50 million in bad loans. More than two-thirds of all DFC loans ended up in default. The annual budget for the entire government of Belize that year was $250 million. The DFC scammers had stolen a sum equal to one-fifth of the nation's yearly budget.

It might not seem unreasonable to assume that at this point international lending institutions like the Inter-American Development Bank and the International Monetary Fund would step in and tell those in charge to knock it off. It's a simple message: Quit funneling development money to your friends. But that's not how these things work. In February 2004, Inter-American Development Bank president Enrique Iglesias visited Belize and gave the country a clean financial bill of health. "Everything looks to be extremely good," he said. Two months later the International Monetary Fund murmured worriedly about the DFC loan defaults and advised "corrective measures" such as wage freezes and tax reform. The IMF thought the best way to solve the kleptomania of Belize's wealthiest cronies was to cut the wages and hike the taxes of Belize's poorest citizens.

Musa and Fonseca agreed with the IMF. Their next budget included a whopping tax hike on everything from tourism to toilet paper to beer.*

Belizeans are notoriously difficult to rile. They have earned their reputation as the most laid-back people in Central America. But even they have a boiling point.

On April 20, 2005, Belize City erupted in riot. It began with a walkout by phone company employees, who were tired of strange men wandering into BTL's headquarters and declaring themselves the new owners. The workers took the phone lines with them. For five days Belize had no phone or Internet service. The strike spread. Students boycotted classes. Government bureaucrats and union workers walked off the job. In Belize City, protesters chanted for Prime Minister Musa's resignation. They blocked the BelCan Bridge. When police threatened them, the protesters sang the Belizean national anthem. Two dozen people were taken to the hospital with injuries. Looters broke into stores and made off with televisions, clothing, and sneakers. Continental and American Airlines canceled flights into Goldson International. Power

---

* Well, not beer, actually. Barry Bowen sells most of the beer in Belize, and he'd written a $500,000 check to reelect Said Musa in 2003. So the beer tax got retracted.

went out across the country. The riots continued that first night and into the next day.

Desperate to stop the uprising, Defence Minister Godfrey Smith called out the Belizean Air Force. The Belizean Air Force consists mainly of one man, Major Ganney Dortch. Most days Major Dorch zips up his green flight suit, hops in his twin-engine Otter, and patrols Belize in search of illegal airstrips, which drug smugglers hide in the jungle. On the riot's second day, Major Dortch took off in his Otter and made a few passes over the angry crowd, which was locked in a standoff with riot police on the Bel-Can Bridge. Ganney Dortch then did something extraordinary. He put on an aerobatics show. Flying low over the crowd, he spun his plane like a corkscrew. After a wide turn over the Caribbean Sea he came back and did a loop-the-loop. People took notice. The rioters settled down into a crowd. The crowd became specta-tors. For ten minutes the riot stopped and an air show broke out. For his finale, Major Dortch executed his signature maneuver, which is to climb straight up and put the Otter into a stall, then plummet silently to earth before pulling out at the last minute. British Forces pilots have seen him do it, and it gives them the creeps. "Every once in a while I'll hear Ganney buzzing by, and I hear that engine go off, and I know what he's doing," a British hel-icopter pilot once told me. "I have to shut the door. I can't bear to listen." Ganney stalled the plane. The Otter hung for a moment, then went into free fall. The crowd gasped. The cops looked sky-ward. The airplane twisted slowly as it raced to the ground. At the last second, just as people were covering their eyes, Ganney started the engine and pulled it out.

Then the riot resumed.

Incredibly, the Musa government survived. The rioters eventually tired and went to bed. The phone workers went back to work. Students went back to class. Ralph Fonseca kept his job.

Sharon was oblivious to the unrest. She didn't know the phones had been knocked out until somebody mentioned it to her two days into the crisis. A week later, as Sharon waited in the airport to catch a flight to Miami for a wildlife conference, a Belizean woman came up to her. "You're the Zoo Lady?"

Sharon nodded.

"I want to thank you," the woman said. "All this going on with government and the protests, it wouldn't have happened if you hadn't done what you did about the dam. You showed everyone it was possible to stand up to government."

CHAPTER 27

AVE YOU EVER SEEN a harpy eagle?" Sharon asked me one day over the phone. Some bird experts with the Peregrine Fund had come by the zoo. They and Sharon got to talking. The Peregrine Fund began years ago as a project to protect peregrine falcons and had expanded to cover a number of birds of prey. Lately they were doing a lot of work with harpy eagles.

"They're the most powerful eagles in the Western Hemisphere," Sharon told me. "They're one of the four largest eagles in the world. The only bird that's bigger is the Philippine eagle, and those birds used to be called Philippine monkey-eating eagles. Because they'd eat monkeys. I mean, Bruce, we're talking about a *big* bird here."

Harpy eagles once thrived from southern Mexico to northern Argentina, but centuries of hunting and deforestation have shrunk their range and dwindled their numbers. Rarely sighted, the birds still exist in Central and South America. Harpy eagles lived in Belize up until the early 1990s. The last known specimen disappeared in 1992.

"Do you know what we're going to do?" she said to me. "We are going to bring the harpy eagle back to Belize." If she couldn't stop the death of the country's scarlet macaws, she would do the next best thing. She would bring another bird back to life.

The Peregrine Fund had a program in Panama that rehabilitated injured harpies and trained captive-bred ones to survive in the wild. If Sharon could find suitable habitat in Belize, they could start releasing the birds. They might survive, they might not. It was worth a try.

She threw herself into the work. The first step was bringing a harpy to the zoo. Fund officials told her they had a bird that might be right for the zoo, a hatchling whose damaged eye made him a poor candidate for wild release. Sharon knew animals couldn't be protected if people didn't know about them. "You put a harpy out there in the Chiquibul Forest, it'll be dead in a couple months," she told me. "People will think it's just another bird and they'll shoot it and eat it. We've got to let the whole country know this bird is something special." She and senior zookeeper Humberto Wohlers designed a harpy eagle exhibit. It was a gorgeous enclosure, lots of space and trees and water and a special ramp so visitors could get up close. When the first bird arrived, Sharon named him Panama, after his place of birth. He was a six-month-old male. "He's blind in one eye, so he'll fit right in here," Sharon said. She fed him by hand every day and spent hours in his cage, talking. The eagle project forced her to rebuild bridges burned during the Chalillo battle. She worked with John Briceño, minister of natural resources, to secure the permits necessary to import harpies and release them on public land. Briceño even showed up for Panama's official unveiling. By then Sharon had posted signs all over the zoo pointing visitors to the harpy's enclosure.

YES! YES!
RIGHT THIS WAY
TO SEE PANAMA
THE FAMOUS
HARPY EAGLE

During a visit in the summer of 2005, I went to meet Panama. Sharon was radiant. "Oh, *Pah-nah-maah*!" she called. The bird screeched back. "Panama, I want you to meet a friend of mine," Sharon said.

The silver-colored eagle landed on a branch two feet from where we were standing. Dear god. Panama was a bear cub with wings. Birds don't have fingers, they have tarsi, and this bird's tarsi were as thick and powerful as a grown man's fingers. His claws were ursine: three-inch knives made for tearing into the vital organs of medium-sized mammals. Panama swiveled his head. Sharon offered him some fresh rat meat.

"The great thing about harpies is that they're an umbrella

species," she said, watching Panama swallow the meat. "They need large areas of forest to hunt and reproduce. To protect them you've got to conserve big forests with a lot of biodiversity. So if you save the harpy, you're saving everything else in the forest. I'm convinced that's the way to go. We can't save animals species by species. We've got to go after big habitats."

I kept Sharon between myself and the bird. "You think they can make it in Belize?" I said.

"We'll see. Down in Panama the main thing they like to eat are two-toed sloths. We don't have those here. But we do have a lot of other things they eat. Iguanas, agoutis, snakes, tayras, deer."

"Deer?"

"They've been known to take deer. Probably small ones. But still."

I took a half step back.

"Oh, Panama won't hurt you. Will you, you big baby. *You big baby.*" Sharon smiled. It was a smile I hadn't seen in a long time.

The dam grew in the valley all that spring and summer. Fuel trucks and flatbeds roared down the Chiquibul road. Chinese dam workers squared off against their Belizean coworkers in Sunday soccer games. Work continued through the rainy season.

I kept tabs on the dam's progress through Donna Hynes, the public relations director at Fortis. "They say it may be completed by the fall," she told me.

I decided to make one last effort to see Chalillo before the dam gates closed. My previous attempts had petered out in a string of unreturned phone calls. Those inquiries had been to BEL, and it occurred to me that going through Fortis corporate headquarters might be more productive. Not returning phone calls was what Belizean business was all about, but BEL officials hopped to when requests came down from the St. John's office. I sent a request to Donna Hynes and she responded promptly and affirmatively. With her blessing, I went to Lynn Young, and he suggested I drive out to the site myself. On a Wednesday morning in August I rented a car in Belize City and did just that.

~

I turned off the main road and followed a sign down the Chalillo spur. At a checkpoint outside the dam site, a security guard looked over my credentials and wrote my name on a clipboard. He glanced over a copy of the e-mail message from Lynn Young, then lifted the gate and waved me through.

When I crested the ridge and caught a full view of the structure, now nearly complete, the sight stopped me cold. The lush green valley I'd paddled with Sharon three years earlier was gone. The soft low contours of the valley stood out in stark relief, like a row furrowed for planting. The topography stood out because the land itself had been skinned and scorched. From ridgeline to ridgeline, all that remained of the lush riverine jungle were charred stumps and blackened bits of palm frond. The burnscape ran upriver as far as the eye could see, a mile or more, until the river bent north and disappeared.

I had known this would happen. It had to happen. It was the environmentally proper thing to do, actually—reservoirs have to be cleared prior to inundation or they'll produce toxic levels of methane, methyl mercury, and other compounds. Even so, seeing it laid bare I couldn't help but feel sick. On the near side of the river, a dam worker was gathering the last of the brush into a small smoky bonfire. Looking closer, I saw others doing the same thing. Whatever this operation had once been, now it came down to a simple work order: seven men, seven machetes, seven matchboxes.

Out of the blackened valley rose the Chalillo Dam, step-toothed and gleaming white. Never mind the nomenclature of the hydroelectric industry: This dam was *big*. A wall of reinforced concrete began at a point midway down the ridge and stretched across a quarter-mile gap. The upriver side was flush and smooth, a formidable 150-foot wall. On the downriver side, the dam sloped steeply away from its thin topsection in a staircase of five-foot-tall blocks. The Chalillo Dam contained within it a half decade of passion, hatred, rancor, and strife. As an aesthetic object, though, it was brutal and magnificent. Fortis had raised a dam that in size and design resembled an ancient Mayan temple stuck in the middle of the Macal River.

A Chinese engineer introduced himself as Mr. Huang. Mr. Huang led me into the gray concrete bowels of the dam. Down two flights of stairs we came upon the intake pipes. Mr. Huang indicated that water from the intake pipes would blast into the turbine blades. His English was so hopelessly mangled that I began miming the action myself, rotating my index fingers around each other, to indicate that I understood. "Yes," Mr. Huang said, and smiled.

The turbines were enclosed in concrete cylinders. The dials and gauges emerging from the turbine housing were all imported from China. The writing on them was in Chinese. I wanted to ask Mr. Huang how the Belizeans who ran the dam were supposed to read the dials, but he was already out of the room and up the stairs.

"Shall we go to the top of the dam?" I suggested. Mr. Huang nodded.

"It is very narrow," he told me as we neared the top. Eighteen feet, to be exact. Just wide enough for a pickup truck to cross. Mr. Huang and I stood on the fresh concrete and took in the view. Despite the 150-foot height, the workers hadn't yet installed a guardrail; bits of scaffolding were all that kept us from pitching over the edge. Although the dam hadn't yet officially closed, a reservoir had already begun to form. It was as ugly as advertised. Dirty water, the color of iced tea, sloshed at the dam's base. The water ran through an intake pipe and exited on the other side of the dam, where downstream fish, plants, and people would draw on it for sustenance. "Water goes back for fifteen kilometers, maybe more," Mr. Huang told me. Tree stumps, branches, palm fronds, and odd bits of debris gunked up the growing lake. The machete-and-matchsticks men were still clearing the hillside. I pointed them out to Mr. Huang.

"Too much forest litter in the water still," he said. The men were working to clear the area before more water rose, he explained. "Not good for the water if not clean." He gestured with his hands. Understand?

Yes, I nodded. I understood.

At this height I noticed something odd about the dam. It was kinked. When you stood on top at the southern bank and looked across the river, the design revealed itself. The dam went straight across and then at the two-thirds point it doglegged left. I asked Mr. Huang why. "The rock over here," he said, indicating the southern bank, "much better than rock on other side." The other side was where Brian Holland had uncovered a slight fault more than two years earlier. So they angled the dam to anchor that side more solidly.

Mr. Huang walked me back to my car. I gave him my business card and told him to look me up if he ever got to Seattle. The prospect excited him. "Seattle?" he said. "They need Chinese engineers there maybe?"

I told him I didn't know. I asked him how much longer he expected to be in Belize.

"Hard to say," he told me. "My manager, he's been here more than two years. He wants to finish the job and go home."

I bade Mr. Huang good-bye, got in my car, and raised a cloud of dust.

On a whim, I turned left at the Chiquibul road and drove all the way to Caracol. The ancient Mayan city was nearly deserted. I strolled the grassy compound, wandering through the limestone ball courts and climbing the thick white blocks of the Caana temple, which rises 145 feet above the central plaza. At the height of its power in the seventh century A.D., Caracol held twice the population of modern-day Belize City. It defeated the great city of Tikal not once but twice. Thirteen hundred years later, we can stand before the city's limestone glyphs and see Caracol still boasting of those victories. This is the kind of place where professors recite "Ozymandias" aloud—*"Look on my works, ye mighty, and despair!" / Nothing beside remains. Round the decay / Of that colossal wreck, boundless and bare. . . .* Even the mightiest among us return to dust, they say. Nothing remains but these shattered fragments of their kingdom.

But that's not really the point, is it? These shattered fragments *remain*—that's the point. We look upon the magnificent temples and stelae and ball courts of Caracol in awe. There's no despair here. The Maya built something astounding and permanent. Look on our works, ye mighty, and revere. The ancient Maya speak to the twenty-first century through those temples and say: We did something amazing here.

What will our descendants think when they come upon Chalillo? When they scrape away the deep layer of dirt covering its stepping-stone façade, what will they make of the dogleg design, the Chinese gauges, the long-stopped turbines? What will they make of the skeletons and fossils of birds long gone? Will they connect the two?

That evening Sharon stopped by. She came draped in a slinky black dress, something you'd wear to a gallery opening. I asked her where she was headed. She shrugged. "Just out for a walk," she said.

She told me about a baby tapir who'd just arrived at the zoo. "Humberto, one of our keepers, heard about some people out by the border keeping it as a pet," she said. "He went out and talked to them and found out they thought it was a paca, which people are fond of eating. They were going to kill it but the neck was too tough to cut. So they kept it as a pet. Humberto convinced them to let the zoo have it, so now I'm raising another baby tapir. I'd forgotten how much fun they are."

She asked about the dam visit.

"I'm glad you weren't there," I said. "It would've killed you."

She nodded. I had offered to bring Sharon along on the dam tour, but she declined.

"It was pretty overwhelming," I said.

She'd heard about the slash-and-burn clearing. "Is it growing back?"

"The idea is not to have it grow back," I said. "It's worse for the river if it grows back before the reservoir floods it."

"They asked me to work on the macaw nesting boxes," she said. "I said no way. They're not going to work, and I don't want to legitimize the dam in any way."

Nesting boxes were a sore point with Sharon. As part of the

dam's environmental compliance plan, BEL agreed to mount artificial macaw nests around the edge of the reservoir. They contracted the nesting-box project to Pepe Garcia, the Belize Audubon Society president who had pushed the BAS to support the dam. To Sharon, mounting nesting boxes was like slapping a bandage on an amputation. Nobody knew whether the macaws would use the fake nests. Experiments in other countries had yielded mixed results. In Costa Rica, researchers mounted thirty-eight artificial nests in an existing macaw brooding site between 1995 and 2000. Over five years a total of eight chicks successfully fledged from the artificial nests. At Chalillo the macaws faced daunting odds. If the nesting boxes succeeded, the macaws still had to survive the threat of pet trade poachers—who now had a dam access road leading straight to the chicks.

Sharon and I listened to a pair of chachalacas *churr* to each other from nearby trees.

"So what's up with the harpy project?" I said.

"It's going great," she said. She'd released the first harpy into the wild a couple of months earlier in the Chiquibul National Forest. Signals from its radio collar indicated the bird was thriving along the Belize-Guatemala border. "And guess what? When I was in Washington, D.C., a while back I found out about this painter, John Ruthven, who's got a bunch of work in the National Gallery. His bald eagle paintings are in the White House. He's the greatest bird artist since John James Audubon. It turns out he did a portrait of a harpy eagle years ago. I've been talking with him about what we're doing to bring the bird back to Belize, and do you know what? John Ruthven is donating a print of that painting to Belize." She looked at me as if to say, What do you think of that!

"Where are you going to put it?"

"That's the thing," she said. "The humidity here will destroy it. We're trying to find a climate-controlled room for it. I offered it to the U.S. embassy. You know, they've got those air-conditioned offices in Belize City. They turned me down. I asked them why. Do you know what they said to me? 'It might contain a wiretap. Or a bomb.' A bomb! Where the hell am I going to hide a bomb in a flat painting?

"So here's what I decided to do," she said. "We're building an art gallery at the zoo. Taking part of the reptile house, sealing it off, and bringing in special lighting, air-conditioning, and a dehumidifier. I've got a big-shot art photographer coming down next month, he wants to spend three weeks shooting the jaguars and he's got some serious bucks, so that'll help pay for the gallery. And here's the best part. We've got to have it done by November because John Ruthven himself is coming down to dedicate it. Not only that. I talked to the Peregrine Fund folks in Panama and it looks like we've got another bird ready to go into the wild. I'm going to take it out into the bush with Ruthven and we're going to release it together."

She looked out over the darkening savannah. "I'm feeling real good about life right now."

CHAPTER 28

*N*EAR THE END OF 2005 I returned to Belize for the last time. John Ruthven had accepted Sharon's invitation to witness a harpy eagle return to the wild. "The Peregrine Fund folks have lined up a bird for us, and we're going to hang Ruthven's painting in the new art gallery," she told me. "I can't wait to see that bird."

At the Belize airport, I picked up a copy of *The Reporter*. "ELEC-TRICITY RATES NEED 20% HIKE, SAYS BEL," the front page said. In the main terminal the government had installed a billboard touting the success of its wildlife conservation programs. What made me stop and drop my bag was the illustration behind the text. It was a giant photo of a scarlet macaw.

Sharon picked me up wearing a pea-green jumpsuit and a Pere-grine Fund ballcap. "They weren't going to allow us to move the harpy from Panama to Belize because of this avian flu thing," she told me. "I told them, come *on*, guys. The bird's been tested, she's clean, what's the hangup? I've got John Ruthven coming in for this, I've got contributors coming in tomorrow. . . ."

She had a big week planned. "We've got a cocktail party tonight, over at Barry Bowen's brewery," she said. "Then we head up to Rio Bravo for the harpy release, and on Friday we're opening up the art gallery with John's harpy print." A couple of Sharon's friends were arriving on a later flight, so we picked up my bags and relaxed on the observation deck. I asked her about the bandage on her arm.

"It happened with Gregory Colbert, that photographer I was telling you about," she said. "He came down to shoot the jaguars and tapirs. It ended up fabulous, but when he first came in I didn't know what to make of the guy. What he does is he comes in with this hot Spanish supermodel and sort of drapes her over a tapir in the middle of the pond. Which is okay with the tapir. But then he wants jaguars and ocelots.

"So two days before Colbert arrives, Ollie the ocelot, who I always hand-feed, jumps at me and sinks his teeth deep into my forearm and won't let go. I mean it *really* hurt. I eventually pried his jaws open and put a bandage on it. I should have gone to the hospital, but who's got the time?

"The day of the shoot arrives. The photographer and his crew want a shot of a jaguar, in a dory, on water, gazing at the Spanish model dangling near the end of the boat. We had one day to get the shot. So I bring in Pete. Pete's an old jaguar that Richard Foster's used for years in his films. He's like an arthritic ninety-year-old man. I bring Pete out, but he's not interested in getting into the water or the boat.

"Then I come up with an idea. We've got a zoo dog named Gordo. One of Gordo's favorite things to do is to go up to Pete's enclosure and tease him. Gordo really gets under Pete's skin. So I call Gordo over to the dory. He hops in. Pete sees Gordo and realizes that finally, after all these years, he's got an open shot at Gordo. No fence between them.

"Pete the geriatric springs into action. He comes straight for me and Gordo. The only thing I could do was jump into the pond with Gordo, who by this time was starting to panic. In that state of panic, his claws found my Ollie wounds and ripped them open again. Blood everywhere.

"I was able to keep Gordo with me. Pete stayed in the dory, eyeing Gordo the whole time. I moved up to the bow, near the model. And *click,* that's when Colbert got the shot. Pete looks like he's gazing at the model—who's doing okay because I don't think she knows what a jaguar can do to a person—but he's really looking at Gordo and me, in the water behind the boat."

Sharon's friends Gil and Lillian Boese arrived on the afternoon flight. Gil was the director of the Zoological Society of Milwaukee and a founder of Birds Without Borders, an international organization that studies migratory birds. He and Lillian have worked on conservation projects in Central America and Africa for nearly thirty years. They supported Sharon in the zoo's early years. "I used to slip her twenty bucks so she could get something to eat," Lillian told me on the ride back to the zoo.

Later that night we met up with John Ruthven at a cocktail party at Barry Bowen's brewery. Bowen maintains a working English pub on the second floor of the Belikin Beer offices. That Sharon chose to host a party in Ruthven's honor in the heart of Bowen's empire indicated how well she had integrated back into Belizean society. "It's the harpy project," she told me. "It's something everybody can get behind. It's not divisive like Chalillo."

A gentle, soft-spoken man in his seventies, John Ruthven wasn't frail, but he moved slowly. He told us that the harpy portrait came about as part of his series on the four great forest eagles. The other three were the African crowned eagle, the New Guinea harpy eagle, and the Philippine eagle. "When I painted the harpy eagle I had only one print made of the finished work," Ruthven said. "That's the one I'm donating to the Belize Zoo."

His words drew a polite round of applause from the guests, a typically eclectic Belizean crowd. Ganney Dortch, the one-man Belizean Air Force, stood in one corner. British helicopter pilots, American aid workers, and staffers from Belize's Department of the Environment gathered around him. The new American ambassador to Belize, a Colorado law professor and a noted fundraiser for George W. Bush, stood by the bar. Kevin Bowen, Barry's son, answered proudly when I asked when his ancestors had arrived in Belize. "1750!" he said. "They were pirates!"

As Ruthven finished speaking, Sharon motioned me over. "Do you think I should bring out my guitar?" she whispered. "I wrote a special song for the harpy."

"Don't you dare," I said. "You need these people to donate money."

"I'll have you know many people enjoy my singing," Sharon said.

A man wearing gold chains came away from the bar carrying two beers. He bumped me as he passed. "Whoa! Excuse me," he said. He introduced himself as Bill Motto. A midwestern industrialist, Motto made his fortune with a brilliant if rather odd product. Years ago he noticed that hospitals had no easy way to

transport stool samples from exam room to lab. So he designed a
convenient hygienic system that became the international standard. His children called him the Crap King. The Crap King was
John Ruthven's patron, protector, and friend.

Sharon spent the next day filling out paperwork to get the harpy
through customs, so I hopped in a truck with Gil and Lillian
Boese and we went looking for a recently discovered cave in the
Runaway Creek Nature Preserve.

Runaway Creek was one of the best kept secrets in Belize. Back
in the 1990s, years before Chalillo became an issue, Meb Cutlack
mentioned to Sharon that he was looking to sell some of his land.
Cutlack owned six thousand acres of raw savannah and jungle
about ten miles west of the zoo. A consortium of Chinese investors wanted to buy the land and plow it into orange groves.
Cutlack needed the money but he didn't want to see the bush bull-
dozed. Sharon contacted Gil Boese, who suggested turning the
land into a nature reserve. Working with conservationists in the
United States, Boese came up with the money and met Cutlack's
price. A sign at the entrance to the site, which lies east of the zoo,
now marks it as the Runaway Creek Nature Preserve.

"Belize likes to talk about the fact that we've designated forty
percent of the country as 'protected' areas," Sharon told me, "but
we've all seen how that protection is dropped whenever some
minister wants to develop a certain area." Sharon had waged her
war against Chalillo with NRDC tactics: using the courts and
the media to force the government to uphold its own laws. With
Runaway Creek, she and the Boeses were trying the Nature Conservancy strategy: buying up private land and preserving it themselves.

It sounded easy: Buy up raw wilderness and leave it alone. But
it wasn't that simple. Wilderness preservation costs a lot of money.
First, there are poachers. Runaway Creek, named after escaped
slaves who took refuge along its banks in the eighteenth century,
flowed in a lush, overgrown plain between low limestone foothills.
Jaguars, peccaries, spider monkeys, and deer flourished in its

roadless expanse. Local men often hunted the area to feed their families. "I stopped one poacher out here a few months ago," Gil told me as we drove. "I'd heard some of the locals were coming out to hunt and selling the meat to the local butcher. So I asked this guy about it. Turns out he *was* the local butcher. He'd come out to restock his shelves."

Gil worked out an agreement with the butcher and hired two local hunters to patrol the area. That meant he had to pay them. But as far as money went, paying the rangers was the least of his worries. The government had appraised the reserve at twice what he'd paid for it. Under the Musa government's new tax rates, the owners of the Runaway Creek Nature Preserve would have to pay $10,000 in property tax—a $9,000 increase over the previous year. "The frustrating thing is, they appraised it using a 'total destruction' model," Lillian Boese told me. "In other words, they totaled up what it would be worth if we leveled everything, sold the timber, and turned it into a gravel pit."

We picked our way through thickets of fiddlewood and bay leaf, taking care not to touch the trunk of the notorious give-and-take palm, which bristles with inch-long thorns. David Tzul and Reynold Cal, the Runaway Creek rangers, led the way. Like most Belizeans who worked on the land, Tzul and Cal were phenomenal naturalists. Over the past few months they had identified 304 species of native and migratory birds within the preserve's boundaries.

"Watch your head," Tzul warned us as we passed through a thickly forested section. He pointed up to a troop of spider monkeys eyeing us warily from branches forty feet up. One of the monkeys screeched and threw a seed pod at us. We kept moving.

We slogged through a knee-deep swamp and regained dry land. Water sloshed out of our boots. David Tzul stopped and pointed out a jaguar track. "Fresh but not today," he said. "Maybe last night."

Once we reached the cave, our eyes took time to adjust to the dim light. The sheer size of the place overwhelmed us. Damp and cool, the cave was as big as a concert hall. Here and there lay evidence of past inhabitation. Lillian turned up a pottery shard. Gil pointed out a glass bottle leaning against a boulder. "That one goes back to 1760," he said. "We had an archaeologist date it." David Tzul pointed out where a jaguar had recently dragged in a peccary and eaten it. Bats clung to the ceiling overhead.

That night Sharon joined Gil and Lillian and some others to talk about what to do with Runaway Creek. Ideally, they said, they'd keep it absolutely pristine. But with the government's new property taxes, they'd have to bring in some serious cash just to break even. To keep it undeveloped, they'd have to develop it.

Gil looked around the room. "Anybody got any ideas?"

The next morning Sharon was all smiles. "We've got the bird," she said. "She's gorgeous. Just like Panama."

We drove out to the Rio Bravo Conservation Area, a 230,000-acre nature reserve near the border where Belize intersects Guatemala and the Mexican state of Quintana Roo. Along the way Sharon told Claudia and me about her latest scheme.

"I was talking to Bill Motto last night," she said. "He told me about these card games. He knows how to play them. He can go into any casino in the world and double his money. He never loses. He plays blackjack and he's got this system. So get this. Bill and I made a plan yesterday. After we release the harpy and get back to town, he and I are going to go down to the Princess Casino and take them for all they're worth." She was proud of herself. "It's perfect. We'll fund the rest of the new art gallery with my casino winnings."

Claudia and I exchanged a look. "Sharon," I said, "you should not do this. This is a very very bad idea."

She looked at me like I was crazy. "Bill can't lose! He's got a system."

"Systems don't work," I said. "The thing about Bill is, he's got enough money to ride out a cold streak. He can just go on playing all night until he starts winning. You'll go in there with a hundred bucks and be wiped out in ten minutes."

"Bruce," she explained to me, "Bill has a *system*."

Claudia weighed in. "Sharon, how do you think those casinos make all their money? Off of people like you."

Sharon was unconvinced. "Well. I'll just go in with a couple of hundred dollars."

"In cash," I said. "No checks. No credit cards. You don't want to tell everyone at the zoo you blew their paychecks playing blackjack with the Poopmaster."

"Crap King," Sharon said. "And he has a system. You'll see. I'll be calling you in a week and the sound you hear will be my thumb strumming through a stack of bills."

We drove on for another half hour in relative silence. Iguanas darted across the road. Wood storks drifted in the air above cattle pastures. After a while the scent of burning rubber floated into the van.

"What's that smell?" I said.

Claudia turned to Sharon. "Are you driving with the parking brake on again?" she said. "Sharon!"

In a world filled with corrupt ministers and paper parks,* the Rio Bravo Conservation Area is a small miracle. It's a conservation program that actually works. Hidden away in a quiet corner of Belize, the quarter-million-acre reserve functions as a scientific research station, a forestry laboratory, and a rough-hewn ecotourism destination for those intrepid enough to find it. The reserve, which encompasses vast swaths of subtropical forest and savannah, came into being in the late eighties when Barry Bowen agreed to sell a portion of his vast estate to the government of Belize for conservation purposes. More acreage was added with the help of NGOs like the Nature Conservancy. Still more land was added in the nineties with money brought in through carbon se-

* Paper parks are conservation areas that exist on maps but aren't protected in practice. They make governments look good in the eyes of international lenders, tourists, and environmentalists, but they're essentially a form of greenwashing.

questration programs. American power companies like Wisconsin Electric and Edison Power offset the greenhouse gases emitted by their coal-burning power plants by donating money to Rio Bravo. Although the reserve exists at the cutting edge of conservation, its funding is strictly hand to mouth. Ten rangers patrol a quarter-million acres with no weapons and a single truck.

We rendezvoused with the rest of our party at La Milpa Field Station, the Rio Bravo headquarters, a small compound of thatch-roof cabanas on a grassy footprint in the middle of the jungle. There's a kitchen and a meeting hall and a bookshelf full of well-thumbed field guides. Wild turkeys peck in the short grass. White-lipped peccaries root at the edge of the compound.

After lunch, Sharon joined Angel Muela and Marta Curti, biologists with the Peregrine Fund, for a briefing on the next morning's harpy eagle release. "Tomorrow morning we'll drive out to a little logging road and then walk about a kilometer and a half to a small clearing," Sharon said. "Then we'll slowly open the transfer kennel and let the bird out."

As the eagles are captive-bred, they have to be taught how to eat and eventually fend for themselves. For months after each bird's release, volunteer researchers hang dead rats on wires to keep the eagles from starving. "After a while they get the hang of it," Ryan Phillips explained to me. Phillips was a young volunteer field biologist from California. "One day we'll see them next to a fresh kill and know they're on their way." Phillips and four colleagues went out in the bush for days on end tracking the reintroduced harpies using satellite transmitters.

"Our bird will be the seventh harpy released in Belize and the first female ever," Sharon said. "We could have a mating pair within three years."

Twenty-pound birds with seven-foot wingspans, harpies aren't great fliers. They perch on sturdy branches high in the canopy, waiting for prey to appear below. The bird's primary method of attack is to pierce and squeeze their prey around the neck or vital organs until death. Harpies kill sloths by choking them, but sometimes they'll just pick up the sloth and drop it to the ground, killing it with the fall. They also eat porcupines, howler monkeys, and collared peccaries.

Late that afternoon I caught up with Sharon at the edge of the compound. "I'm going for a walk," she said. "Want to come along?"

I nodded. Twilight had touched down but it looked as if we might have another half hour before dark. We walked down a dirt road. Our shoes left light impressions on the damp earth.

At a clearing we came upon a great spreading oak tree. Oropendola nests dripped from its branches. "How many do you count?" I said.

"Fifteen, twenty," said Sharon. We listened to the birds gackle. We kept on walking.

Sharon got to talking about birds. The harpy eagles made her so happy, she said.

"A year ago I didn't think I'd ever feel like this about a bird again," she said. "Not after the macaws."

Over the past few weeks Chalillo's reservoir had risen to inundate the macaw nesting sites along the Macal and Raspaculo. It was November, and the year's newborn chicks had long since left the nest. The birds could still be seen feeding in the hills above Red Bank, but they seemed to be staying away from the dam and its reservoir.

"You know, the last two great auks were shot by men who knew they were killing the last two," she told me. "They shot them, crushed the last egg, and sold the bodies to collectors. That amazes me. When I think about people who take the last of a species like the scarlet macaw, I wonder what lets them do it."

I thought about what keeps most people from *not* doing it. "Partly it's something we learn as kids," I said. "Long-term benefit is better than short-term gain. It's something we know intellectually but it's hard to resist the impulse. It's a form of altruism. It's saying, I won't take this even though I could—even though I want to—because I want others to share in its glory. It's something we try to teach children. Not to take and destroy by taking, but to let things be."

We walked farther down the road. At a muddy spot we turned around and headed home.

"You know, with all this harpy eagle stuff, you're going to earn yourself a new name," I told her. "They're going to start calling you the Bird Lady."

That raised a smile.

"Why do birds fascinate us?" I asked her.

Sharon shrugged. "They fly. We don't. We're jealous."

I said there had to be more to it than that.

"They're graceful," she said. "Beautiful. I think we respond to an animal that cares for its young so fully. It reaches the hearts of people. Why do you think?"

"I think we respond to their beauty. I think part of it is the fact that they've got access to a world beyond us. They're up there in the air, where we can't go. They're like sea creatures that way. We can't see most sea creatures, though. We can look up and see birds in the sky. They go into a world we can see and yet can't access. They go through that glass window keeping us out. They're so fragile, yet we can't grasp them. All those things."

We returned past the oak tree. The setting sun turned the branches and oropendola nests into a lacy black silhouette.

"They could take this away from you, too," I said.

"Who take what?"

"Government. Shut the harpy project down."

"Nahh," she said. "No way. And even if they did, I'd find something else. You don't stop. If you lose a battle, that doesn't mean you stop. You keep fighting. You find other battles. The work to save what's left of nature is endless. You can really get down and depressed. But you can't stop and stand aside and let the wheels keep rolling in the wrong direction."

We reached the edge of the compound. Ryan and some other young biologists were playing a game of Ultimate Frisbee. "Sharon!" they called. "Come on. We need another player!" She kicked off her shoes and ran across the grass to join them.

After dinner that night, Claudia called the zoo to get her messages.

"One you should know about," she told Sharon. "The American ambassador left a message saying he's sorry he can't make it up for the bird release because he's going to the dam opening."

"The dam's opening?" she said. "When?"

"Tomorrow," I said. I'd known about it for a few days but hadn't said anything to Sharon. No sense spoiling the harpy release. "They're having everyone up for a dedication ceremony. Stan Marshall, Musa and Fonseca, Lynn Young, Joseph Sukhnandan. I hear they might trot out George Price."

"Funny, I didn't get an invitation," Sharon said. She looked at me and smiled. "Screw 'em. We've got a harpy eagle to release."

We all got up the next morning and ate breakfast and piled into the van. Angel and Marta followed in a truck, carrying the harpy eagle in a kennel in the back seat. It was a little past ten in the morning. Opening ceremonies were just getting under way at Chalillo.

We hiked down an old overgrown logging road. Vines draped down from acacia trees and gumbo limbos. Spider monkeys swung in branches above us. It was a dank and hot morning and all of us were sweating.

We gathered at a small clearing at the edge of the forest and watched Sharon, Angel, and Marta position the closed kennel. John Ruthven clasped his hands. Angel cautiously opened the kennel door and stepped away.

Nothing happened. The bird cowered in the kennel. Angel gently rocked and tapped it from behind. Then at once the harpy emerged, wheeled at us, and spread her great wings.

We drew in our breath. The bird rotated her silvery head, crouched once, and flew to a branch twenty feet above. She ruffled her feathers audibly. I caught a glimpse of white feathers under the dark black cloak. Then the bird shat.

"I love it when they poop," Sharon said. She hugged John Ruthven and leaned over to me.

"Look at that magnificent bird," she said. And then, more to the eagle than to me: "Go now." In a whisper, she said "Fly," and the bird flew.

NEARLY A CENTURY BEFORE Sharon Matola began fighting the Chalillo Dam, a remarkably similar battle took place in the American West.

In 1900, San Francisco needed more water. The growing port city's three hundred thousand citizens demanded more than private companies could supply. So the mayor commissioned a study of nearby watersheds. The consultants identified the most attractive site for a dam and reservoir: the Hetch Hetchy Valley, a spectacular mountain valley 190 miles east of San Francisco in California's Sierra Nevada. There was only one problem. The Hetch Hetchy Valley was located inside Yosemite National Park. The Sierra Club described it as the Yosemite Valley's little sister, "a great and wonderful feature of the Park," full of magnificent groves, flowery meadows, and popular camping grounds.

John Muir, by then a well-known naturalist, writer, and conservationist, led the fight to stop the dam. "Dam Hetch Hetchy!" he wrote. "As well dam for water tanks the people's cathedrals and churches, for no holier temple has ever been consecrated by the heart of man." His Sierra Club argued that invading a national park for private water use "would, to a great extent, defeat the purpose and nullify the effect of the law creating the Park." Alternatives were available, Muir pointed out. Other watersheds could be tapped. The only reason San Francisco wanted Hetch Hetchy was because it was the city's lowest-cost option.

Muir defeated the dam, for a while. President Theodore Roosevelt's secretary of the interior denied the city's application to develop the valley. Then the great San Francisco earthquake and fire of 1906 destroyed the city. Proponents of Hetch Hetchy seized the moment. San Francisco would not have burned, they claimed, if Hetch Hetchy Valley water had been available.

Nearly all the city's water mains had been broken by the earth-quake, but no matter. The city found allies in Congress and the White House, and in 1908 a new interior secretary gave the dam the green light. San Francisco started raising money for construction.

Faced with the imminent flooding of the valley, John Muir tried a desperate ploy. In 1909 he invited newly elected president William Howard Taft to spend a day with him in the Hetch Hetchy Valley. Taft accepted. Muir's plan worked. Taft came, he saw, he turned against the dam. San Francisco's great reservoir scheme stalled for four more years.

Taft's successor, Woodrow Wilson, rekindled the dam fight by appointing San Francisco's former city attorney, Franklin Lane, as his interior secretary. Lane immediately pressed for the dam's construction. After a year of politicking, a bill authorizing the construction of a Hetch Hetchy dam was approved by Congress and signed by President Wilson. Construction of the O'Shaughnessy Dam took ten years, but John Muir never saw it completed. He died in 1914 at the age of seventy-six, one year after Wilson authorized the flooding of Muir's beloved valley. In environmental circles they often say the old man died of a broken heart.

John Muir lost the battle over Hetch Hetchy, but his valiant defeat inspired thousands of others to fight ten thousand more campaigns. Hetch Hetchy is commonly regarded as the beginning of the modern American environmental movement. Imagine that: One of the greatest social awakenings of the past century started when a few people fought a dam and lost.

The Macal River valley is no Hetch Hetchy. Or is it? It may be for Belize and Central America. We'll know in ten or twenty years. The issues today are more complicated. The weight of history and colonialism can't be denied. The idea of an outside group like the NRDC coming down to a poor developing country and "telling us what to do," as one Belizean put it, makes many environmentalists uneasy. A certain amount of corruption was endemic to John Muir's time, as it is to Sharon Matola's time. Hush-hush deals were signed in back rooms. Some men were made wealthy. Others lost a big piece of their heart.

In his classic essay "The Tragedy of the Commons," Garrett Hardin offered a principle that I often found helpful in navigating the competing claims that surrounded Chalillo. "The morality of an act," Hardin wrote, "is a function of the state of the system at the time it is performed." Shooting a hundred passenger pigeons while millions fly overhead is not an unconscionable crime. Killing the last surviving great auk and selling its body is. John Muir fought the flooding of Hetch Hetchy during a time of great abundance. Wondrous scenes of natural beauty abounded in the American West of 1900, although many were already succumbing to development. Men of his age firmly believed in what former U.S. interior secretary Stewart Udall once called the "myth of superabundance," the idea that the trees in the forest and the fish in the sea are so limitless that the greatest efforts of man could never deplete them.

Sharon Matola fought the construction of the Chalillo Dam at a time when the system was crashing. Animals like the scarlet macaw are disappearing at unheard-of rates because humans are turning their homes into reservoirs and coffee plantations. Habitat destruction doesn't usually happen on a scale that makes headlines. It happens acre by acre, often in remote and unknown places like the Macal River valley of Belize. It happens because too many people are willing to serve up half-truths, erase fault lines, and rig studies in order to get paid. It happens because too few people have the courage or capacity to stand against powerful institutions on behalf of powerless creatures like red seed-eating birds.

The state of the system in the early twenty-first century was also this: The world has more than seventy years of experience with mammoth concrete dams. We know that they kill rivers. We know that they often serve as boondoggles for corrupt governments. The NRDC's position in the Chalillo battle wasn't perfect. But consider the alternative. Is it better for First World citizens to withhold our hard-won experience and scientific knowledge from our Third World counterparts simply to avoid the specter of postcolonial guilt? We built easeful lives of luxury here in the United States, but our environment paid a high price. The developing world pioneered the concept of technological leapfrogging by bypassing land-line phones and moving straight to cellular service. The same idea must be applied in the environmental realm. Others can get to where we are, and they don't have to take the same steep mountain passes. There are wider, easier, and better roads now.

People like Sharon are rare and strange and sometimes aggravating. They don't calm choppy waters. They barge in and stir things up and make people frown when they'd rather smile. But sometimes all that smiling acts as cover for a lot of wicked acts. For a good portion of my life I believed that a law of benevolent action held sway in the world. This law maintained that if you did the right thing and worked hard, eventually things would work out; that the world generally trended toward fairness, decency, and wisdom. But of course the world doesn't work that way. The people who learn that lesson through crushing experience and still refuse to bow to it astound me. They go on fighting, again and again and again. These people aren't perfect. They aren't simple heroes. They are complex human beings. And we need them. Because without them the world would be lost.

The Chalillo Dam was officially commissioned on November 15, 2005.

The 150-foot-high dam required 200,000 cubic yards of concrete to retain 157 million cubic yards of water. In early cost-benefit analyses, BEL and Fortis calculated that a 6-megawatt dam would be economically feasible at a construction cost of $25 million. According to Fortis, the dam's final bill came to $34 million. At maximum capacity, Chalillo produces 6 megawatts of power. Its reservoir keeps the 25-megawatt powerhouse at the Mollejon Dam working year-round.

Said Musa's government continues to borrow money to paper over its incompetence and graft. Despite frequent calls for his ouster, Ralph Fonseca remains Musa's chief minister and the most powerful man in Belize.

By the end of 2005, Belize's debt level had reached 100 percent of its GDP, which meant Musa had borrowed more money than it was possible to pay back through the combined labor of every citizen of Belize for an entire year.

Musa sought debt relief, blaming his country's financial calamity on the weather. Hurricanes, he said, had devastated Belize's economy.

BEL continues to be a profit center for its parent company, Fortis.

In 2005, BEL recorded a record profit of nearly $10 million on revenues of $60 million.

BEL and its sister subsidiary, BELCO, continue to seek new sources of energy within Belize. BEL has signed a power purchase agreement with Belize Sugar Industries (BSI), which will supply BEL with 13 megawatts of power from burning bagasse. In 2006 BEL signed a new power-purchase agreement with CFE, the Mexican national power utility. Because of the volatility of the natural gas market, the new contract calls for a fluctuating price based on the daily cost of fuel. BEL estimated that the new contract would raise the wholesale price of Mexican power by as much as 59 percent. The company hopes to purchase less Mexican power when the third dam at Vaca Falls comes online in 2009.

Belize's demand for electricity did not rise as fast as BEL planners anticipated. By early 2007, peak demand had grown to 63 megawatts, a 6 percent annual increase over the previous five years, or about half as much growth as BEL had planned for.

In 2006, Fortis released an environmental impact assessment for the Vaca Dam, six miles downstream from Chalillo. The proposed two-hundred-foot-high structure would flood 150 acres of subtropical forest and produce 18 megawatts of power. Fortis estimates construction cost at $50 million. Amec was not hired to produce the dam's EIA.

Occasional blackouts continue to hit Belize's national power grid.

~

Shortly after Chalillo closed, the quality of Macal River water downstream of the dam began deteriorating.

Mick and Lucy Fleming installed a $10,000 water filtration system at Chaa Creek Resort Lodge so they and their guests could continue to drink and shower. With its sediment trapped in the reservoir, the river turned hungry and began scouring sediment from its banks below the dam. At some resorts downstream of Chalillo, the Macal has swept away sandy bankside beaches that had been a natural part of the landscape for centuries.

Meb Cutlack left *The Reporter* and cofounded a new weekly paper, *The Independent Reformer,* in early 2007. The newspaper is the intellectual home for a "good government" movement trying to start a third political party to challenge the PUP and the UDP.

Brian Holland continues to sell dolomite to banana farmers through his company, Belize Minerals. He and his wife, Anne, also work with the National Garifuna Council on economic development projects in Punta Gorda.

Tony Garel left the Belize Zoo in 2005 to pursue his dream of opening a reptile house on his own in Belmopan.

Jacob Scherr directs international campaigns for the Natural Resources Defense Council. He continues to work closely with Ari Hershowitz, director of the NRDC's Latin American BioGems program. In his spare time, Hershowitz is earning a law degree at Georgetown University.

Kimo Jolly lives in San Ignacio and works as an ecotourism guide and environmental consultant.

Ambrose Tillett left the Belize Senate at the end of his four-year term. He is now the chief consulting officer for BSN Digital, a computer software company in Belize City.

Candy Gonzalez and her husband, George, formed an environmental watchdog group, We Belizeans Against the Dam (WeBAD) that monitors BEL's work at Chalillo, Mollejon, and Vaca Falls.

Chief Justice Abdulai Conteh presides over Belize's highest court. His seven-year tenure has, by most accounts, been marked by unusual fairness and wisdom. He continues to be active in Sierra Leonean politics.

Lord Michael Ashcroft and the government of Belize remain embattled over the ownership of BTL, the phone company. With the demise of Intelco, Glenn Godfrey's rival start-up telecom, BTL regained its position as a private monopoly and continues to charge exorbitant rates. In 2005 a former company official admitted that BTL illegally traded nearly $100 million on the currency black market between 2001 and 2005. The Belizean government took no action against the company.

Belizean founding prime minister George Price enjoys an active retirement in Belize City. He lives in a humble wooden house in the center of town. It is said that he attends Mass every morning before dawn.

Adult scarlet macaws continue to be seen in the hills above the village of Red Bank and in the Macal River valley. Their nests upriver from the Chalillo Dam are now under water.

In 2005 BEL hired Tunich-Nah Consultants, an environmental engineering company owned by former Belize Audubon Society president Jose "Pepe" Garcia, to place thirty nesting boxes in the hills around the reservoir. Tunich-Nah's contract called for annual monitoring of the nesting sites for five years. After one year, BEL chose not to renew Tunich-Nah's contract for monitoring services. When reached by phone in Belize, Garcia said the macaws were doing fine. He was unable to release any specific data to confirm that assessment, however, under the terms of his nondisclosure agreement with BEL.

In a press release issued shortly after Chalillo's commissioning, the Belize Audubon Society reiterated its position that "the population of scarlet macaws in Belize is stable."

In May 2007, BirdLife International updated its survey of the world's birds for the IUCN Red List. BirdLife officials found 1,221 of the world's 9,956 species of birds threatened with extinction, an increase of 35 species since 2007. A further 812 species were considered "near threatened," an increase of 82 species in the same period. The scarlet macaw continued to be listed as a species of least concern. That status was based on the same early-1990s data that has been used for the past ten years. No updated studies were sourced. BirdLife and the IUCN have no specialist tracking the macaw, and have no plans to reconsider the bird's Red List status.

Sharon Matola remains the director of the Belize Zoo, where she continues to oversee all operations of the zoo and the Tropical Education Center.

In 2006 more than eighty thousand visitors passed through the zoo's turnstiles. To date, ten harpy eagles have been reintroduced to Belize. Satellite tracking and radio telemetry indicate that seven of the birds are alive and flourishing. Sharon lives in a small bungalow in the Belizean bush, where she continues her work to conserve the habitat and wildlife of Central America. She is happy.

Acknowledgments

This book would not have been possible without the generosity of Sharon Matola. Sharon allowed me into her life while the Chalillo whirlwind was swirling around her, and continued to welcome me back to Belize for more than five years. She answered my questions and assisted my reporting long after others would have banned me as a nuisance. I'm grateful for her courage, her strength, and her kindness.

A number of Belizeans educated me in the ways of their country: Meb Cutlack, Tony Garel, Mick and Lucy Fleming, Ambrose Tillett, Lynn Young, Lois Young, Yasser Musa, Richard Holder, Emory King, Godsman Ellis, Candy and George Gonzalez, Martin Meadows, Jan Meerman, Claudia Duenas, and Brian and Anne Holland. Thank you all.

I owe a great professional debt to the journalists of Belize. They turn out tough, lively investigative pieces under difficult circumstances. Some of the source material for this book was published in Belize's four weekly papers: *Amandala, The Reporter, The Guardian,* and the *Belize Times.* Harry Lawrence's heroic *Reporter* and Evan X. Hyde's mighty *Amandala* were especially valuable guides to the ins and outs of Belizean politics and culture. Meb Cutlack's bold, indefatigable reporting inspired me. Jules Vasquez at Belize's Channel 7 often asked questions nobody else had the guts to ask.

A number of crucial documents came to light through the persistence of Grainne Ryder and her colleagues at Toronto's Probe International. Ryder uncovered CIDA's development payments to Amec and shed light on an aspect of the project that would otherwise have gone unnoticed.

Many people in Newfoundland were generous with their time, including Fortis CEO Stan Marshall, Fortis spokesperson Donna Hynes, and actor/activist Greg Malone.

Ari Hershowitz first alerted me to the Chalillo project, and he continued to be a valuable source throughout the reporting of this book. Many of the documents upon which this story relies were made public by Hershowitz, Jacob Scherr, and their colleagues at the NRDC.

Thanks to Hal Espen and Jay Stowe at *Outside* magazine for taking a flyer and sending me to Belize to chase down the Zoo Lady. I'm especially grateful to Hal for nourishing a generation of adventurous writers at *Outside*. Without his vision and support we would be nowhere.

During the book's late stages I benefited from a Ted Scripps Fellowship in Environmental Journalism at the University of Colorado. The fellowship's patron, Cindy Scripps, has been quietly supporting the development of environmental journalism for more than a decade. At CU, Len Ackland, Tom Yulsman, Charles Wilkinson, Patty Limerick, Leslie Dodson, Keala Kelly, Anne Raup, and Jerd Smith provided excellent guidance and deepened my understanding of the natural world.

At Random House, Jonathan Karp perceived the heart of the book from the very beginning, Ben Loehnen edited and shaped it, and Jonathan Jao brought it home. My wife, Claire Dederer, gave me invaluable advice and provided wise, pitiless edits. My agent, Elizabeth Wales, fought to bring the book to life, and she succeeded spectacularly.

Best for last: Claire and our children, Lucy and Willie, endured my many trips to Belize with grace and good cheer. I am blessed to have their love and support. The next one, I promise, will be closer to home.

Notes on Sources

The Last Flight of the Scarlet Macaw grew out of an article commissioned by *Outside* magazine editor Hal Espen in early 2002. Bits and pieces of that original piece, as well as phrases from an earlier *Outside* feature on dams, survive in this book.

The historical works of O. Nigel Bolland and Assad Shoman were essential sources for much of the material about Belize's past. Those books include *Thirteen Chapters of a History of Belize* (Shoman); *Land in Belize, 1765–1871* (Bolland and Shoman); *The Formation of a Colonial Society* (Bolland); and *Colonialism and Resistance in Belize* (Bolland). Also helpful were Robert A. Naylor's *Penny Ante Imperialism* and the popular histories of Emory King, including King's memoir *I Spent It All in Belize*. Evan X. Hyde's weekly editorials in *Amandala* were also informative, as were Karla Heusner's *Reporter* columns and Lan Sluder's reports on his "Belize First" website (www.belizefirst.com). Many of Hyde's best pieces are collected in his book *X Communication*; Heusner's are in her anthology, *Food for Thought*.

Other sources consulted include: *A History of Belize: Nation in the Making*, edited by Robert Leslie; *The Environment of Belize: Our Life Support System*, by Kimo Jolly and Ellen McRae; *Environmental Statistics for Belize, 2000* (Central Statistical Office, Ministry of Finance, Belmopan); *A Geography of Belize: The Land and Its People*, by Sydney Campbell; *Belize and Northern Guatemala: The Ecotravellers' Wildlife Guide*, by Les Beletsky; *Jaguar*, by Alan Rabinowitz; *Sastun: My Apprenticeship with a Maya Healer*, by Rosita Arvigo; *The Upper Raspaculo River Basin, Belize, Central America: Report of the Joint Services Scientific Expedition to the Upper Raspaculo, January–February 1991*, by Major Alastair D. F. Rogers and David A. Sutton; *The Columbia River Forest Reserve: Little Quartz Ridge Expedition*, edited by Jan Meerman and Sharon Matola; *The Mammals of Belize*, by Sharon Matola; and *The ABC's of the Vegetation of Belize*, by Sharon Matola.

Sources for Belize's Mayan period included Peter Harrison's book *The Lords of Tikal: Rulers of an Ancient Maya City*; David Webster's *The Fall of the Ancient Maya*; Rafael Girard's *People of the Chan*; Charles Gibson's *The Aztecs*

Under Spanish Rule; Tzvetan Todorov's *The Conquest of America;* Nigel Hughes's *Maya Monuments;* Grant D. Jones's *Maya Resistance to Spanish Rule;* and Lauren A. Sullivan's "Dynamics of Regional Integration in Northwestern Belize" in *Ancient Maya Political Economies,* by Marilyn A. Masson and David A. Freidel. Information on Christopher Columbus came from *The Diario of Christopher Columbus's First Voyage to America, 1492–1493,* abstracted by Bartolomé de las Casas; *The Voyage of Christopher Columbus,* translated by John Cummins; and *The Conquest of Paradise,* by Kirkpatrick Sale. More information on John Lloyd Stephens and Frederick Catherwood can be found in Stephens's travelogue, *Incidents of Travel in Central America,* and in *Maya Explorer: John Lloyd Stephens and the Lost Cities of Central America,* by Victor Wolfgang von Hagen. For information on logwood dye, see *The Art and Craft of Natural Dyeing,* by J. N. Liles, and *Dyes from Plants,* by Seonaid M. Robertson. Two essential sources for the sections on Spanish conquest and the British Empire were Mark Crocker's *Rivers of Blood, Rivers of Gold* and Niall Ferguson's *Empire: The Rise and Demise of the British World Order and the Lessons for Global Power.*

The research of Sharon Matola, Greg Sho, Elizabeth Mallory, and Katherine Renton yielded much of the information about Belize's scarlet macaws. Mallory and Matola's "Scarlet Macaw Distribution and Movements in the Maya Mountains of Belize" (in draft) includes both historical and current data on the species in Belize. Renton's studies "Diet of Adult and Nesting Scarlet Macaws in Southwest Belize" (*Biotropica,* v. 38, no. 2, 2006), and "Seasonal Variation in Occurrence of Macaws Along a Rainforest River" (*Journal of Field Ornithology,* v. 73, no. 1, 2002) were especially helpful, as was the research of Christopher Vaughan and Charles A. Munn. Other general sources about the birds of Belize included *Birds of Belize,* by H. Lee Jones; *A Checklist of the Birds of Belize,* by Jaime Garcia, Sharon Matola, Martin Meadows, and Charles Wright; "Ornithology in Belize Since 1960" (*Wilson Bulletin,* v. 110, no. 4, 1998) by Bruce and Carolyn Miller; and *Macaws,* by Elizabeth Butterworth. José A. Gonzalez's "Harvesting, Local Trade, and Conservation of Parrots in the Northeastern Peruvian Amazon," in *Biological Conservation* (v. 114, issue 3, December 2003), provided an extraordinary firsthand look at parrot poaching. Also helpful were "The Wild Bird Trade: When a Bird in the Hand Means None in the Bush," a 1992 policy report by Wildlife Conservation International; and "Trade in Neotropical Psittacines and Its Conservation Implications," by J. B. Thomsen and T. A. Mulliken, in Beissinger and Snyder, *New World Parrots in Crisis: Solutions from Conservation Biology.* David Wiedenfeld's discovery of the subspecies *Ara macao cyanoptera* was published in "A New Species of Scarlet Macaw and Its Status and Conservation" (*Ornitología Neotropical*, v. 5, no. 2, 1994). The World Parrot Trust and its 2004 Parrot Action Plan were valuable resources. Information about both can be found at www.worldparrottrust.org.

On dams: It's been more than ten years since the publication of Patrick McCully's *Silenced Rivers: The Ecology and Politics of Large Dams*, and still nothing approaches its breadth and authority. All of us who write about rivers and dams owe McCully a note of thanks. I drew on a number of sources besides *Silenced Rivers* for this chapter, including Jacques Leslie's *Deep Water: The Epic Struggle over Dams, Displaced People, and the Environment*; John Warfield Simpson's *Dam!—Water, Power, Politics, and Preservation in Hetch Hetchy and Yosemite National Park*; Norman Smith's *A History of Dams*; and Nicholas J. Schnitter's *A History of Dams: The Useful Pyramids*. Material on ancient dams came from those sources and from Louis Delaporte's *Mesopotamia: The Babylonian and Assyrian Civilizations*. For material on Hoover Dam, I found Joseph E. Stevens's *Hoover Dam: An American Adventure* especially useful. Terry S. Reynolds's *Stronger Than a Hundred Men: A History of the Vertical Water Wheel* is one of those great nonfiction gems that I considered myself lucky to discover. The IUCN/World Bank report *Large Dams: Learning from the Past, Looking at the Future* (1997) provided an institutional overview of the issues. For information about rivers, I often turned to *Lifelines: The Case for River Conservation* by Tim Palmer, and *River Ecology and Management*, edited by Robert J. Naiman and Robert E. Bilby. If you really want to get technical, dive into *The Rivers Handbook: Hydrological and Ecological Principles*, edited by Peter Calow and Geoffrey E. Petts. Philip Fearnside's research on Brazilian dams can be found in a number of scientific journals, including *Environmental Management* and *Environmental Conservation*. Billy Frank's classic quote can be found in Charles Wilkinson's *Crossing the Next Meridian: Land, Water, and the Future of the West*. Richard White's "organic machine" concept comes from his book of the same name, *The Organic Machine*. Finally, it must be acknowledged that the letter and spirit of Marc Reisner's *Cadillac Desert* permeates everything written by a western American about rivers and dams. Or at least it's been so for me.

Sources for the sections on former Belizean prime minister George Price included the historical work of Bolland and Shoman, and also Rudolph I. Castillo's biography, *Profile of the Rt. Hon. George Price, P.C.: Man of the People*. Castillo's book in particular is a great source of information about Price's political talents and personality.

From 1999 to 2001, a number of London newspapers put Michael Ashcroft, the Baron of Belize, under public scrutiny. I benefited greatly from their reporting. The *Sunday Times, The Observer,* and the *Financial Times* all covered Ashcroft's empire during this period, but Dominic Kennedy and Paul Durman of *The Times* and Rob Evans, David Hencke, and David Pallister of *The Guardian* turned out extraordinary pieces on Lord Ashcroft and his strange ties to Belize. *Amandala* reporter Adele Ramos also published a number of enlightening articles about Ashcroft's phone company, BTL, and its private monopoly in Belize. In 2005, Ashcroft answered his critics in the autobiography *Dirty Politics, Dirty Times: My Fight with Wapping and New Labour.* That, too, proved to be a valuable source of information.

Information about the NRDC's Washington, D.C., office can be found at www.nrdc.org/cities/building. For more dismal reading on Ferdinand Marcos's kickback-laden scheme for a nuclear power plant, see Karl Wilson's July 1, 2004, story in the journal *Energy Bulletin,* and Raul Dancel's piece, "Foreign Debt: The Price of Greed," in the September 21, 2002, issue of *The Nation.*

The literature on extinction fills entire libraries. I'll mention a few sources that were helpful to me. The works of Edward O. Wilson (*Biodiversity; Biophilia; The Diversity of Life; The Future of Life*) and Jared Diamond (*Guns, Germs, and Steel;* and *Collapse*) are great places to start. If you like Diamond, you'll love Charles L. Redman's *Human Impact on Ancient Environments,* an outstanding exploration of prehistoric loss of biodiversity and habitat. Editor Ross D. E. MacPhee's *Extinctions in Near Time: Causes, Contexts, and Consequences* contained a number of insightful essays on previous extinctions. Martin Rudwick's classic work *The Meaning of Fossils* was very helpful, as was *Quaternary Extinctions: A Prehistoric Revolution,* edited by Paul S. Martin and Richard G. Klein, and *No Turning Back: The Life and Death of Animal Species,* by Richard Ellis. I relied on Martin Garretson's book *The American Bison* for information about the bison slaughter, and Errol Fuller's *Extinct Birds* for data and anecdotes about avian loss. More information on the Tasmanian tiger can be found in *Tasmanian Tiger: The Tragic Tale of How the World Lost Its Most Mysterious Predator,* by David Owen. Two other helpful sources were "Predicting Extinction Risk in Declining Species," by Andy Purvis et al., in *Proceedings of the Royal Society of London,* October 7, 2000, and "Ecological Basis of Extinction Risk in Birds," by Ian Owens and Peter Bennett in *Proceedings of the National Academy of Sciences of the United States of America,* v. 97, no. 22, 2000.

Further information about climate change and extinction risk can be found in the U.N. Intergovernmental Panel on Climate Change's 2007 report "Impacts, Adaptation and Vulnerability" (Working Group II summary for policymakers); "Fingerprints of Global Warming on Wild Animals and Plants," by T. L. Root et al., in *Nature,* v. 421, January 2, 2003; "Extinction Risk from Climate Change," by Chris Thomas et al., in *Nature,* v. 427, January 8, 2004; "Human Impacts on the Rates of Recent, Present, and Future Bird Extinctions," by Stuart Pimm et al., in *Proceedings of the National Academy of Sciences of the United States of America,* v. 103, no. 29, 2006.

The debate over species definition is at once fascinating and head-spinning. A few sources were particularly helpful. They included "Species Concepts and Species Limits in Ornithology," by Jurgen Haffer, in volume 8 of Josep del Hoyo's *Handbook of the Birds of the World;* "Taxonomic Stability and Avian Extinctions," by George Sangster, in the April 2000 issue of *Conservation Biology;* the books *Species: The Units of Biodiversity,* edited by M. F. Claridge et al., and Ernst Mayr's *Systematics and the Origin of Species.* E. O. Wilson's quote about subspecies came from his book *The Diversity of Life.* Information about the IUCN's Red List of Threatened Species can be found at www.iucnredlist.org. BirdLife International posts Red List bird updates at www.birdlife.org.

More information on the Privy Council can be found in *The Judicial Committee of the Privy Council, 1833–1876,* by P. A. Howell.

For more background and updates on the harpy eagle, see the Peregrine Fund's site, www.peregrinefund.org.

Further information on Sharon Matola and the best little zoo in the world can be found at www.belizezoo.org.

PHOTO: ROGER SCHREIBER

BRUCE BARCOTT, author of *The Measure of a Mountain: Beauty and Terror on Mount Rainier,* is a contributing editor at *Outside* magazine. His feature articles have appeared in *The New York Times Magazine, Mother Jones, Sports Illustrated, Harper's, Utne Reader,* and other publications. He contributes reviews to *The New York Times Book Review* and the public radio show *Living on Earth,* and is a former Ted Scripps Fellow at the University of Colorado. He lives in Seattle with his wife and their two children.